Threats to the

International

Civil

Service

To friends and former colleagues

in international secretariats

and to Mandy Eggleston

for all her assistance

Threats to the

International

Civil

Service

Yves Beigbeder

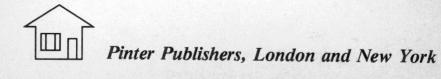

Pinter Publishers, London and New York

© Yves Beigbeder, 1988

First Published in Great Britain in 1988 by
Pinter Publishers Limited
25 Floral Street, London WC2E 9DS

British Library Cataloguing in Publication Data

A CIP catalogue record for this book is
available from the British Library

Library of Congress Cataloguing in Publication Data

Beigbeder, Yves.
    Threats to the international civil service : past pressures and
    new trends / Yves Beigbeder.
    p. cm.
    Bibliography: p.
    Includes index.
    ISBN 0-86187-953-8 : $39.00 (U.S.)
    1. International officials and employees. 2. United Nations-
    Officials and employees. I. Title.
    JX1995.B427 1988
    354. 1'6--dc19

                                                                88-10137
                                                                CIP

Typeset by Arjan Ltd, Erith, Kent DA8 1NP, England
Printed by Biddles of Guildford Ltd, England

The author has written this book in a personal capacity:
the views and conclusions are his own responsibility.

Contents

List of tables

List of abbreviations

ACC	Administrative Committee on Coordination
CCAQ	Consultative Committee on Administrative Questions
CCISUA	Coordinating Committee for Independent Staff Unions and Associations of the United Nations System
CERN	European Organization for Nuclear Research
CPC	Committee for Programme and Coordination
ECA	Economic Commission for Africa
ECLA	Economic Commission for Latin America
ECOSOC	Economic and Social Council
EEC	European Economic Community
FAFICS	Federation of Associations of Former International Civil Servants
FAO	Food and Agriculture Organization of the United Nations
FICSA	Federation of International Civil Servants' Associations
GATT	General Agreement on Tariffs and Trade
GDR	German Democratic Republic
IAEA	International Atomic Energy Agency
ICAO	International Civil Aviation Organization
ICJ	International Court of Justice
ICM	Intergovernmental Committee for Migration
ICSAB	International Civil Service Advisory Board
ICSC	International Civil Service Commission
ILO	International Labour Organisation
ILOAT	ILO Administrative Tribunal
IMO	International Maritime Organization
ITC	International Trade Centre
ITU	International Telecommunication Union

JIU	Joint Inspection Unit of the United Nations
ONUC	Opération des Nations Unies au Congo
PAHO	Pan-American Health Organization
PLO	Palestine Liberation Organization
SWAPO	South-West African People's Organization
UN	United Nations
UNAT	United Nations Administrative Tribunal
UNCTAD	United Nations Conference of Trade and Development
UNDOF	United Nations Disengagement Observer Force
UNDP	United Nations Development Programme
UNESCO	United Nations Educational, Scientific and Cultural Organization
UNFPA	United Nations Fund for Population Activities
UNHCR	United Nations High Commissioner for Refugees
UNICEF	United Nations Children's Fund
UNIDIR	United Nations Institute for Disarmament Research
UNIFIL	United Nations Interim Force in Lebanon
UNITAR	United Nations Institute for Training and Research
UNJSPF	United Nations Joint Staff Pension Fund
UNOG	United Nations Office at Geneva
UNRWA	United Nations Relief and Works Agency for Palestine Refugees in the Near East
UPU	Universal Postal Union
WHO	World Health Organisation
WIPO	World Intellectual Property Organization
WMO	World Meteorological Organization

Introduction

And so the the dreamers, the idealists, the pragmatists, the artisans in the vineyards of human betterment, the indefatigable apostles in the cause of peace, to all who are tenacious, and unrelenting, I wish you well and ask you never to be cowed.

Stephen Lewis[1]

It is likely that many of the men and women who initially joined the League of Nations and the United Nations organizations did so as pioneers trekking into new territories: they were mostly idealists, international missionaries dedicated to building a better, more peaceful world. No doubt later recruits also included pragmatists, artisans, careerists and those who wanted, simply, a good job.

Whatever their initial motivation, they were joining a new type of human enterprise, the global intergovernmental organization and a new type of public service, the international civil service. As noted by Mailick,[2] in the long-range perspective of the political history of the world, the emergence of the phenomenon of the international organization is likely to appear as a major development of the twentieth century, comparable in importance to the emergence of the nation-state in Europe at the end of feudal civilization. The organizations' staff member, the international civil servant, is also a product of this century: 'As a species of the *genus homo* he would not have been identified by a political Darwin as recently as forty years ago'.[3]

The first modern intergovernmental organization, the Central Commission for the Navigation of the Rhine, was created by the Congress of Vienna in 1815. In 1914 intergovernmental organizations numbered about fifty, in 1939 about eighty and in 1980 more than 600.[4] This impressive growth includes the global and the regional organizations, such as the UN and the European organizations grouping most of the international staff.[5]

The structure of intergovernmental organizations includes intergovernmental bodies composed of member states' representatives (assemblies, conferences and boards) and secretariats. The creation of permanent international secretariats was the main feature of the evolution from international conferences into intergovernmental organizations.

International civil servants now number approximately 100,000, half of whom serve in the UN family of organisations.

A service in crisis

The international civil service, particularly in the UN organizations, is in crisis. For the Federation of International Civil Service Associations (FICSA), it is the target of increasingly violent attacks, directed against the staff's integrity, efficiency, their conditions of employment and against the very existence of the international civil service.[6] Attacks against the UN organizations' staff are attacks against the organizations themselves.

These attacks emanate mostly from conservative American circles who question the need for UN organizations; challenge their programmes; criticize their budgets and management; and expose their bloated, overpaid, ineffective bureaucracies. These circles successfully encouraged the United States' withdrawal from UNESCO in 1985, followed by the British withdrawal in 1986 and the US legislation adopted in 1985, which has caused severe financial crises in the UN and in the specialized agencies in 1986, 1987 and 1988. Other Western countries agreed with the United States on the need for financial restraint, but do not question the need for international organizations: they have not shared in the United States' financial blackmail against the UN organizations. While generally supporting the UN organizations' programmes, the socialist countries have allied themselves with the West in effectively curbing UN budgets and staff. In opposition with these two groups, developing countries want the organizations to grow and provide more financial and operational assistance; however, their own financial contributions to the organizations' budgets are minimal.

In several internal UN reports the Joint Inspection Unit (JIU) has from time to time alerted governments and organizations to staff problems. In his 1971 report on 'Personnel Problems in the UN',[7] Inspector Bertrand found that 25 per cent of the UN professional and higher categories personnel had no university education, and that recruitment processes and searches were highly inadequate. He formulated a number of reform proposals, including longterm manpower planning, the use of competitive examinations, and a reorganization of personnel services. Thirteen years later, Bertrand noted that the staff policy reforms had been implemented in part, sometimes cautiously, more often with a slowness that served no purpose and could hardly be justified.[8] In the more recent 'Staff Costs' reports,[9] other JIU inspectors have criticized the excessive salaries and benefits of UN staff and their alleged declining efficiency. They have recommended against any increase of their remunerations and against the establishment of any new post.

In 1986 the Group of 18[10] proposed, and the General Assembly agreed, that the UN staffing should be reduced by 15 per cent over three years.

According to the former president of FICSA, forty years after the establishment of the UN, a genuine international civil service based on career and merit and free from political interference was still a dream.[11]

Previous crises and pressures

The present crisis has been preceded by several others. During the late 1920s and in 1930s the internationalist obligations of some of the League of Nations' staff members were openly breached by a few governments, including fascist Italy and Nazi Germany.

In the 1950s, during the McCarthy witchhunts, the United States exercised an unsavory and unstatutory interference in the personnel management of the UN organizations by demanding the dismissal of a number of US citizens employed by the organizations.

The socialist countries are in constant, more or less avowed, opposition to the internationalist view of the international civil service, which causes periodical, but often hidden, tensions. The Soviet Union created a public crises after its violent attacks against the first two secretaries-general, Trygve Lie and Dag Hammarskjold, in the 1950s and in the 1960s.

Since the 1970s observers have often been critical of the UN bureaucracies; however, most criticisms have been addressed to the UN in New York, while relatively less attention has been given to the specialized agencies, with the exception of UNESCO.[12]

In 1974, the Finger Study[13] found that the quality of UN professional staff was not what it could be because of the UN's personnel policies and because of the policies and practices of many member states, including political pressures and 'cronyism'. A UN official was quoted to have said, 'It is not so much that the political pressure is intense, but that our resistance is so low'. In a follow-up report[14] the authors concluded that the situation at the UN had deteriorated: disorganization, inefficiency, waste or resources, personal disputes, useless transfer of incapable employees from one department to another, a decline in motivation and in the independence of the international civil service.[15]

For Weiss[15] the deterioration of the concept of an autonomous international civil service is particularly distressing because the international staff has acquiesced in the erosion of its essential *raison d'être*. He found plausible the hypothesis that the activity of international administration was not efficient or effective even according to the low standards usually applied to measure their behaviour.[16]

In 1981 Jordan, wondering 'What happened to *our* International Civil Service',[17] referred to a high degree of dissatisfaction among employers (the senior secretariat officials responsible for personnel matters and the Fifth Committee of the General Assembly) and employees alike.

In 1983 Meron[18] exposed the politicization of the international staff, the decline of its quality, its balkanization into national enclaves and the sharing of important posts between powerful countries and blocs. He prophesied that the international civil service would probably become intergovernmental (instead of international), its staff giving their allegiance to their governments and no longer to the international organization.

In 1985 Inspector Bertrand again deplored the inadequacy of qualifications of the staff, the lack of definition of qualifications required for recruitment and promotion to higher grades, the indifference shown towards standards of work and competence, and the absence of a system of in-service training. These inadequacies create a deplorable working environment in which the best staff members can no longer find the motivation needed to dedicate themselves to their tasks.[19]

Some of these criticisms are no doubt justified, but they do not necessarily apply to all staff working in all UN organizations. Are the WHO staff, who have eradicated smallpox and now fight against AIDS, so incapable? Do the field staff working for UNICEF or for the High Commission for Refugees lack faith and motivation? Do the specialists of the World Meteorological Organization and the International Telecommunication Union lack expertise? The staff of UN organizations resent the lack of public support, and they feel that these constant criticisms are often unfair. They are also concerned about their deteriorating employment conditions. The staff of two UN agencies, the International Labour Organization (ILO) and the General Agreement on Tariff and Trades (GATT) went on a symbolic, short strike in 1987 to protest against reduced salaries and pensions, a sign of staff unrest.

Some of these crises and the staff malaise have been caused, entirely or in part, by political and financial pressures. International organizations are not living in a secluded ivory tower: global, regional and country ideological, political, economic and social problems are reflected in the debates of their assemblies, and these problems affect the organizations' performance and autonomy, the staff's independence, morale and well-being.

As noted by Nerfin,[20] the current crisis of the UN is a reflection of the crisis of multilateralism, an image and an identity crisis. One reason is that the Western democracies no longer recognize their creature, over which they have lost some of their control; for them, the organizations have thus become politicized. Another more fundamental and justified reason is the apparent lack of clear and tangible results obtained by some organizations, that is mainly the impotence of the UN in maintaining peace and meagre progress in the economic development of the Third World.

In spite of the organizations' fragility, failures and weaknesses, the concept and practice of international organizations has endured as the concretization of the dream for a better, more united and peaceful world and as the only tool available for international cooperation. At the same time the international civil service has also survived more than seventy years of crises, hidden and open pressures and criticisms.

Who is an international civil servant?

A broad legal definition of an international agent has been given by the International Court of Justice in its Advisory Opinion of 1949: 'The Court understands the word 'agent' in the most liberal sense, that is to say, any person who, whether a paid official or not, and whether permanently employed or not, has been charged by an organ of the Organization with carrying out, or helping to carry out, one of its functions—in short, any person through whom it acts'.[21]

Bastid, in her pioneering book written in 1931, has defined the international civil servant as 'any individual entrusted by representatives of several States or by an organ acting in their names, following an inter-State agreement and under the control of one or the other, to fulfil, under specific legal rules, continuously and exclusively, functions in the interest of all those States'.[22]

For our purposes, the international civil service may be considered as a body of persons employed by intergovernmental organizations to fulfil international functions. The service therefore includes all temporary and permanent employees, local or international recruits, professional and general service (support) staff, and officials seconded from national civil services or other public or private organizations, under the condition that they declare their allegiance to the international organization for the duration of their international employment.

With regard to UN organizations, the UN Charter (Art.97) states that 'The Secretariat shall comprise a Secretary-General and such staff as the Organization may require'. The constitutions of the other UN organizations use a similar language.[23]

Under UN Staff Regulation 1.1, members of the secretariat are 'international civil servants', although special employment conditions apply to specific categories of staff.[24]

National and international administrations

International secretariats have common characteristics with national administrations: they also have their own specificity.

Like national administrations, international organizations render a public service: they are both part of the public, government, sector, in contrast with the private, profit-making, sector. Both types of organization are financed from public funds.[25]

The staffing of intergovernmental organizations is generally much smaller than that of national ministries in medium or large countries. The largest UN organization, the UN itself, employs approximately 14,000 staff members, a small number in comparison with the 990,000 employees of the United States Department of Defense and the 1.6 million employees of the Indian railways.[26]

While governments change, national administrations remain. They represent the permanent element of public action, and ensure executive and administrative continuity. International administrations play the same role in relation to the organizations' governing bodies, which normally meet for only limited periods. Thus the international secretariats represent the organizations in their permanency. The organizations cannot function without them: secretariats prepare programme and budget proposals, and implement them when the governing bodies give their approval.

National administrations are durable, while international organizations are fragile and expendable. International organizations are created by states and can be destroyed by them. They are legally and financially dependent on their member states for their existence and survival. National administrations can grow and decrease, some may be merged with others, and departments may be transferred from one ministry to another. However, in every country there will always be ministries of the interior, of external relations, of defence, of economy, and so on. National administrations fulfil long-established, expressed national needs of governments and populations. International administrations respond to such needs as world peace, security, economic and social cooperation and development, the protection of human rights and refugees, and so on. However, these needs are usually more general, indirect and sometimes abstract: they usually relate to governments rather than to individual citizens. Intergovernmental organizations are the creatures of states (non-governmental organizations are created by citizens), they have no 'right' to life.[27]

As a consequence of the fragility of the international organizations, international staff do not enjoy the assured, comfortable security of employment of national civil servants. Like their organizations, and even if they hold a 'permanent' appointment, they are expendable.

Another obvious distinction is that international secretariats are made up of staff of multinational origin (and not only of one nationality) and that they are to serve, not one country, but a multiplicity of countries (twelve for the European Community, 159 for the UN), or more precisely, the 'collective will' expressed by the majority of these countries in decisions and resolutions of the organizations' governing bodies.

In principle, managing heterogeneous multinational staff with different cultural and administrative backgrounds—different education, work experience and career expectations, and varying linguistic skills—is more complex than managing homogeneous national staff (but some national societies, and therefore their administrations, are also multicultural). Problems of leadership styles, communications, motivation, loyalty, efficiency and accepted behaviour, are to be expected. Problems are compounded by geographic distribution requirements, the need to show no discrimination towards particular nationalities, races or national or group ideologies. Personnel management is made more difficult by the problems caused by expatriation[28] and mobility, with their demands on the staff members and their families to adjust periodically to another duty station, another country, its climate, its political, economical, social and cultural conditions, its language and other factors.

National administrations' staff may also have to be mobile, but mostly within their own country, while professional staff of UN organizations may be assigned to any country in the world. Diplomatic personnel are assigned to various countries, but they continue to work for their own country, for their home ministry, and they work mainly in their own language: they work in the national, protected enclaves of their country's embassies and consulates. Their natural allegiance is to their country, while international staff are expected to develop a new, additional loyalty to an international, abstract and contested entity without historical or emotional substratum.

International organizations are a recent phenomenon, in contrast with the centuries-old British, French or German civil services. The international administrations have had to invent their structures, policies, rules and procedures and to set up records and archives.

In fact, the newly established international secretariats borrowed administrative principles, institutions and processes from national administrations and adapted them to their own requirements.

Thus concepts and methods of the British Civil Service were applied by the League of Nations, while practices of the United States Federal Civil Service influenced most UN organizations. The creation of the UN International Civil Service Commission was inspired by the former United States Civil Service Commission—the concept of the UN Joint Inspection Unit was based on a French model, UN Staff Ombudsmen were copied from the original Swedish prototype, the establishment of the League of Nations, ILO and UN Administrative Tribunals inspired by similar national institutions in continental Europe, while their jurisprudence owes much to French administrative law. However, the national organs thus grafted onto international bodies acquired their own characteristics which differentiated them progressively from their national models.[29]

While the employment conditions of national civil services are based on national criteria and standards, those of the international civil service constitute an autonomous, extra-territorial system unrelated to national labour legislation and regulations. Such systems, which are promulgated by the organizations' governing bodies, include all aspects of personnel policies and practices: salaries, allowances, benefits, contracts, social security, discipline, pensions, grievance settlement, and so on. They constitute the internal legal administrative system of the international organizations.

However, no salary and benefits system is created *ab nihilo*: national or local employment conditions serve as references for the initial setting of the international employment systems and later adjustments. The United States Federal Civil Service is the comparator for the compensation scheme of the UN professional and higher categories staff. The employment conditions of the best local employers are the basis for determining the salary scales and allowances of the UN general service staff in the various duty stations.

National civil services work in an administrative hierarchy, where strategies and policies are decided upon by a minister, or by the government or by parliament. International civil servants are also part of an administrative structure under the direction of the head of the secretariat. Major broad decisions are made by the governing bodies during their temporary sessions; in practice, international secretariats are usually less supervised and controlled by the decision-makers than national bureaucracies.

National civil servants exert a degree of public authority over citizens and institutions, by delegation from the legislative and executive authorities. Most international organizations have no such powers, except for the European Community institutions. The UN organizations' governing bodies cannot take binding and enforceable decisions. Failing a world government, an effective world justice and an international police with coercive powers, the organizations mostly adopt resolutions, formulate recommendations and advise. Thus the UN civil servants have no public executive authority. They study, compile, report, advise, circulate information, set norms, control performance, but they do not sanction member states nor take decisions enforceable by citizens. In the international civil service the decision-making authority is that of the head of the secretariat, under the terms of the organizations' charter or constitution, which may be delegated to subordinate managers. Thus functions in national administrations may include executive and enforceable decision-making, while those in international secretariats are more of an advisory nature.

In the same way as there are specialized national ministries, there is a diversity of intergovernmental organizations which relate to these ministries.

Intergovernmental organizations include the global UN organizations, the regional organizations, the all-purposes organizations, the political, military, economic, social, technical, cultural, scientific organizations.

There is a diversity among UN organizations: varying missions, budget and staffing levels, geographic locations, professional types of personnel, leadership and management styles, and so on, Their personnel includes generalists, specialists, administrators, language staff, operation officers, secretarial and custodial staff.

In spite of this diversity, all the UN organizations participate in a 'Common System of Salaries and Allowances', although there are some minor variations in employment practices in some of the organizations.

While international and national administrations belong to separate systems, their interaction is constant. Jéquier has noted than an international organization is a juxtaposition of three bureaucracies, one international and two national, which complement each other, conflict with each other and interact in an extremely complex system of relations.[30] The first bureaucracy is the international secretariat. The second is that of the national diplomatic delegations of member states to the organization's headquarters.[31] The third bureaucracy consists of the civil servants, experts and politicians who deal in the capital of each member state with the business of each organization.

There are also interchanges between national and international bureaucrats or specialists, mostly through the appointment or secondment of national civil servants from home services and from the diplomatic corps to international organizations.

In summary, the international civil service is a branch of the public service, with its own characteristics—in particular, the international allegiance, the multinational composition of the staff, the relative fragility of the organizations and their dependence on the member states' goodwill and subsidies, the relatively precarious employment tenure of its staff.

Assumptions and limitations of this book

The assumptions are first that there is and will be a continuing need for international cooperation through institutions and other processes to help solve regional and global problems; second, that this need is recognized and accepted by most or all of the world's government, with the support of public opinion;[32] third, that the secretariats play a key role in the effective funtioning of the organizations; fourth, it is acknowledged that the original concept of the international civil service has been challenged and eroded, and is now under pressure. Finally, it is believed desirable, possible and timely to consider adjustments to past concepts and practices of the international civil service, in order to meet new needs.

This book will focus on UN secretariats as the largest part of the staff of intergovernmental organizations. The concept of the international civil service, created by the League of Nations and later embodied in the UN organizations, has been a model for other intergovernmental organizations; references will be made, from time to time, to such organizations.

This book is not a technical book on international personnel rules and practices.[33] It is, or hopes to be, a critical review of the traditional concept of the international civil service, of past and new pressures, of current challenges and solutions. The international civil service was created after the First World War to staff the League of Nations and the International Labour Organisation: the same employment concepts were applied to the staffs of the UN organizations after the Second World War. After seventy years there is a need for a critical review of the paradigm of the international service, in view of political, economic, social and administrative changes which have affected universal organizations over this period.

In Chapter 1 we will recall the traditional concept of the international civil service and the assumptions on which this service is based: an independent service, and élite corps, enjoying comfortable employment conditions, privileges and immunities, serving the community of nations under the leadership of the secretariat head.

In Chapter 2 the action and words of the second secretary-general of the UN, Dag Hammarskjold, will be recalled, as the prototype of the independent international civil servant. By comparison, brief references will be made to the other secretaries-general of the League of Nations and the UN.

Chapter 3 will expose the US pressures on the UN secretariats. In the 1950s the Korean War and McCarthyism triggered American interference with the executive heads' staffing perogatives. In the 1980s United States conservative circles have criticized UN Organizations' programmes, budgets and staff, and the United States Congress has adopted legislation which has severely curtailed the organizations' funding. The American withdrawal from UNESCO has hardened and added to, these pressures.

Chapter 4 will turn to the socialist countries' minority views on international secretariats: for them, allegiance to the socialist dogma and state prevails over internationalist ideals. Socialist countries' practices conflict with the international requirements of the UN Charter and Staff Regulations.

In Chapter 5 we will assess if the international civil servant is still 'pampered', in spite of the increasing erosion of his employment conditions imposed by member states, of zero-growth budgets and staffing reductions.

Chapter 6 will review the theory and practice of staff immunities. The protection of the international civil servant by quasi-diplomatic immunities has been shown to be an ineffective armour: a number of UN employees have been subjected to violations of human rights, like ordinary citizens.

In Chapter 7 the role of staff associations and unions will be examined. They support the internationalist concept, career service and the rule of law in internal staff-management relations. Do they exercise an abusive influence over the administrations by submitting exorbitant claims for better, costly employment benefits?

In Chapter 8 we will examine examples of new employment practices which deviate from the traditional international service concept. What needs do these fulfil and should they be made part of a broader 'new employment package'?

In the Conclusion, we will try to show that innovation is needed to face new pressures and constraints. There is a need to integrate a core of loyal, devoted and effective career staff with a variety of other alternative employment schemes. There is also a need for executive heads and member states to restore the morale of their staff and their faith in the organizations' usefulness and effectiveness.

This book is based on UN organizations' documentation, staff associations' publications, jurisprudence of the UN and ILO Administrative Tribunals, books and articles, comments from active or retired UN officials and the personal experience of the author, a former UN organizations' official.

Notes

1. 'The Defensible United Nations', by Stephen Lewis, in *International Perspectives*, Ottawa, September-October 1985, p. 6.
2. Sidney Mailick in *Public Administration Review*, Washington, DC, May-June 1970, no. 3, p.206.
3. Philip Jessup, 'The International Civil Servant and His Loyalties', *Columbia Journal of International Affairs*, vol. IX, no. 2, 1955, p. 55.
4. Harold J. Jacobson, *Networks of Interdependence*, Alfred A. Knopf,

New York, 1984, p. 9.

5. Staff of UN organizations numbered 51,654 on 31 December 1986. The European Community had a staff of 19,700 in 1986.

6. FICSA React Communiqué no. 1, in ILO's *Union*, no. 161, May 1986.

7. UN Doc. JIU/REP/71/7, pp. 17, 51-2.

8. UN Doc. JIU/REP/84/11, in A/40/34, p. 8.

9. UN Doc. JIU/REP/84/12 and JIU/REP/85/8.

10. The 'Group of High-Level Intergovernmental Experts to Review the Efficiency of the Administrative and Financial Functioning of the UN' was created by UN General Assembly Resolution 40/237. Its report (Doc. A/41/49), was generally approved by Resol. 41/213.

11. Wytold Zyss' statement is in Doc. FICSA/C/39/9, para. 22.

12. Exceptions include the following scholarly studies: Robert Berkov, *The World Health Organization: A Study in Decentralized International Administration*, Droz, Geneva, 1957; Thomas George Weiss, *International Bureaucracy*, Lexington Books, Lexington, Mass., 1975; Robert J. McLaren, *Civil Servants and Public policy: A Comparative Study of International Secretariats*, Wilfrid Laurier University Press, Waterloo, Ontario, 1980; Norman A.Graham and Robert S. Jordan (eds.), *The International Civil Service: Changing Roles and Concepts*, UNITAR, Pergamon Policy Studies, New York, 1980. The more critical and controversial studies of *Heritage Foundation*, Washington, DC, have referred to UNCTAD, UNESCO, UNICEF, WHO, the World Bank and the International Monetary Fund, besides the UN proper.

13. Seymour Maxwell Finger and John Mugno, *The Politics of Staffing the UN Secretariat*, the Ralph Bunche Institute on the UN, the Graduate School and University Center of the City University of New York, Dec. 1974, pp. 5, 6, 8, 11.

14. Seymour Maxwell Finger and Nina Hanan, *The UN Secretariat Revisited*, Ralph Bunche Institute on the UN, 1980, pp. 2, 4.

15. Weiss, p. 75.

16. Weiss refers to an observer's calculation that 'international organizations are 20 to 25 per cent less efficient than a national organization' (p. 85, note 92). One wonders as to the basis for such a calculation, and as to what international organization (or department of an international organization) was compared with what national organization (or department) in what country.

17. My emphasis. The great majority of UN staff, in the 1950s and 1960s, was made up of staff members from Western countries. See Robert S. Jordan, 'What Happened to Our International Service? The Case of the UN', in *Public Administration Review*, March-April 1981, p. 236.

18. 'L'Independance de la fonction publique internationale et son avenir', in *L'Avenir des organisations internationales*, Economica, Paris, 1984, pp. 221-40. See also Theodor Meron, *The UN Secretariat: The Rules and Practice*, Lexington Books, Lexington, Mass. 1977.

19. UN Doc. JIU/REP/85/9, *Some Reflections on Reform of the UN* by Maurice Bertrand, 1985.

20. Marc Nerfin 'The Future of the UN System' *Development Dialogue*, Dag

Hammarskjold Foundation, Uppsala, 1985/1, p. 9.

21. Advisory Opinion of 11 April 1949, 'Reparation for Injuries Suffered in the Service of the UN', ICJ Reports, 1949, p. 177.

22. Suzanne Bastid, *Les Fonctionnaires internationaux*, Recueil Sirey, Paris, 1931. My translation.

23. For instance, Article 30 of the WHO Constitution: 'The Secretariat shall comprise the Director-General and such technical and administrative staff as the Organization may require'.

24. UN Staff Rule 101.1 identifies Technical Assistance Project Personnel Conference and other short-term staff as a separate category of staff to whom specific rules apply.

25. With minor exceptions, such as private donations and the sales of UNICEF Greeting Cards.

26. Quoted by Nicholas Jéquier in 'La Triarchie des trois bureaucraties', *Les Organisations internationales entre 1' innovation et la stagnation'*, Presses Polytechniques Romandes, Lausanne, 1985, p. 220. On 31 December 1986 UNDP staff numbered 6,096, FAO 7,141, WHO 4,456, UNICEF 3,538, ILO 2,636. UPU had only 161 staff members.

27. However, the UN replaced the defunct League of Nations. If WHO or ITU disappeared, other similar organizations would probably need to be set up in order to fulfil the nations' need for international cooperation in public health and telecommunications.

28. As of 31 December 1986, 86 per cent of professional staff at headquarters and other established offices were expatriated; 94 per cent of professional project staff were expatriated in UN organizations; see *Personnel Statistics*, UN Doc. ACC/1987/PER/R.35/Rev.1 of 14 September 1987.

29. 'L'Influence de modèles administratifs nationaux sur le système administratif des institutions des Nations Unies', *International Review of Administrative Sciences*, Brussels, 2/1984, pp. 148-56, Yves Beigbeder.

30. Jequier, pp.221-3.

31. Practically all of the 159 member states have a delegation at the UN headquarters in New York. 124 permanent delegations service the UN Office in Geneva, which is also the headquarters of ILO, ITU, ITC, GATT, WIPO, WHO and WMO. In Paris seventy four permanent delegations are attached to the UNESCO headquarters.

32. Since 1986 UN organizations have been undergoing a critical phase, due to a large extent to United States criticisms and their withholding of part of their obligatory financial contributions to the organizations' budgets (see Ch. 3 below). An allied question is that of the respect and implementation by member states of resolutions and policies voted by them in the organizations' governing bodies. Some governments support the organizations' positions verbally while denying them financial support, or in ignoring their obligations and commitments. Dr Halfdan Mahler, Director-General of WHO, challenged the representatives of member states by asking, 'is WHO to be the Organization you have decided it should be, the Organisation that will

lead the people of this world to health for all by the year 2,000? ...Is it to be merely a congregation of romanticists talking big and acting small; or just another international group of middlemen, giving pocket money to ministries of health and keeping a percentage for its own survival?'

33. Recent technical books include Alain Plantey's *Droit et pratique de la fonction publique internationale*, Editions du CNRS, Paris, 1977, and Henry Reymond and Sidney Mailick, *International Personnel Policies and Practices*, Praeger, New York, 1985.

Chapter 1

The internationalist view of the international civil service

That the concept of an international civil service should be 'internationalist' appears tautological and obvious. However, the internationalist view was not shared by all when the Secretariat of the League of Nations was set up. Furthermore, as will be seen in Chapters 3 and 4, this view has been attacked in the past and is still challenged today.

In this chapter we will recall the steps which led to the creation of the international civil service, prior to the League of Nations—then the League rules and records—followed by the UN experience. We will try to identify the basic elements of the international civil service, the required obligations and standards of conducts and their justification, with a few references to relevant judgments of the administrative tribunals. Finally, we will point to some of the limitations of the idealistic, generous, internationalist concept.

Before the League of Nations

The origin of international secretariats dates back to the nineteenth century, in relation to international conferences and institutions.

International conferences

International political conferences and congresses held in Europe, the then political centre of the world, had secretariats during their sessions, directed by national diplomats. The secretariats were initially composed of national civil servants of the host country, while some became multinational.

A Prussian diplomat in the service of Austria assumed all the tasks of the secretariat of a multilateral diplomatic meeting at the 1814—15 Congress of Vienna. The secretary of the 1856 congress of Paris was a French diplomat, the secretaries of the London Conferences of 1867 and 1871 were British diplomats. The chief and members of the secretariat of the Congress of Berlin were all German, except for the assistance of one French diplomat. It was customary to entrust the secretariat of an International conference to the Foreign Affairs Ministry of the host country.

The multinational process began with the Hague Conference of 1899, when the president of the Conference, the Russian ambassador to London, appointed a Dutch secretary-general, a Russian assistant secretary-general and six secretaries chosen among Dutch, French and Belgian diplomats. The 1907 Conference extended the number of nationalities to nine.

The practice of appointing secretaries among diplomats of all participating countries was applied at the Bucharest Conference of 1913, at the Naval Conference of 1908-09 and the Conference of 1912-13 for the settlement of the Balkan problems.

The Peace Conference of 1919 confirmed the principle and practice of multinational secretariats: it was composed of one representative each from the United States, the British Empire, France, Italy and Japan.[1]

International institutions

Conferences and congresses are time-limited events: one of the key elements of the future international civil service, permanency, also occurred in the nineteenth century, mainly in Europe, but also in the Americas. Permanency and multinationality were then progressively combined and evolved towards the international secretariat.

Between 1865 and 1914, thirty-three intergovernmental and 182 non-governmental organizations were created.[2] Commissions were formed to regulate travel by river on the European continent: in 1804, the 'Convention de l'octroi' concluded between France and the German Empire created the first administration common to states bordering on the Rhine. Initially a centralized, supranational administration, the 'Central Commission for the Navigation of the Rhine' was later converted into a periodical diplomatic conference, with controlling, administrative, judicial and legislative functions.[3] In 1856 the European Commission of the Danube was created by the Treaty of Paris. The Commission was composed of representatives of Great Britain, France, Austria, Russia, Sardinia and the Ottoman Empire. Its staff was recruited from the administrations of member states. Their international character was recognized only in 1878: its officials were granted varying immunities and privileges, as the Commission had an extraterritorial status.[4]

International unions were the direct predecessors of the contemporary intergovernmental organization. In view of increasing trade exchanges and wider communications, nations felt the need for international regulations and cooperation in various economic, technical and social fields. Among these:

(1)   In the field of communications, the International Telegraph Union (renamed the International Telecommunications Union in 1934) was founded in 1865 and the Universal Postal Union in 1874: both are now specialized agencies of the UN.

(2)   In the cultural field, the International Union for the Protection of Intellectual Property and the Union for the Protection of Literary and Artistic Works were founded in 1883 and 1886; these were later integrated in the World Intellectual Property Organization, another UN specialized agency.

(3)   In the health field, the International Office of Health, created in 1907, was one of the predecessors of the World Health Organisation.

The staff of these international administrative unions was usually composed of civil servants loaned by the host country and sometimes by several member states; staff members were therefore all national civil servants on secondment to the union. For example, the staff of the Universal Postal Union (a small secretariat of up to forty-three persons) was administered by the Swiss Federal Council and had the status of Swiss civil servants. However, the staff gave evidence of exemplary impartiality in its action.[5] For seventy-three years, its personnel had no immunity or privileges; it acquired an international status only in 1947.

The International Institute of Agriculture, founded in 1905 in Rome the predecessor of the Food and Agriculture Organization of the United Nations (FAO), obtained an international status for itself and for its staff, independent from the member states; its staff, and the staff of the European Commission of the Danube, were the first international civil servants.

The Organization of American States (OAS) is the oldest regional society of nations in the world. It dates back to the first International Conference of American States, held in Washington, DC, which, on 14 April 1890, established the International Union of American Republics. When the UN was created the OAS joined it as a regional organization. Founded for economic purposes, it became a union with multiple aims, with an international secretariat in Washington.

The League of Nations

The slow transformation from national to multinational to international secretariats, finally matured into the latter concept with the League of Nations.

While the UN organizations' basic texts refer explicitly to the staff members' international obligations, the League Covenant makes no such reference. It refers to a 'permanent secretariat', comprised of a secretary-general and such secretaries and staff as may be required. The secretary-general is appointed by the Council with the approval of the majority of the Assembly. The secretaries and staff are appointed by the secretary-general with the approval of the Council. Officials of the League (presumably senior staff) when engaged in the business of the League enjoy diplomatic privileges and immunities. Secretariat positions are to be open equally to men and women.[6]

Lacking a clear mandate, the newly appointed secretary-general, Sir Eric Drummond, was facing a dilemma: should the secretarial work of the Assembly, the Council and the other League organs be entrusted to a staff composed of national delegations or was an international secretariat a realistic possibility?

The post of secretary-general had first been offered to Sir Maurice Hankey, who had been the first secretary of the British War Cabinet; he refused the post. Many observers[7] felt that Hankey would have appointed nine national secretaries with their own staff. The League secretariat would then have operated according to the traditional methods of international conferences with delegations representing national interests. It would also have followed the pattern of the successful inter-Allied war effort, also based on national representation, admittedly of only a few countries.

The French and the British then offered the post to the prestigious Greek politician Eleutherios Venizelos. The post would have been that of a chancellor with wide political powers, as a quasi-independent institution to be filled by an international statesman. When he refused, the nature of the post was modified and assimilated to that of the permanent and non-political under-secretary of a British government office.[8]

Sir Eric Drummond, a former British diplomat, boldly decided from the first 'to organize his staff as an international civil service, each official being supposed to act only on the instructions of the Secretary-General and in the interest of the League, without regard to the policy of his own government'.[9]

This was a quiet revolution, the passage from national, bilateral and multinational diplomacy to an internationalism embodied into a human and administrative structure.

This momentous individual decision was later confirmed by the League bodies. The 1920 Balfour Report identified the essential principles of an international civil service:

By the terms of the Treaty, the duty of selecting the staff falls upon the Secretary-General ... . In making his appointments, he has primarily to secure the best available men and women for the particular duties which have to be performed; but in doing so, it is necessary to have regard to the great importance of selecting the officials from various nations. Evidently, no one nation or group of nations ought to have a monopoly in providing the material for this international institution. I emphasize the word international, because the members of the Secretariat once appointed are no longer the servants of the country of which they are citizens, but become for the time being the servants only of the League of Nations. Their duties are not national, but international.[10]

These principles include (1) the prerogative of the head of the secretariat to select and appoint his staff, (2) the identification of competence as the first selection criterion, (3) as a complement, the need to recruit from various nations, (4) as a corollary, no staff monopoly or domination by any nation or group of nations, (5) the staff's allegiance to the organization, not to their country, (6) their international duties.

In 1921 the Noblemaire Report defined the principles of the secretariat's administrative and budgetary organization.[11] The report and the Fourth Committee expressed their high opinion for the work of the secretariat, the individual quality and high standard of culture of the staff, their unbounded faith in the great ideals of the League, their unremitting zeal and their unshaken confidence in its ultimate success. At the same time, they recommended that the secretariat should not extend the sphere of its activities, that in the preparation of the work and the decisions of the various organizations of the League, it should confine itself to collating the relevant documents, and the preparation of decisions without hazarding suggestions; finally, that once these decisions had been taken by the bodies solely responsible for them, it should confine itself to executing them in the letter and in the spirit, and should refrain as far as possible from interpreting them.

The concept of the international secretariat as a purely administrative, neutral organ, avoiding political judgements and actions, had been adopted by Drummond on the basis of his own experience of the British Civil Service. In the United Kingdom, as in other West European countries, political decisions are to be taken by the government and parliament, while the civil servant is the non-partisan administrator of these decisions. In fact, Drummond himself played a self-restraining role in public, while also playing a role behind the scenes, acting as a confidential channel of communication to governments engaged in controversy and dispute.[12]

The Noblemaire Report is better known for having formulated the so-called 'Noblemaire principle': the League officials' salaries can only be calculated on the basis of salaries granted to the highest-paid officials in the various member states of the League; otherwise, the League secretariat would be deprived of the services of civil servants of these countries, which would have been unacceptable. The British administration's salary scale was then chosen as the comparator, the scale to be supplemented by an expatriation factor. League emoluments would be exonerated from income taxation by member states.

Recruitment should be effected by competitive selection, on the basis of a review of the applications or by an examination. Candidates should be recruited, as much as possible, in a equitable proportion from the various member states. The Noblemaire Commission envisaged a mix between short-term and long-term contracts. High-level staff (secretary-general, assistant-secretaries-general, under-secretaries-general and directors) would be appointed for a maximum of seven years. Manual workers and low-level clerks would be employed locally according to local terms. Secretaries and other middle-level employees would be employed as international staff with long-term contracts (up to four seven-year contracts). Part of the senior personnel would be seconded by national administrations to the League for limited periods. However, most of this category of personnel would be recruited by the League for twenty-one years (three seven-year terms) with retirement at 55. Those provisions would afford sufficient security to enable the League's staff to devote themselves to their work without any anxiety as to their future, 'for only the hope of a definite career will attract them to the service of the League'.

The League had therefore opted for a mainly, but not exclusively, career service, with a relatively high level of remuneration. The career trend was reinforced by the creation in 1923 of a Pension and Retirement Fund with compulsory participation, and, in 1927, the institution of an Administrative Tribunal to hear complaints of officials against the League.[13]

The staff's international obligations were embodied in Article 1.1 of the

League's Staff Regulations of 1922: 'The officials of the Secretariat of the League of Nations are exclusive international officials and their duties are not national but international'. In 1932 the staff were required to pronounce and sign the following declaration:

I solemnly undertake to exercise in all loyalty, discretion and conscience the functions which have been entrusted to me as an official of the League of Nations, to discharge my functions and to regulate my conduct with the interests of the League alone in view and not to seek or receive instructions from any government or other authority external to the Secretariat of the League of Nations.[14]

In 1930 the Committee of the Thirteen confirmed the principles concerning the staff's international obligations and the duration of appointments.[15]

The League's experience

Notwithstanding the League's weaknesses, errors and failures as a peacekeeping organization, observers agree that the concept of an international civil service responsible only to the organization, as created and applied by the League, was workable and efficient.[16]

In 1919 Carl Hymans had asked, 'How can men and women of forty different nations work together beneath a single roof? It will be not only a Tower of Babel, but a Bedlam too'. Philip Noel-Baker testified at the last meeting of the League in July 1946 that, proud as he was of his British Civil Service, he could say with truth that 'in none of our departments did I find a higher standard of technical efficiency, a higher level of personal and official probity, a greater industry and devotion to their cause'.[17]

In 1930 the Committee of the Thirteen was of the opinion that, in the course of the first ten years, proof had been given over and over again that it is possible to reckon on the existence of a body of good international officials, loyal to the League and ready to discharge faithfully the obligation which they accepted on entering its service.[18]

Of course, all could not be hard-working, efficient, idealists.[19] The internationalist spirit and obligations of the staff were challenged mainly by the interference of authoritarian governments with the secretary-general's staffing prerogatives. Progressively, the international majority of the staff became aware that colleagues from non-democratic countries (Italy, Germany, Japan, Poland) served as agents of their governments within the secretariat and were loyal, not to the League, but to their own government.[20]

Critics of the League's secretariat have shown that the staff geographical distribution was not equitable: there was initially a strong European, mostly French and British, domination. In 1920 there were seven European staff members to one non-European. In 1938 this proportion improved slightly: five Europeans to one non-European.[21] Some progress also occurred in the proportion of senior officials, citizens of permanent member states of the League Council: the proportion decreased from 75 per cent in 1922 to

25 per cent in 1938.[22]

In spite of these tensions and shortcomings, and in spite of its modest size,[23] the League's secretariat experiment is generally considered to be a successful pioneering venture: it demonstrated that international administration is possible, and that it can be successful 'up to a certain point', even under particularly unfavourable conditions.[24]

The substantial administrative experience gained by the League assisted in the creation and running of the new UN organizations; in particular, a number of former League staff members were appointed to the UN organizations, which benefited from their experience.[25]

In the UN organizations

The Preparatory Commission of the UN affirmed that the UN secretariat could not be composed, even in part, of national representatives responsible to governments. For the duration of their appointments, the secretary-general and the staff will not be the servants of the state of which they are nationals, but the servants of the UN alone.[26]

In the same vein, the constitutions of the UN organizations assert the international nature of their secretariats, thus continuing the tradition established by the League and confirming the internationalist principle. In the words of the UN Charter, 'In the performance of their duties, the Secretary-General and the staff shall not seek or receive instructions from any government or from any other authority external to the Organization'. As a necessary innovation, the UN staff's obligation is linked to an obligation on the part of member states: 'Each Member of the UN undertakes to respect the exclusively international character of the responsibilities of the Secretary-General and the staff and not to seek to influence them in the discharge of their responsibilities'.[27]

These texts also make the head of the secretariat, appointed by the organization's governing body, responsible as chief administrative officer, for the appointment of all staff in the secretariat under regulations approved by the governing body:

> The paramount consideration in the employment of the staff and in the determination of the conditions of service shall be the necessity of securing the highest standard of efficiency, competence and integrity. Due regard shall be paid to the importance of recruiting the staff on as wide a geographical basis as possible.[28]

Integrity, a criterion which needs clarification,[29] was thus added to the 'efficiency and competence' as the primary requirements for UN employment. The 'geographical basis' is listed as a secondary, desirable requirement.

In 1946 the UN General Assembly approved the proposal of the Preparatory Commission that all new staff subscribe to an oath or declaration undertaking to discharge their functions and regulate their conduct with the interests of the UN only in view.[30] The Commission also supported the career concept and the unity of all the staff in the UN family of organizations.

Rules and standards

The Staff Regulations and Rules of the UN organizations give more explicit guidance as to how these general principles should be applied. Furthermore, the International Civil Service Advisory Board (ICSAB) reported in 1954 on standard of conduct expected of international staff.[31]

All staff are subject to the authority of the head of the secretariat and to assignment by him to any of the activities or offices of the organization. This refers to the normal hierarchical authority principle found in national administrations and private-sector organizations. For international organizations, the assignment of duties may involve, for professional and higher-category staff, the acceptance of mobility, that is transfer to different duty stations in different countries, 'in the interest of the Organization'. *In re* Verdrager the ILO Administrative Tribunal (ILOAT) sustained the decision of the WHO director-general to terminate the appointment of the defendent who had refused an instruction to be transferred to Bangladesh, for family and health reasons. The appellant had served the organization well for eighteen years and had been transferred many times during his career. The UN Administrative Tribunal has also ruled that staff members have an obligation to accept assignments to a specified duty station at a given time.[32]

Staff Regulations emphasize what international staff should *not* do: they should not engage in any activity incompatible with the proper discharge of their duties. They should avoid any action and in particular any public pronouncement which may adversely reflect on their status, or on their integrity, independence and impartiality. They should exercise reserve and tact concerning their religious and political convictions, and exercise the utmost discretion regarding all matters of official business. For instance, the arrival of a newly appointed ILO staff member in Chile gave rise to an incident reported to the press and followed by students' demonstrations: this had been caused by the individual's political activities in the country prior to his international employment. ILO then decided to transfer him to Geneva. The ILOAT supported the ILO's 'consistent policy whereby it avoids keeping on any staff member in any area where he has become a controversial figure, whatever the controversy may be, since the activities of international organizations can be effective only if their officials are above all suspicions. In another case submitted to the ILOAT, a UNESCO staff member was summarily dismissed for serious misconduct for having addressed written statements containing grave allegations against one of his colleagues, and indirectly against the organization itself, to bodies outside the organization, including governments. By accusing publicly his colleague of incompetence and subversion, he brought the international civil service into disrepute and acted contrary to the duty of discretion.[33]

International staff will not accept any honour, decoration, favour, gift or remuneration from any government, without the approval of the head of the secretariat.[34] The immunities and privileges granted to them by virtue of Article 105 of the UN Charter are only conferred in the interest of the organization in so far as they are necessary for the independent exercise of the staff's official functions.

The ICSAB Report defines several concepts.

Integrity includes such elementary personal or private qualities as honesty, truthfulness, fidelity, probity and freedom from corrupting influences. The international staff's private interests should be subordinated to those of the organization. Jonah defined integrity as 'implying such rectitude that one is incorruptible or incapable of being false to a trust, to a responsibility or to one's own standards'. Dishonest acts committed by international staff in their official functions or in their private life have usually been sanctioned by dismissal. For instance the ILOAT has sustained the following dismissal decisions: *In re* Amonfio, the appellant had repeatedly submitted medical and education grant claims supported by forged and falsified documentation, resulting in significant financial losses to WHO; *in re* Giannini, for embezzlement of the organization's and colleagues' funds; *in re* Karakalos, for embezzlement of his colleagues' monies, sanctioned by a conviction by a local tribunal.[35]

The international civil servant should be loyal to the objectives of the organization. Loyalty, in ICSAB's view, involves willingness to try to understand and be tolerant of different viewpoints, different cultural patterns and different work habits, willingness to work without prejudice or bias with persons of all nationalities, religions and cultures. What is essential is not the absence of personal, political or national views, but rather restraint at all times in the expression of such views.

Impartiality implies objectivity, lack of bias, tolerance, restraint—particularly when political or religious disputes or differences arise. The potential conflict between such international obligations as integrity, independence, impartiality and reserve, and an individual's moral conscience and dedication to human rights was brought to light in the van Boven affair. Van Boven, a Dutch citizen, had been appointed as director of the UN Human Rights Division in May 1977. His contract was not renewed in April 1982 because he had made public statements 'not wholly in keeping with his status as an international civil servant'. According to van Boven, there was a difference of views between the UN leadership and him. His role was, in his view, to defend the rights and freedoms of peoples and individuals, while the UN leadership and system were more concerned with maintaining friendly relations with all governments, including those with the most repressive regimes. Van Boven's high 'Human Rights' profile, which had antagonized, among others, the Soviet Union repressive Latin American countries, was clearly not compatible with the UN desirable standards of conduct. Van Boven is now an expert from the Netherlands in a UN Human Rights Sub-Commission.[36]

Social relations with colleagues of different races, religious and cultural backgrounds are desirable. Staff members should avoid any action which would impair good relations with governments or destroy confidence in the secretariat, such as public criticism or interference. *In re* Mojfeld, the ILOAT has affirmed that, as a result of unavoidable conflicts between international staff in the field and members of the counterpart staff of national authorities, a government may declare the international official *persona non grata*. In such a case there may be grounds for termination of the staff member's appointment, in view of the deterioration of his relations with the host government.[37]

Any direct or indirect activity to overthrow a government by force is one of the gravest forms of misconduct. It is inexcusable for a staff member to lobby with governmental representatives in order to secure support for improvements in his personal situation. International civil servants cannot be candidates for public office of a public character, nor can they support publicly a political party. They cannot belong to a political party which is illegal in the country of which they are citizens. No outside activity is permissible which would interfere with the international civil servant's work, or which is incompatible with his status.

In his private life the staff member should set himself a high standard of personal conduct. He should scrupulously comply with the laws of the host country and of his own country. The application of a temporary staff member of the Universal Postal Union for permanent appointment was rejected by the Union as he had defaulted on his obligations as a US citizen: he had refused to present himself when called up for military service, because this would have been 'inconvenient' to him and would have 'interrupted his literary career.'[38]

Personal attributes

To these exacting statutory standards, several former or acting staff members have added the following desirable characteristics. Ranshofen-Wertheimer has remarked that the denationalized cosmopolitans and globe-trotters are less qualified for international service than typical Frenchmen, Englishmen, Poles or Czechs.[39] Only the blending, in one person, of national characteristics with a belief in the necessity of the international work of the League enabled a person to serve with real usefulness within an organization, the task of which was to reconcile national aspirations with international action:

Jenks confirmed this view:

A lack of attachment to any one country does not constitute an international outlook. A superior indifference to the emotions and prejudices of those whose world is bounded by the frontiers of a single state does not constitute an international outlook. A blurred indistinctness of attitude toward all questions, proceeding from a freedom of prejudice born of lack of vitality, does not constitute an international outlook. The international outlook required of the international civil servant is an awareness made instinctive by habit of the needs, emotions and prejudices of the peoples of differently circumstanced countries, as they are felt and expressed by the peoples concerned, accompanied by a capacity for weighing these frequently imponderable elements in a judicial manner before reaching any decision to which they are relevant.[40]

For Loveday, 'Blind loyalty is not enough. The loyalty must spring from an understanding of and the belief in the ultimate value of the work and purposes of the institution'.[41] Dr Brock Chisholm, first director-general of the World Health Organisation, included among the ideal qualifications of an international civil servant a knowledge of history, semantics, the world's major religions and its local variations.[42] He should know something of the attitudes of the sociologist, something of social psychology and minor psychopathology. He should have some knowledge of law, political science and the art of teaching. For Chisholm, the personality of the international civil servant is immeasurably more important than advanced qualifications (although these are required for the job). He should have empathy, sympathy and fellow-feeling, but no rigid attitudes. He should have patience, persistence, humility and self-reliance. One of his objectives should be to enhance the prestige of local authorities and national government employees. He has to accept the particular culture in the country of his work or the mixed composite culture of his organization's headquarters. Missionary zeal in the sense of trying to convert people to a particular way of life is entirely out of place. We must recognize all cultures, including our own, as experimental.

Finally, Breycher-Vauthier adds to these many qualities and requirements a spirit of international understanding, dynamism, flexibility, negotiating skills, a sense of initiative, hard work and linguistic skills.[43]

Justification for the internationalist view

For the UN founders, the staff member's responsibilities are exclusively international. The international official should be loyal to the organization, competent, impartial and independent from governments. The staff, recruited on a wide geographical basis, should be mainly career officials. They should enjoy comfortable employment conditions as well as functional privileges and immunities. In brief, the international civil service is an élite corps at the service of the world community.

As noted by Barnes, the international civil service has traditionally been based on the conviction that it should protect the interests of all parts of the world community equitably and dispassionately, and the recognition that the staff itself should be insulated from partisan pressure by the assurance of secure, lifetime employment.[44]

Employment conditions are designed to allow the international official to be independent from his own government and any outside source for his subsistence and professional future. The recruitment and career system, the compensation and pension schemes should be able to attract and retain competent candidates from all countries. Internal disputes between staff members and the organization should be settled by independent international jurisdictions. Member states should respect the independence of the secretariat, the exclusive staffing prerogatives of its head as well as the ratified Conventions on Privileges and Immunities.

Besides this ideological argument, there is a technical justification for having a staff appointed by and reporting to the head of the secretariat, united in its loyalty to the international organization and its objectives, rather than having a cluster of national groups reporting to their own governments. The internationalist option conforms with the management principle that unity of command is beneficial to an organization: it avoids duplication, confusion, contradictions, deviations, loss of time and of resources. The 'national sections' option would create semi-autonomous groups with their own, possibly conflicting objectives which the secretariat head would be at pains to reconcile.

Finally, the internationalist concept corresponds to the historical evolution towards more international cooperation and, for the European Community, more integration. The international secretariats thus represent the visible hopes of a more united world, the materialization of the future world (or European) citizen.

Limitations

International civil servants are no more perfect than national civil servants or employees in the private sector. They have their foibles, their deficiencies, their ambitions, their frustrations. A staff member of a UN organization who feels that his merits have not been recognized, or whose contract is terminated, may, contrary to his oath, ask his government to intervene. A few may serve as overt or covert government agents, allowing their national obligations to prevail over their international allegiance.

Governments may be at fault in exacting obedience (forced or voluntary) from their citizens employed by an international organization. Under the guise of 'improving the geographic distribution' of the staff, some of them not only recommend or nominate candidates for employment, but they also insist on their placement in a specific post, at a specific grade. Some intervene more or less openly to facilitate contract extensions and promotions. Inversely, some demand that the executive head terminate the contract of their citizens considered disloyal or unrepresentative.

Government pressures and attacks on the international status of UN organizations' staff have come mainly, but not exclusively, from the United States and from the socialist countries. They will be described in Chapters 3 and 4.

In Chapter 2 we will recall the exemplary experience of the second secretary-general of the UN, Dag Hammarsjkold, a man fully devoted to internationalism in action and in words, the paragon of the international civil servant. Brief references will also be made to other secretariat heads.

Notes

1. Jean Siotis, *Essai sur le secrétariat international*, Librairie Droz, Geneva, 1963, pp. 23-31.
2. See F.S.L. Lyons, *Internationalism in Europe, 1815-1914*, Leyden, Sythoff, 1963, quoted by Thomas George Weiss in *International Bureaucracy*, Lexington Books, Lexington, Mass., 1975, p. 44 note 10.
3. Communication of Mr Doerflinger to the Colloque of the Société Française pour le Droit International in Strasbourg, 21-3 May 1987: 'La Commission centrale pour la navigation du Rhin'.
4. Siotis, pp. 33-8.
5. George Langrod, pp. 35-41. The same comment could be applied now to the staff of the International Committee of the Red Cross, aSwiss (International) organization composed of Swiss citizens.
6. Covenant of the League of Nations, Art. 2, 6 and 7.
7. Weiss, p. 35 and p. 44, note 12.
8. Siotis, p. 63,
9. Egon F. Ranshofen-Wertheimer, 'International Administration: Lessons from the Experience of the League of Nations', *American Political Science Review*, vol. 37, 1943, p. 874.
10. League of Nations *Official Journal*, June 1920, p. 137.
11. From the name of the president of the Commission of Experts, M. Georges Noblemaire, France. See 'Report Submitted by the Fourth Committee to the Assembly on the Conclusions and Proposals of the Commission of Experts', 26 September 1921, Doc. A.14(0). The report was adopted by the Assembly on 1 October 1921.
12. Dag Hammarskjold, 'The International Civil Servant in Law and in Fact', Oxford Lecture, 30 May 1961, Clarendon Press, Oxford, pp. 5-7.
13. Langrod, p. 116.
14. Articles 1 and 3.1 of the Staff Regulations of the Secretariat of the League of Nations, 1945.
15. League Doc. A.16.1930.
16. Weiss, p. 38, Hammarskjold, p. 7.
17. David Owen 'Reflections of an International Civil Servant', *Public Administration Review*, no. 3, May-June 1970, pp. 209-10.
18. League Doc. A.16.1930, p. 9.
19. See *Belle du Seigneur*, a novel by Albert Cohen, Gallimard, Paris, 1968, for an inside story of an ambitious, but less than zealous, League official and a critical description of the Geneva international bureaucracy.
20. Ranshofen-Wertheimer, pp. 882-5.
21. Siotis, p. 119-20. Siotis also notes that (a) during its five years of membership, the Soviet Union only had one staff member in the League, an under-secretary-general, (b) in 1930 Germany had ten staff members, while Switzerland had nine and the Netherlands seven, (c) from 1920 to 1938 the number of member states increased from thirty-eight to fifty-four, and the number of nationalities of staff from fifteen to forty-three.
22. Langrod, p. 133.
23. The League secretariat numbered 659 staff members in 1930; its maximum size was 706. The ILO had a maximum of 425 staff members in 1939. See Langrod, pp. 137 and 149.
24. Ranshofen-Wertheimer, p. 886.
25. For instance, Adrien Pelt and Thanassis Aghnides, two former senior League

officials, presided on committees of the UN Preparatory Commission, which met in London in 1945 (Langrod, p. 169). Many others were recruited by the new UN organizations.

26. Quoted by Adrien Pelt in 'Peculiar Characteristics of an International Administration', *Public Administration Review*, vol. VI, spring 1946, p. 110.

27. Art 100.1 and 100.2 of the UN Charter. A similar wording is found, for instance in Art. 37 of the WHO Constitution.

28. Arts. 97 and 101.1 and 101.3 of the UN Charter.

29. See below. 'Integrity' was a controversial issue during the McCarthy investigations in the UN secretariats; see Ch. 3.

30. UN Staff Regulation 1.9. See UN General Assembly Resolution 13(I) of 13 February 1946.

31. The Staff Regulations and Rules of the UN are in the UN Doc. ST/SGB/Staff Rules/1/Rev.6, Geneva, 1984. ICSAB was created by UN General Assembly Resolution 13(I) on 13 February 1946: ICSAB reported to the Administrative Committee on Coordination. It was replaced in 1975 by the International Civil Service Commission. Its 'Report on Standards of Conduct in the International Civil Service' of 1954 (Doc. COORD/Civil Service/5) was reissued in January 1982.

32. See ILOAT Judgment No. 325 and UNAT Judgments Nos. 92, 165 and 241.

33. See ILOAT Judgments Nos. 154 and 63.

34. See UN Staff Regulation 1.4, 1.5 and 1.6.

35. See Jonah's article on 'Independence and Integrity of the International Civil Service: The Role of Executive Heads and the Role of States', in *New York University Journal of International Law and Politics*, vol. 14, no. 4, Summer 1982, The Meller Conference on the International Civil Service, p. 849. See ILOAT Judgments Nos. 539, 79 and 513.

36. See *UN Special*, Geneva, March 1982.

37. See ILOAT Judgment No. 260.

38. See ILOAT Judgments Nos. 122 and 135.

39. Ranshofen-Wertheimer, p. 878.

40. C. Wilfred Jenks, 'Some Problems of an International Service', *Public Administration Review*, spring 1943, p. 95.

41. Alexander Loveday, *Reflexions on International Administration*, Clarendon Press, Oxford, 1956, p. 32.

42. WHO Doc. 'Working for WHO', WHO, Geneva, pp. 9-13.

43. A.C. Breycha-Vauthier, *Le Fonctionnaire international*, La Diplomatie contemporaine, Graz, 1959, pp. 276-7.

44. Roger Barnes, 'Tenure and Independence in the UN International Civil Service', *New York University Journal of International Law and Politics*, vol. 14, no. 4, summer 1982, p. 767.

Chapter 2

The archetype of the international civil servant: Dag Hammarskjold

The precarious and lonely role of the Secretary-General[1]

For many long-serving staff members and retirees of UN organizations, the name of Dag Hammarskjold remains as a symbol of internationalism—the little-known Swedish fonctionnaire, proposed by the United Kingdom and France for his administrative and diplomatic (rather than political) skills, raised to the stature of an influential international diplomat in a period when the UN was in the news. His support for decolonization and non-alignment aroused the hostility of both East and West. His accidental death in Zaire reinforced the myth of the independent, but lonely, international middleman, dedicated to peace, supporter of small nations, whose fragile power of influence failed when faced with the major states' real power and interests, and the realities of national and international politics.

The secretary-general of the UN is of course not a typical international civil servant: secretaries and clerks in a UNICEF field office, WHO nurses in Nepal, FAO agronomists in Egypt, IAEA inspectors, UN accountants, ICAO or WMO specialists or bureaucrats and thousands of others are fulfilling less exalted but necessary functions. Most of the organizations' staff have no influence over international politics, no contact with representatives of member states on political issues. Their role is either internal to the secretariat or their relations with nationals are, in principle, limited to administrative, financial and technical matters, although these may have political connotations. Their international obligations are rarely at risk, their own government or other governments have no intention or interest in trying to seduce or intimidate them into betraying their international allegiance.

Threats and risks are only present at the higher levels of the secretariats (secretaries-general, directors-general and their direct assistants), or in some exposed positions such as chiefs of personnel, directors of administration, legal advisers and organizations' representatives in countries. In most UN organizations, most powers are centralized in the hands of the secretariat head himself, the visible figurehead of his organization, a target of honours, pressures and criticisms.

In most national bureaucracies, bureaucrats remain (and want to be) anonymous. Only the changing ministers acquire and lose fame, as accountable elected politicians.

Heads of UN secretariats are selected and elected by member countries, their political constituency on which they depend for re-election. Many start as technicians (the education specialist in UNESCO, the medical doctor in WHO) or as career diplomats, and acquire progressively the skills required for their new job. They also discover the limitations, the political, technical and human constraints of their role.

An executive head has some power within his organization as chief administrative officer: he prepares the organization's programme and budget, appoints his staff, directs and controls the activities of the secretariat, allocates funds, approves or rejects claims. Externally, in the arena of world politics, he may have influence but no real power. He may have influence as a moral voice, or as expressing a majority view (at the risk of being censured by the minority), or because he is well informed, being at the centre of diplomatic exchanges, or because he is able to facilitate contacts between leaders who wield real power.

The former ILO director-general, David A. Morse, has noted that, when it comes to exercising influence, there are differences between the UN and an organization like ILO.[2] In Morse's experience it was possible to change an organization almost exclusively concerned with international standards into one which was mainly operational, to introduce extensive manpower activities and to launch a World Employment Programme. Such strong executive leadership and initiatives would, however, be less acceptable in the UN, where governments are more directly concerned with the political issues and less likely to leave the initiative to the secretary-general.[3]

The secretary-general of the UN is in a unique, visible and exposed position. What he makes of that position depends on his own skills, temperament, competence and hard work, on the world's political climate, the attitude of member states (particularly those of the major powers), political opportunities and luck. As the most senior and politically visible and exposed staff member of all the UN organizations (although he is not the chief of the executive heads of the specialized agencies), he can be used as a standard and as a model. Dag Hammarskjold has been cast in that role.

We will first recall the reasons for Hammarskjold's lasting reputation, and then refer briefly to other past and present heads of UN secretariats.

Dag Hammarskjold's deeds

On 7 April 1953 the UN General Assembly approved the Security Council's recommendation to appoint Hammarskjold as its second secretary-general. On 17 September 1961 he died in an accidental plane crash on his way to meet with the secessionist Tschombé at Ndola in Northern Rhodesia, to negotiate a ceasefire between UN forces and the mercenaries-led Katanga forces.[4]

Hammarskjold's experience as a Swedish civil servant was initially in the economic and financial fields, then in foreign affairs, to which was added exposure to European and UN cooperation. In 1930 he was appointed a secretary of the Royal Commission on Unemployment; in 1936, at age 31 he was appointed under-secretary in the Ministry of Finance, the youngest to hold so high an office in Sweden. From 1941 to 1945 he served also as chairman of the Board of Governors of the Bank of Sweden. From 1945 to 1947 he was appointed as under-secretary in the Foreign Office; in 1949 secretary-general and in 1951 vice-minister of Foreign Affairs with cabinet status. From 1947 he was Sweden's representative to the Organization for European Economic Cooperation (the predecessor to the present Organization for Economic Cooperation and Development), a member of the OEEC Executive Committee and a delegate to the new Council of Europe. In 1952 he served with the Swedish delegation to the UN.

A brilliant intellect, the successful public administrator was also a shy and lonely man, deeply religious if not mystical, totally devoted to his work and intellectual and artistic interests. He loved and practised literature and poetry, and enjoyed modern art and nature.

Hammarskjold's nomination as secretary-general was formally proposed by France, seconded by the United Kingdom,[5] without objections from the United States and the Soviet Union. The choice of a quiet economic technician from neutral Sweden was acceptable to all, as a replacement for the flamboyant and fallen Trygve Lie: the preferred choice was for a secretary-general who would concentrate on administrative problems, avoid public involvement in political questions and who would not seek to develop the political importance of his office, nor of the UN. These expectations were later disproved by the new incumbent of the 'most impossible job on this earth', in the words of his predecessor.

Any secretary-general of the UN has dual responsibilities: he is its chief administrative officer (Art. 97 of the Charter) and thus accountable for the effective functioning of the institution, its financing, staffing and general administration, including the management of peacekeeping operations. He is also an international diplomat, secretary to the General Assembly, the Security Council, the Economic and Social Council and the Trusteeship Council, a central agent in multilateral relations, a sometimes negotiator and mediator. Hammarskjold was both an administrator and an international politician, although for him and for his predecessor and successors, the latter tasks took precedence over the former under the pressure of international crises. He was also an ideologist of international cooperation and of the international civil service.[6]

Hammarskjold inherited from Trygve Lie's period the secretariat's unrest caused by the American interference in staffing matters linked to the McCarthy loyalty investigations (see Ch. 3). The anxiety of the international staff was allayed by the decisive and skilful diplomatic action of Hammarskjold and of a few heads of specialized agencies. The staff's confidence was restored when the fundamental principles of the independence of the international civil service were firmly upheld by the Administrative Tribunal of the UN and by the International Court of Justice.[7] Characteristically he had taken an equally tough line with the US government and with the UN staff. The members of the secretariat had a right to protection as international civil servants, but they also had an obligation to deserve that right by their integrity and conduct. As noted by Urquhart,[8] some of Hammarskjold's decisions reflecting this point of view were far from popular with the UN staff until they realized that only this uncompromising approach would in the end enhance their status.

In order to stabilize and rationalize the organization's personnel management, Hammarskjold undertook various reforms. The staff regulations were revised and staff rules drafted: one objective of this revision was related to the US pressures to terminate the appointments of UN staff members, US citizens, accused of disloyalty towards their country. The revision attempted to find a compromise between the staff's legitimate desire for security of tenure, the organization's need to be able to terminate an appointment for reasons defined in the regulations and the legal requirements of due process. Various measures concerning the UN Pension Fund, salaries and leave conditions were adopted and applied to the staff of all the UN organizations. Permanent appointments (89 per cent in 1956) gradually replaced temporary appointments.[9] Advisory bodies with staff participation were set up to advise the secretary-general on appointments, promotions and regrading. The International Civil Service Advisory Board (ICSAB) prepared in 1954, while the secretariat crisis was at its height, a 'Report on Standards of Conduct in the International Civil Service', an ethical code and a detailed guide to behaviour. As a protective and prescriptive device also related to the US pressures, the report defined basic standards of integrity, loyalty, independence and impartiality (see Ch. 1). Internal structures were reorganized,[10] there was a gradual improvement of recruitment methods and procedures, including geographical distribution.

However, neither internal administrative reforms nor the improvement of staff morale would have been sufficient to transcend the secretary-general from a cautious non-political bureaucrat into an acclaimed, and then contested, international statesman: only his treatment of international crises achieved this result.

Hammarskjold's political action

Hammarskjold's position in the Guatemala affair strained his initial relationship with the United States. In June 1954 the regime of President Jacobo Arbenz Guzman, in power in Guatemala since 1951, was overthrown by a coup supported by the United States and the Central Intelligence Agency (CIA), and replaced by a dictatorial regime. Before Arbenz's fall, Guatemala asked the Security Council to consider its complaint that it was being invaded by troops from Nicaragua. The United States ambassador Henry Cabot Lodge claimed that under Article 52 of the UN Charter the complaint could not be considered by the Security Council because the Organization of American States (OAS) had primary responsibility for threats to the peace in the Western hemisphere and that the United States would never have signed the UN Charter if this understanding had not been accepted.[11] Although the Security Council decided in favour of the United States' position, Hammarskjold expressed his disapproval in a statement on the relative jurisdictions of the UN and regional organizations, gave to Lodge a legal study of the position and stated in the introduction to the 1954 report that the right of a member nation to a hearing under the Charter should be fully preserved. Latin American states involved directly or indirectly in disputes with the United States tend to prefer the global forum while the latter presses for action in the OAS, a forum which it dominated with less difficulty than the world organization.[12] This episode showed that Hammerskjold placed more importance on principles than on opportunism, at the risk of jeopardizing his position vis-a-vis one of the two major powers.

In 1955 Hammarskjold obtained the release of fifteen American pilots who had manned UN planes in Korea, were detained in China and condemned to long prison terms as spies. Faced with congressional pressures for military retaliation, the Eisenhower administration decided to use the UN as an instrument for negotiation. At the American initiative, a General Assembly resolution (A/L 182, 7 December 1954) had requested the secretary-general to seek the release of all captured UN personnel 'by the means most appropriate in his judgement'. Hammarskjold based his mandate on the general authority provided by the Charter to the Office of the UN Secretary, rather than, more narrowly, on the Assembly resolution, thus providing himself with more discretion (the 'Peking Formula').

Hammarskjold's success, after taking great risks, restored his position in relation to the United States and demonstrated to the international community the potential capacity of the Office of the UN Secretary-General to act as an effective, neutral and independent international mediator. It also revealed to the world the exceptional diplomatic talents of the relatively unknown Swedish civil servant who had come to occupy this office.[13] No doubt Kurt Waldheim's rating as secretary-general (leaving aside the current criticisms against him) would be higher if his efforts to obtain the release of the American hostages held in Teheran in 1980 had borne fruit.[14]

In 1948, following the creation of the state of Israel, the UN had appointed a mediator to help promote a peaceful adjustment of the situation in Palestine and set up a Group of Military Observers (the UN Truce Supervision Organization, UNTSO) to supervise the truce.

Hammarskjold's greatest achievement is to have expanded the UN role in peacekeeping through the creation, organization and deployment of peacekeeping forces in Egypt in 1956 and in the ex-Belgian Congo in 1960-4. He then took much bigger risks for the UN and for himself than in the China case.

Following President Nasser's nationalization of the Suez Canal Company in July 1956, Israel, France and the United Kingdom intervened militarily against Egypt. The UN General Assembly called for a ceasefire and withdrawal of the invading forces. The Canadian representative, Lester B. Pearson, proposed the establishment of a truly international peacekeeping force to serve as a buffer between the contending parties, while a political settlement was being worked out. This provided a face-saving device for the British and French withdrawals while preventing the Soviet Union from gaining a foothold in the Middle East. Convinced by Pearson, Hammarskjold proposed the creation of the UN Emergency Force (UNEF), providing that none of its officers or troops would be nationals of the great powers. The General Assembly approved the plan and delegated to Hammarskjold discretionary power to organize and administer the force. The force would exert a supervision based on the voluntary compliance of the ceasefire resolution by the parties themselves; it would be more than an observers' corps but in no way a military force temporarily controlling the territory in which it was stationed.

Hammarskjold had thus turned the UN from the impossible concept of collective security towards the notion of a third-party, neutral intermediary which could serve as a buffer keeping hostile states apart while simultaneously ensuring that greater power intervention did not create a threat of world war.[15]

Although the British, French and Israeli interventions were stopped more by the American and Soviet pressures on the invaders than by the UN, the UN resolutions and peacekeeping intervention did not endear the organization nor its secretary-general to the Israeli, British and particularly the French governments and public opinion. On the other hand, emancipated colonies of the Third World applauded.

The UN was only a critical observer of the Hungarian uprising of 1956: the Security Council was blocked by the Russian veto, and the General Assembly could only condemn the Russian intervention. There is no role for the UN in a crisis occurring within the empire or zone of influence of one of the superpowers and when the latter's vital interests are at stake.

Hammarskjold's action in the 1958 Lebanon crisis confirmed that the UN and its dynamic secretary-general could play an effective role in a sensitive region as a focal point for a search of reasonable compromises, as a neutral third-party independent from the big powers, and as the protector of newly independent countries, able to isolate areas from the East-West ideological conflict. Hammarskjold was instrumental in setting up promptly the UN Observation Group in Lebanon (UNOGIL), formed of personnel of countries not involved in the crisis.

In 1959 Moscow became irritated with Hammarskjold's independent initiatives to encourage the neutralization of Laos, then torn between the United States' support for its government, and Soviet, Chinese and North Vietnamese support for the Pathet Lao movement. For the Soviet Union, the secretary-general could not be allowed to act without the positive backing of the great powers as expressed by Security Council's authorization.

In June 1960 the independence of the Belgian Congo brought a dramatic challenge to the UN, called upon to provide military and civilian assistance to the new country, unprepared for self-government, in a state of civil war. This was a formidable task and an almost impossible challenge, under the conflicting external interventions of the former colonial power, Belgium, wanting to maintain political and economic influence for itself, an American policy of working through the UN in order to maintain a Western-orientated government in Léopoldville (now Kinshasa); De Gaulle's scorn for the stateless 'Machin' and its insolent interference in the domaine of sovereign countries; traditional British coolness towards an independent UN initiative and its rejection of the use of military force by the UN; Soviet efforts to gain political access and influence in Central Africa; the Third World countries' goal of restoring the unity of the country and of protecting it against outside interference.

Technically, this was the UN's most impressive operation: in less than forty-eight hours after the Security Council resolution, contingents of a UN force (Opération des Nations Unies au Congo, ONUC) provided by Asian, African and European states arrived in the Congo. At the same time the UN and the specialized agencies rushed civilian experts to the Congo to help ensure the continued operation of essential public services. The maximum strength of the UN force totalled nearly 20,000 officers and men. The UN civilian aid programme employed some 2,000 experts at its peak in 1963-4. The creation, transport, maintenance and supervision of both the military and civilian forces, under the ultimate but distant and sometimes uncertain overview of the Security Council, remained as the direct and immediate responsibility of the secretary-general and of his assistants.

While the military force was not to intervene in internal Congolese politics, its presence and action in fact caused or allowed the political defeat of the Soviet-supported Premier Lumumba (and his later assassination) and the seizure of power by the pro-Western Kasavubu and Mobutu. Hammarskjold's insistence on a peaceful resolution of the secession of Katanga was an additional bone of contention for the Soviet Union. At the same time the UN was criticized in many Western states, particularly in the United Kingdom, for using military force in an unsuccessful attempt, in September 1961, to end the Tschombé-led secession. A year before, Nikita Khrushchev had taken Hammarskjold to task and proposed the setting-up of a 'troika', a tripartite secretary-generalship representing East, West and the Third World, to replace the potentially biased single secretary-general. In February 1961, when learning of the death of Lumumba, the Soviet Union withdrew its recognition from Hammarskjold, labelling him 'an accomplice and organizer of the murder' of the ex-premier.[16]

Hammarskjold died in a plane crash on 17 September 1961 on official duty.

In spite of the conflicting pressures and the break of the Soviet Union with the secretary-general, by 1964, the UN's main objectives had been reached in the Congo: interventions by the big or medium powers had been stopped or avoided; the civil war had ended; the Cold War had not extended to the area. These results were due to a large extent to the personal action of Hammarskjold.

Hammarskjold's views

Hammarskjold was a man of action, a political leader and a risk-taker. He was also a theoretician of the role of the universal international organization and of its staff.

As his League predecessor, Drummond, he developed the notion of 'quiet diplomacy': the critical work of diplomacy had to be done quietly, and the UN could be used as a structure for discreet international negotiations. Furthermore, the effectiveness of the secretary-general's action, in a good-offices or mediation role, depends on his discretion. In Walter Lippman's words, Hammarskjold conducted this quiet diplomacy with 'a finesse and courtliness in the great traditions of Europe', although 'never before and perhaps never again has any man used the intense art of diplomacy for such unconventional and novel experiments'.[17]

Hammarskjold is credited with the notion and practice of preventive diplomacy. His aim was to use the UN in order to eliminate, reduce or limit local conflicts, by preventing both a power vacuum and the consequent intervention by big powers, thus keeping such areas out of the Cold War. The UN should protect the independence and rights of small nations. The UN presence necessitated an activist role for the organization, including the innovative use of military forces, not to make war, but to make peace.

The UN activist, interventionist, role could only be justified if the organization and its servants remained 'wholly uninfluenced by national or group interests of ideologies'.[18] In spite of his desired neutrality, the secretary-general could be entrusted by the Organization's bodies with tasks that have required him to take action which unavoidably may have to run counter to the views of at least some of the member states.[19] In the absence of clear instructions, the secretary-general may have to solve a problem on his own and at his own risk. For Hammarskjold, 'it is possible for the secretary-general to carry out his tasks in controversial political situations with full regard to his exclusively international obligation under the Charter and without subservience to a particular national or ideological attitude',[20] contrary to Khrushchev's assertion. To this end, the political judgement of the secretary-general should be guided and assisted by the UN Charter and resolutions, international law, consultations with permanent missions and guidance from advisory committees; additionally, his personal judgement needs to be based on integrity, self-analysis and conscience.[21]

Hammarskjold has stressed the need for a strong UN chief executive, with a right to initiate autonomous action even without the guidance of the Security Council or the Assembly if such a course were essential for the maintenance of peace and security. A choice had to be made between two concepts of the UN:

> Certain Members conceive of the Organization as a *static* conference machinery for resolving conflicts of interests and ideologies with a view to peaceful coexistence within the Charter...; other Members have made it clear that they conceive of the Organization primarily as a *dynamic*

instrument of government through which they, jointly and for the same purpose, should seek reconciliation, but through which they should also try to develop forms of executive action undertaken on behalf of all Members, and aiming at forestalling conflicts and resolving them, once they have arisen, by appropriate diplomatic or political means, in a spirit of objectivity and in implementation of the principles and purposes of the Charter.[22]

Hammarskjold's hopes for a dynamic role for the UN, after initial successes were frustrated: they met the limits imposed by the powers of the main states. Still, his contributions to multilateral politics and international organization, his imaginative use of peace-building and peacekeeping devices, his quiet, preventive diplomacy, his advocacy of a neutral and dynamic international civil service, his idealism controlled by realism, his moral and physical courage, his intellect and competence, his integrity, make him an unforgettable example and a beacon for those who believe in the necessary progress of international cooperation.

Hammarskjold was a man of the 'next generation'.[23]

Other secretaries-general

Singling out Hammarskjold as the paragon of international civil servants may appear somewhat unfair to the other secretaries-general of the League of Nations and of the UN. The justification for this selection has been made in terms of the personal qualitites of Hammarskjold, his competence and diplomatic skills, his international activism, his visibility, his successes, his ability to formulate and promote his claims for the UN's neutral but active role in peace and security matters and in assistance to developing countries. Of course, these talents could only be exercised in a particular set of political circumstances, in a particular historical period, with the support of, or lack of strong opposition on the part of, the major powers. Other secretaries-general did not always enjoy similar conditions: some did not possess the necessary personal talents to enable them to exploit unfavourable circumstances to the benefit and advantage of the UN, and of peace.

Most other secretaries-general have adopted a neutral internationalist stance, have generally been competent and tried to promote the organization's role. The international reputation of a few has suffered from actions or revelations which occurred after their international tenure. Hammarskjold's successors were not allowed or not able to assume an effective and visible role in international politics, on account, in part, of the lack of agreement of the big powers on political issues and of their unpublicized agreement to restrain the field of activities of the universal organization.

The League's secretaries-general

The first secretary-general of the first global organization, Sir Eric

Drummond[24] remained true to the tradition of the British Civil Service, as a discreet but efficient administrator. He is rightly credited with having established the foundations and defined the principles of the international civil service. The creator of 'quiet' multilateral diplomacy, later adopted by Hammarskjold and his successors, Drummond enjoyed considerable political prestige on account of his competence, his discretion in his consultations with national delegates, his imagination in formulating porposals to contending parties. He invented a political role for the secretary-general. A former member of the British Foreign Office, Drummond was later accused of having kept too close relations with his former ministry for an international civil servant.[25] It was also somewhat unfortunate that Drummond served his country as ambassador to Rome from 1933 to 1939, when Great Britain was trying to convince Mussolini that she would not insist on the economic sanctions decided upon by the League. This was a complete reversal of role and loyalty which tended to erode the concept of an independent international civil servant and the obligations of international staff (even after cessation of the international employment), a concept to which Drummond had personally and effectively contributed. It also reflects unfavourably on Drummond's reputation and otherwise distinguished achievements as the League's first secretary-general.

The French Joseph Avenol succeeded Drummond.[26] An ultra-conservative, he kept close links with the Quai d'Orsay and the high French administration during his League appointment. He supported the appeasement strategy of the French and British governments, to the point of refusing support to the League sanctions against Italy. His sympathies leaned more towards the dictatorships' 'New Order' than towards the democracies.[27] His unindustrious nature, lack of political competence and his partiality contrasted with Drummond's strengths: they decreased the moral authority of the Secretary-General's Office. In July 1940 he offered his resignation as secretary-general of an international organization to the chief of the French state, Marshall Philippe Pétain. He was thus subordinating his position to the interests and authority of his own country, in total ignorance of, or in contempt for, the principles of an international secretariat.[28] As stated by Barros,[29] Avenol will be defended by no one.

The other UN Secretaries-General

The first secretary-general of the UN, Trygve Lie, was a Norwegian Social-Democrat politician and a labour lawyer.[30] He was Minister of Foreign Affairs from 1941 to 1945. Anti-fascist and anti-Nazi during the Second World War, he was also anti-communist. In contrast with Drummond's and Hammarskjold's reserved personalities, he was truculent and outspoken. Elected through an agreement between the United States and the Soviet Union, he initially tried to follow a line of action not in opposition with the political line of the two superpowers. He regarded himself as 'a spokesman for a world interest overriding any national interest in the councils of nations'.[31] However, Lie irritated the United States by supporting the Soviet stand for Communist China's representation in the UN. By giving vigorous support to the UN-sponsored United States military intervention to counter the North Korean aggression, he antagonized the Soviet Union, who vetoed the renewal of his appointment. His mediation efforts had been more successful in the Palestine question (through the UN mediators Count Folke Bernadotte and Ralph Bunche) than in the Berlin blockage crisis. His personal, unnegotiated initiative for a twenty-year peace programme was received coldly by the leaders of Western countries and by the Soviet Union.

His attitude with regard to the US pressures on the UN secretariat during the McCarthy era, was seen to be detrimental to the independence of the international staff. It created a serious malaise in the secretariat.

On the positive side, Lie can be credited for the initial building-up of the organization and of its secretariat. By expressing his political views in strong terms, he legitimized the political functions of the Secretary-General's Office. He emphasized the need for an active programme of technical assistance for economic development, the expansion of world trade, vigorous UN work on human rights and peaceful decolonization. However, the Korean War and the McCarthy episode had made him almost totally ineffective.[32]

Following the tenure of two European secretaries-general, the appointment of the Burmese U Thant[33] was symbolic of the evolution of a UN dominated by the West to a UN where the Third World concerns for economic and social development, neutralism and anti-colonialism would be strongly expressed. A diplomat and a Buddhist. Thant was a mild-mannered and soft-spoken pragmatist whose base of influence was mainly the neutralist countries of Africa and Asia. In 1962 he assisted the negotiations between the Netherlands and Indonesia, which resulted in the temporary administration of West New Guinea by the UN prior to its transfer to Indonesia. His role in the Cuban missiles crisis, although modest, served as a face-saving device for the Soviet Union tactical retreat. Both Kennedy and Khrushchev thanked him for his efforts. In the midst of intense conflicting pressures from East and West, Katanga's secession was ended by UN forces in 1963. Also in 1963, Thant served as a fact-finder and arbitrator in the dispute involving Indonesia, the Philippines and Malaya; his report facilitated the creation of the Malaysian Federation. He established a peacekeeping force in Cyprus in 1964 as a buffer between Greek and Turkish Cypriots. In May 1967 the UN Emergency Force (UNEF) was withdrawn by Thant from the Middle East at Nasser's request, which was followed by a new outbreak of Arab-Israeli warfare. The withdrawal decision was perceived as a stunning reverse for the UN peacekeeping role and capacities, and caused severe criticism of Thant's action. He played a useful, insistent, if not conclusive, role as a messenger and active agent in trying to bring peace to Vietnam. The Soviet Union and France's insistence on maintaining Security Council control over peacekeeping activities limited Thant's, and even more his successors', area of independent political initiatives and activities.[34]However, in spite of the UNEF withdrawal fiasco and without Hammarskjold's charisma, Thant has been an activist secretary-general committed to a stronger role for his office, who obtained results without antagonizing the two Big Powers.

Kurt Waldheim also had a diplomatic background. He had been Minister of Foreign Affairs of Austria in 1968—70.[35] Like his predecessor, he practised quiet diplomacy, which some have considered too quiet. On the Security Council's instructions, a second UNEF was created and dispatched swiftly to the Middle East in 1973 to seperate Egyptian, Syrian and Israeli forces.[36] Waldheim offered his good offices repeatedly to the Greek and Turkish Cypriots in unsuccessful attempts to resolve the continuing dispute. His mission to Iran in 1980 to try to obtain the release of the American hostages failed. The UN was impotent in the face of the Soviet intervention in Afghanistan in December 1979, and to prevent or stop the Iran—Iraq War started in September 1980. Waldheim helped repair a diplomatic break between France and Guinea. He helped India and Bangladesh resolve a dispute over the Ganges river, and he helped Bangladesh and Burma solve a crisis over refugees. He organized relief operations in Bangladesh and Cambodia. One of his close assistants, Brian Urquhart said that 'in terms of usefulness, not glamour, he's actually been the best Secretary-General'.[37]

In his memoirs, Waldheim referred to the 'Tarnished Image' of the organization. Unfortunately, his own image was tarnished after his UN tenure. Following a succession of press revelations and admissions on his part, it was shown that he had hidden his presence as an officer in the German Wehrmacht in 1942 in Yugoslavia and in Greece.[38]

Javier Perez de Cuellar took over in 1982 from Waldheim, who was reluctant to leave. A former diplomat from Peru, former chairman of the Group of 77, he had the reputation of being as cautious as Waldheim. He was re-elected for a second term in 1987. It is premature to attempt any assessment of his role. While his own 'quiet diplomacy' has been active, he has not been able, yet, to achieve nor record any progress in the priority issues he listed when he was first appointed: Afghanistan, the Middle East, Iran-Iraq and Namibia,[39] to which Cyprus could be added. In spite of his efforts, the adversaries in the Falklands/Malvinas war did not avail themselves of his proffered good offices. The UN condemned the Israeli intervention in Lebanon in 1982, but the UN Intervention Force in Lebanon (UNIFIL) was brushed aside by the Israeli forces. In 1986 Perez de Cuellar firmly faced the financial crisis of the UN aggravated by the United States withholdings of their obligatory contributions, by imposing courageous economies on the bureaucracy. He is implementing the structural and administrative reforms proposed by the Group of 18 and approved by the General Assembly, including a 15 per cent staffing reduction over three years.[40]

Other international models

The directors-general of UN specialized agencies play a role very similar to that of the UN Secretary-general, except that their domaine is, theoretically, non-political, or rather not directly concerned with peace and security. As directors of global technical, economic or social institutions, they have the dual role of programme and administrative manager, and that of an international politician dealing with member states' representatives, other intergovernmental bodies and non-governmental organizations. They have to deliver a programme, administer the secretariat, satisfy the governing bodies and individual countries (and particularly the major powers), while remaining true to their international obligations.

Their attitudes may be those of an extraverted Trygve Lie or those of a reserved Hammarskjold or Thant. They may be loyal and independent international officials, or, like Avenol, ignore their international allegiance.

The first director-general of the International Labour Organisation, Albert Thomas from France, earned a reputation for 'electric leadership'.[41] He was a socialist politician,[42] a trade unionist, a social campaigner and a reformer. He assumed an independent, dynamic, personalized role for his office by proposing specific measures to the ILO Conference, even when government disagreed with their substance, and by giving his own views in public reports.[43]

The former director-general of the World Health Organisation (WHO), Dr Marcolino Candau, from Brazil, was, in the words of his successor, a legendary figure, a brilliant health stateman, a courageous leader, a man of foresight.[44] He initiated the now completed, successful, WHO Smallpox Eradication Campaign, as well as the ongoing Onchocerciasis Control Programme in West Africa. He recruited his personnel without giving in to government pressures; he showed equity and wisdom. In twenty years he led the organization firmly and without major crises in its growth.[45]

International organizations need leaders as figureheads, as international politicians and diplomats and as managers. However the executive heads could not fulfil their functions adequately without the help of hundreds or thousands of administrators, specialists, technicians, clerks, secretaries and their own personal assistants. Among the latter, Brian E. Urquhart should be singled out. He served loyally and effectively all the UN Secretaries-general until he retired in 1984. He had assumed responsibility for the UN peacekeeping operations. Widely respected for his cool effectiveness, his intelligence and his bluntness, he showed that an international civil servant need not be a 'coward or a neutral to succeed at the UN'.[46]

It is a credit to the international civil service that it has produced or revealed such exceptional international statesmen as Hammarskjold, such memorable chiefs of specialized agencies as Thomas and Candau, such able executive officers as Urquhart.

No doubt many other trusted, enthusiastic, capable, dedicated, men and women, of various nationalities, working behind the scenes, could be found in many of the UN organizations at various levels and in various countries. The knowledge that persons of such quality serve or have served the organizations might help correct the damaging, distorted image cast in recent years by some Western Media on the international staff.

Notes

1. Evan Luard, *A History of the United Nations*, Macmillan, London, 1982, vol. 1, p. 360.
2. 'A More Powerful Secretary-General for the UN', *American Journal of International Law*, Proceedings of the American Society of International Law, vol. 66, no. 4, September 1972, p. 85.
3. In 'Bureaucratie internationale et détermination de la ligne générale des organisations internationales: le cas de l'UNESCO', *Etudes internationales*, December 1985, Quebec, pp. 757-70, Daniel A. Holly argues that in general international organizations' secretariats wield considerable power over the definition of the institutions' strategies and exercise tremendous control over the content of the programme. His hypothesis is based on an analysis of the role of the UNESCO secretariat. Robert I. McLaren showed with empirical data that international organizations which are secretariat-oriented (including such small organizations as ICAO, IMO, ITU, UPU and WMO), rather than programme-oriented organizations, do not have a significant policy-making role for their international secretariats: *Civil Servants and Public Policy: A Comparative Study of International Secretariats*, Wilfrid Laurier University Press, Waterloo, Ontario, 1980.

   It is probable that the secretariats of programme-oriented organizations like ILO, FAO, UNESCO and WHO play a significant policy-making role in defining objectives and strategies. In WHO, the role of the directors-general (Dr M. Candau and Dr H. Mahler, respectively, and their staff) in launching the successful Smallpox Eradication Campaign and in formulating the 'Health for All by the Year 2000' objective and strategy, could be shown as essential.
4. See Arthur W. Rovine, *The First Fifty Years: The Secretary-General in World Politics, 1920-1970*, A.W. Sijthoff, Leyden, 1970, Ch. 5; Mark W. Zacher, *Dag Hammarskjold's United Nations*, Columbia University Press, New York, 1970; Brian Urquhart, *Hammarskjold*, Alfred Knopf, New York, 1972; Robert S. Jordan (ed.), *Hammarskjold Revisited: The UN Secretary-General as a Force in World Politics*, Carolina Academic Press, Durham, NC, 1983—a bibliographic essay on Hammarskjold, by Larry Trachtenberg, is in Ch. 8.
5. According to James Barros, in Jordan, p. 29. The initial proposal was made by Sir Gladwyn Jebb. See also Rovine, p. 274, and Jean Siotis' *Essai sur le secrétariat international*, Lib. Droz, Geneva, 1963, pp. 222 and 223.
6. See Georges Langrod's *The International Civil Service*, A.W. Syjthoff, Leyden; Oceana Publications, Dobbs Ferry, New York, 1968, Ch. 10.
7. Langrod, pp. 229-30.
8. In *Jordan*, p. 139.
9. According to Resol. 1095(XI) of 27 February 1957 and Doc. A/3558 (pp. 31-3), the General Assembly adopted the figure of 20 per cent temporary appointments (see Langrod, p. 242).
10. General Assembly Resol. 343 (IX) dated 17 February 1954.
11. See Zacher.
12. Inis L. Claude, *Swords into Plowshares*, Random House, New York, 1971, p.114.
13. See Rovine, p. 279-83; Urquhart, pp. 94-131.

14. Kurt Waldheim, *In the Eye of the Storm: A Memoir*, Adler & Adler, Bethesda, 1985, Ch. 11, pp. 156-69.
15. Rovine, pp. 271-340.
16. Ibid., p. 321.
17. *New York Herald Tribune*, 21 September 1961, as quoted by Oscar Schachter, in article 'The International Civil Servant' in Jordan, pp. 49-50.
18. Dag Hammarskjold, *The International Civil Servant in Law and in Fact*, Clarendon Press, Oxford, 1961, p. 14.
19. Ibid., p. 22
20. Ibid., p. 24.
21. Ibid., p. 27.
22. *Introduction to the Annual Report of the Secretary-General for 1960-1961*, p. 1.
23. As expressed by Barbara Ward, and quoted by Zacher, p. 249.
24. See Langrod, pp. 309-10; Siotis, pp. 106-7; Claude, pp. 193-4, Rovine, pp. 100-3; Barros, in *Jordan*, pp. 35-7. Sir Eric Drummond was secretary-general of the League from 1919 to 1933.
25. 'Sir Eric Drummond and Mr Avenol were accustomed to consider the Chiefs of the Ministries of Foreign Affairs of their respective countries as their sole masters'. *Proceedings, Exploratory Conference on the League of Nations Secretariat*, Carnegie Endowment for International Peace, New York, 1942, pp. 48, 49 and 65. Quoted by Siotis, p. 106.
26. Avenol was secretary-general of the League from 1933 to 1940. His successor, Sean Lester from Ireland, served the League from 1940 to 1947. His role is not mentioned here, in view of the twilight existence of the League during the Second World War and its later liquidation. See Rovine, pp. 105-72 and Siotis, pp. 107-9.
27. According to Siotis (p. 109), he made proposals to the German and Italian governments with a view to fitting the League machinery (physically and politically) in the inevitable 'New Order'.
28. Siotis, pp. 108-9.
29. Barros, in *Jordan*, p. 37, and in, *Betrayal from Within: Joseph Avenol, Secretary-General of the League of Nations, 1933-1940*, Yale University Press, New Haven, Conn., 1969.
30. See Trygve Lie, *In the Cause of Peace*, Macmillan, New York, 1954, p. 12; Rovine, pp. 201-69; Siotis, pp. 220-2; Claude, pp. 91, 141, 144, 157-8, 178, 186-7, 190-3. Trygve Lie was secretary-general of the UN from 1946 to 1953.
31. More realistically, he realized that 'this concept is in many ways far ahead of our times, when nationalism is stronger than ever, and national sovereignty still the ruling force'.
32. Urquhart, in Jordan, p. 137. For Barros (in Jordan, p. 29), Lie's Memoir presents a lamentable picture of Lie as secretary-general, showing his partiality and prejudices.
33. U Thant was secretary-general from 1961 to 1971. See Rovine, pp. 341-414; Claude, pp. 158, 192; U Thant, *View from the UN,* Doubleday & Co., New York, 1978; Barros, in Jordan, pp. 29, 32-3, 36.
34. U Thant did not subscribe to the view that the secretary-general should be a 'glorified clerk'. For him, political and diplomatic initiatives are an essential part of the secretary-general's functions: see UN Press Release SG/SM/567, 19 September 1966, p. 4.
35. Kurt Waldheim was Secretary-General of the U.N. from 1971 to 1981. See 'La Fonction de Secrétaire Général de l'O.N.U. à travers l'expérience de M. Kurt Waldheim', by Olivier Pirotte and Pierre-Marie Martin, *Revue internationale de Droit International Public*, Ed. Pedone, Paris, January-March 1974, no.1.

36. Waldheim was proud that it took less than thirty hours to transfer UN troops from Cyprus to Egypt (Waldheim, p. 65).

37. 'Waldheim's Rules of Diplomacy', by Jane Rosen, *New York Times*, reproduced in *UN Special*, Geneva, November 1981, pp. 13-15.

38. On 27 April 1987, the US Department of Justice placed Kurt Waldheim on a Watchlist prohibiting his entry to the United States on the basis of a *prima facie* case of having assisted or otherwise participated in activities amounting to persecutions during the Second World War *(Diplomatic World Bulletin*, New York, 27 April 1987). There is not, at the time of this writing, any evidence that Waldheim was a war criminal, an allegation which he has constantly rejected. However, there is evidence that he attempted to hide his presence in the Balkans as an Officer in a German Army Unit implicated in war atrocities. An international commission of historians reported in February 1988 that he must have known about war crimes and that he bore a moral responsibility of what occurred in areas where he was stationed (International Herald Tribune of 24 February 1988). There is no evidence that his past influenced his attitude or actions while he served the UN, although some have accused him, retrospectively, of having been 'easily pressured' or biased: see Elaine Sciolino's article 'UN Recalls Waldheim as Open, Easily Pressured' in the *International Herald Tribune* of 16 June 1986, also giving Arkadi N. Shevchenko's views; other articles in the same newspaper on 31 October 1986, 4 and 20 May 1987; and *Le Monde* of 30 April 1987, 'Une sixième version des faits?' His memories do not refer to his presence in the Balkans in 1942 (Waldheim, pp. 17-18). In his book *A life in Peace and War* (Harper & Row, New York, 1987), Urquhart wrote, 'Waldheim emerging as a living lie, has done immense damage not only to his own country, but to the UN and to those who have devoted, and in some cases sacrificed, their lives for it'. See also the *Diplomatic World Bulletin*, 19-26 October 1987.

39. *Newsweek*, 21 December 1981.

40. See *Report of the Group of High-Level Intergovernmental Experts to Review the Efficiency of the Administrative and Financial Functioning of the UN*, UN Doc. A/41/49, 1986. Most of the Group's recommendations were approved by the General Assembly in Resol. 41/213.

41. Langrod, pp. 311-12; - Claude, p. 194.

42. Contrary to the normal requirements of the international civil service, he continued as a member of the French Chamber of Deputies during part of his tenure as director-general of the ILO.

43. Rovine, pp.26-27.

44. See WHO Doc. A/36/VR2, pp. 35-40. Dr. Candau was director-general of WHO from 1953 to 1973.

45. Ibid., p. 37. In 1953 WHO had eighty-one member states, 1,500 staff members and a budget of $9 million. In 1973 WHO had 138 member states, 4,000 staff members and a budget of $106 million.

46. In the words of an Asian diplomat. See B.D. Nossiter,'UN's Top Peace Troubleshooter Is Respected as Cool and Canny', *International Herald Tribune*, 21 August 1981. He was Waldheim's senior executive officer 'during some of the worst crises' and a 'most trusted colleague of sterling character': see Waldheim p. 47.

Chapter 3

US PRESSURES ON UN SECRETARIATS

Among UN member states, the United States is particularly critical of the performance of most UN organizations, which it attributes in part to the alleged inefficiency and the politicization of the organizations' staff. The United States is now exerting political and financial pressures on the organizations in an apparent effort to bring about 'reform'. In the 1950s it applied direct pressure on the executive heads in personnel matters, thus importing its national politics into the secretariats.

Authoritarian or totalitarian countries may be expected to exert political pressure on UN secretariats in order to ensure that only citizens loyal to the political authorities are hired by the organizations, to promote the UN career of those loyal citizens, and to insist on the dismissal of those considered disloyal: fascist Italy, Nazi Germany and authoritarian Poland applied such pressures to the League secretariat between the two world wars. The Soviet Union and other socialist countries maintain strict and close control over the temporary appointments of their nationals in the UN organizations and insist on the predominance of socialist loyalty over an ignored or rejected international allegiance (see Ch. 4).

On the other hand, the US gross interference with the statutory staffing prerogatives of the UN heads of secretariats in the 1950s appears at odds with the expected behaviour of the leader of the Western democracies, the land of freedoms and of the rule of law, one of the founders of the UN, a permanent member of the Security Council and the major contributor to the organizations' budgets.

It also appears paradoxical and out of character that the United States should now be creating an organizational and financial crisis which threatens the viability, and perhaps the survival, of the UN system.

The ambivalence of the United States

To foreign observers the United States appears ambivalent with regard to international organization and international law.

The second Hague conference, which met in 1907, was proposed by Theodore Roosevelt, who had received the Nobel Prize for peace for his successful efforts to bring to a close the Russo-Japanese War. Woodrow Wilson was the inspirer of the League of Nations. Franklin D. Roosevelt made his country join the International Labour Organization in 1934 and contributed decisively to the foundation of the UN organizations. In 1946 the United States, which alone possessed the atomic bomb, offered to turn it over to the UN for the purpose of maintaining world peace.[1] The United States sponsored the creation of the Organization for European Economic Development in 1948, to overview the implementation of the Marshall Plan. in 1950 it placed its armed forces in Korea under the UN flag. The United States supported and used the UN during the Suez crisis and most of the 1960-4 Congo crisis.

At the same time, as a Big Power, the United States can and often prefers to carry out its foreign relations on the basis of unilateralism or bilateralism, rather than on a multilateral basis, which would submit its sovereignty, even in a modest way, to collective majority debates, agreements, recommendations and decisions. It has been said that for at least the past quarter of a century, American governmental decision-makers have repeatedly tried to base their foreign policies on Machiavellian power politics,[2] the scarcely used antidote being international law and organization. Following the influx of Third World countries, the United States and other Western states found themselves in a minority in the UN organizations, and the United States often adopted a defensive posture in the organizations.[3]

The Wilsonian dream was shattered by the US Senate's rejection of the League of Nations Covenant. The absence of the United States from the League contributed to its weakness and final bankruptcy.

The United States is prompt to apply financial pressures as a leverage against the UN organizations fallen in disfavour, thus violating its constitutional obligations: in October 1970 the US Congress reduced the American contribution to the ILO by 50 per cent, on the grounds that the Soviet Union was becoming disproportionately influential in the organization. In 1974 the Senate suspended payment of the American contribution to UNESCO as a protest against the UNESCO Conference decision not to include Israel in the European regional group.[4] As an even stronger gesture, the United States withdrew from the ILO from 1977 to 1980 and has not been a member of UNESCO since 1985.[5] The 1985 American legislation has begun to financially debilitate the UN organizations while making demands on them which cannot be satisfied (see below).

The United States applies internally its fundamental belief that law and not force should be the basis of public order but appears reluctant to apply the same principles to the international sphere. A Soviet writer[6] contrasts the American 'mask' as a defender of human rights with its failure to ratify thirty of the forty human rights international treaties and conventions.[7] Many countries ratify international conventions and fail to observe them. Rather than claiming domestic juridiction and the rights of states, adhesion to such conventions would give the United States the right to request compliance of other states with the set standards, without fear of international scrutiny of American behaviour. Ratification would bring credibility and a chance for true international leadership.[8] True to its rejection of international regulation, the Reagan administration made the United States the only country to vote against the WHO International Code of Marketing of Breast-milk Substitutes, and it has refused to sign the 1982 Law of the Sea Convention.

In April 1986 the United States withdrew its acceptance of the compulsory jurisdiction of the International Court of Justice on the grounds that the Court had been abused for political reasons: the United States was then expressing its dissatisfaction with the Court's assumption of jurisdiction over the Nicaragua application.[9] The United States has also recently shown an open disregard for the UN Charter and international law in its unilateral military action in Grenada and Libya and its military support to the Contras in Nicaragua.

The United States is not loath to apply pressures on international organizations and secretariats in order to change policies, programmes or rules. As many of these pressures are discreet, they are difficult to substantiate.[10] Quite openly, the United States expressed its opposition to UNCTAD by sending a middle-level Foreign Service Officer (describing himself as a travelling insult) to the Seventh Conference in July 1987, while other countries sent high-level officials—French President Francois Mitterand addressed the conference. The United States refused to attend the French-inspired and UN-sponsored International Conference on the Relationship between Disarmament and Development in August 1987.[11] Even more openly, the American Alternate Representative to the UN, Charles Lichtenstein, declared in the Committee on Relations with the Host Country that members of the UN should 'seriously consider removing themselves and this Organization from the soil of the US.[12]

American public opinion is also somewhat ambivalent: a 1980 Roper Survey showed that 53 per cent of those surveyed believed that the UN was doing a 'poor job', while two-thirds or respondents favoured maintaining or increasing American participation in the UN. In other words, the UN is not doing well, so it should be reinforced, not abandoned nor dissolved.[13] In 1983 the Roper Survey showed by a margin of two to one that respondents felt that the UN is compatible with American interests, not inimical to them. Again, a majority favoured maintaining or increasing the present level of American involvement in the UN rather than decreasing it.[14] It would therefore seem that the current malaise about the UN is more pronounced among the decision-making élite in the United States (executive and legislative) than it is within the public at large.

The United States and the International Civil Service

The United States strongly favoured an autonomous, energetic administrative arm for the newly founded UN. The United States also supported the overtly political role given by Article 99 of the UN Charter to the secretary-general.[15] However, the United States was insisting on responsiveness and cooperation from the secretary-general towards its positions. The British rather favoured the notion of an international civil service doing its work in the background, following the tradition established by Sir Eric Drummond. The United States and the other Western democracies support the independence granted by the

Charter to the secretariats.

While the principles were clear, the anti-communist McCarthy wave triggered by the Korean War affected official American behaviour towards the UN secretariats. The principle of the independence of the international civil service was sacrificed by the American authorities on the altar of anti-communist opportunism, against the generally weak resistance of several of its guardians, and particularly the UN secretary-general, Trygve Lie and the UNESCO and FAO directors-general.

The international civil service suffered deeply from this frontal attack, but recovered with the assistance of Dag Hammarskjold and such other executive heads as the WHO directors-general Dr Brock Chisholm and Dr M.G. Candau, and the staunch support of the UN and ILO administrative tribunals and of the International Court of Justice. The American international prestige suffered from its overt, albeit temporary, abuse of power over the exposed and fragile international secretariats.

The Loyalty Crisis in the UN

The first breaches in the principle of independence were brought to the UN by Trygve Lie himself.

The initial policy of the United States towards the UN secretariat had been fully in accordance with the Charter. Without regard to his own staffing prerogatives, Lie imprudently requested the US government to help in finding well-qualified personnel of American nationality. The United States categorically refused to recommend candidates for posts in the secretariat 'owing to the fact that according to the Charter and the rules laid down by the General Assembly, the Secretary-General alone has full and exclusive authority to appoint and dismiss officials of the UN'. In his Statement to the resumed Seventh Session of the General Assembly,[16] Lie recognizes, without apparently realizing the seriousness of his initative, that 'in the appointment and *retention* of staff it has often been necessary for me to ask the assistance of Member Governments in checking the character and record of applicants and *staff members*' (my emphasis). He thus deliberately allowed governments to clear the appointments of candidates for UN employment and, even worse, the retention of staff members. This practice should in principle be limited to the employment of national civil servants seconded to the international organization, and not extend to all 'free' (non-civil servants) candidates and staff members. At present only a few UN organizations require that all candidates for employment be cleared by their government before they are allowed to be recruited by the organization.[17]

In September 1948 Lie concluded with the State Department a secret, highly confidential agreement: the US Government was to identify for the secretary-general the American officials in the UN and the American candidates who appeared either to be members of the Communist Party or to be under communist influence. The secretary-general's freedom of decision was, by his own action, severely curtailed, as he could hardly go against the laconic, unsubstantiated United States' replies. Lie had agreed to the introduction of a 'loyalty clearance' for American citizens before the American government imposed it.

The Federal Act of 23 September 1950 obliged all communist organizations in the United States, and all their members and former members, to report themselves to the federal authorities, subject to penalties in case of non-registration. The Special Federal Grand Jury of New York stated publicly that there was 'infiltration into the UN of an overwhelmingly large group of disloyal United States citizens': this group was later shown not to have exceeded 1 per cent of the American citizens employed by the UN. Certain UN officials of US nationality, summoned as witnesses by the Internal Security Sub-Committee of the United States Senate, refused to give evidence invoking either their immunity as international civil servants, the prohibition to give evidence concerning their official secretariat activities or the Fifth Amendment against self-discrimination. This was held by the Sub-Committee to constitute contempt of the Senate. Congressmen made violent attacks against the UN, 'an instrument conceived by the diabolical brain of the international agents of the USSR'.[18]

The secretary-general then dismissed eighteen US staff members because they had refused, on the basis of the Fifth Amendment, to answer questions during the investigation, or because after their testimony they had been charged with actual subversive activities against their country. The reason given for the dismissals was that the officials concerned had been guilty of a fundamental breach of their service obligations and were therefore unfit to remain in UN employment.

On 9 January 1953 the US government published Executive Order 10422 laying down a loyalty clearance procedure as a requirement for the recruitment of American nationals by the UN. Lie welcomed the order as a step forward in establishing 'orderly' procedures.

Twenty-five years earlier, the League of Nations secretariat had undergone a similar experience as the fascist government of Italy insisted upon government clearance for Italians, in order to prevent the employment of opponents to Mussolini by the League.[19]

Lie justified his position by stating that he had tried to uphold and defend the international character of the secretariat.[20] The US actions had to be related to the Korean War, which had cost over 130,000 US casulaties. Korea, together with the growing fear of a Third World War, contributed to the prevailing mood in the United States and to its authorities' and media's preoccupation with internal security. Lie's position was that no staff member should engage in subversive activities against his own government or the government of any member state. In view of the US laws and regulations concerning the Communist Party, no American national who was a member of the American Communist Party and who was, thereby, barred from employment in the service of his own government, should, as a matter of policy, be employed in the secretariat: Lie acknowledged that a major consideration for such a policy was the fact that the United States is the host country of the UN headquarters.

The Secretary-general received support from a group of three jurists: their report, dated 29 November 1952, concluded that the invocation by an international official in a national inquiry of the guarantee against self-incrimination constituted a fundamental breach of his obligations, such behaviour furnishing presumptive evidence of an activity incompatible with the proper discharge of his duties. Another jurist, engaged by the Federation of International Civil Servants' Associations (FICSA) found otherwise; he was later supported by the administrative tribunals of the UN and ILO.

Lie also agreed to the American request that loyalty questioning of staff members of American nationality by the Federal Bureau of Investigation, including finger-printing, would take place on the secretariat's premises with the help of UN staff and during office hours— in contradiction with the principle of extra-territoriality of UN grounds. He asked the staff concerned to submit these investigations.

Trygve Lie resigned and was replaced by Dag Hammarskjold on 10 April 1953.[21] The new secretary-general ordered the FBI agents off UN premises, feeling their presence a challenge to the international character of the secretariat.[22]

Hammarskjold's position was firmer than Lie's; he wrote that his administration

was only prepared to accept information from governments concerning suitability for employment, including information that might be relevant to political considerations such as activity which would be regarded as inconsistent with the obligations of international civil servants. It was recognized that there should be a relationship of mutual confidence and trust between international officials and the governments of member states. At the same time, the Secretary-General took a strong position that the dismissal of a staff member on the basis of the mere suspicion of a government of a member state or a bare conclusion arrived at by that government on evidence which is denied the Secretary-General would amount to receiving instructions in violation of his obligation under Article 100, paragraph 1, of the Charter not to receive in the performance of his duties instructions from any government.[23]

In the second place, the UN judicial process provided a fair hearing and rendered justice to some of the UN victims of the McCarthy witchhunt. They won a moral victory, accompanied by a financial compensation, but they were not reintegrated into the UN service. The stage changed from acrimonious public debates and media, Congress and government pressures, to the quieter and slower judicial process.

The UN judicial cases

In its Judgments of 21 August 1953, the UN Administrative Tribunal (UNAT) found that the opinion of the three jurists — namely that the Secretary-General could without reference to any particular clause of the Staff Regulations dismiss an official on the basis of contractual relations existing between himself and that official — disregarded the nature of permanent appointments. For the UNAT, the fact of having invoked the Fifth Amendment in order to avoid self-discrimination and of having refused to answer certain questions asked by the American authorities, did not constitute 'serious misconduct', which alone could have justified the dismissal of the international official without notice and without observing the guarantees offered by the statutory disciplinary procedure. An official could be dismissed only for 'unsatisfactory services', under the Staff Regulations, if the services in question were connected with the official's professional activities at the UN and not with his general obligations. Any dismissal should, in any case, be based on an express clause of the Staff Regulations.

The ten complainants holders of permanent appointments won their cases and, in view of the secretary-general's refusal to reinstate them, received financial compensation.[24]

The United States and other governments launched an offensive at the Eighth Session of the General Assembly in order to 'correct' the Tribunal judgments and to prevent the payment of the financial compensations granted. The American Permanent Representative at the UN, Henry Cabot Lodge Jr, insisted that 'the finding of this Tribunal is not final' and that 'the General Assembly has the power to overrule it, on the ground that the Administrative Tribunal is a subsidiary body of the UN General Assembly'[25] — a curious conception of the independence of the judiciary.

At the General Assembly's request, the International Court of Justice rendered an advisory opinion on 13 July 1954, declaring:

As this final judgment of the UNAT has binding force on the UN as juridical person responsible for the proper observance of the contract of service, that organisation becomes legally bound to carry out the judgment and to pay the compensation awarded to the staff member. It follows that the General Assembly as an organ of the UN must likewise be bound by the judgment.[26]

The loyalty crisis in the UN specialised agencies

The American investigations extended to the UN organizations outside the United States. As in the UN secretariat, these investigations brought American pressures on UNESCO in Paris, FAO in Rome and ICAO in Montreal, caused personal dramas for the American staff concerned, and malaise and insecurity in the secretariats. They also caused strong reactions from the staff associations and from their federation, FICSA. The issue was finally resolved, in principle, through the judicial process of the ILO Administrative Tribunal (ILOAT), to which most specialised agencies have adhered in preference to the UNAT, and by the International Court of Justice.

The UNESCO cases

In February 1952 the State Department warned the acting director-general of UNESCO that, without the organization's cooperation in the investigations undertaken, it would be impossible for his government to give continued support to UNESCO.[27] The American pressures continued until 1955.

The best-known UNESCO case was that of David Leff. Leff had been employed by UNESCO since 1949. He held a fixed-term appointment. In August 1951 his American passport and the passports of his wife and two children were withdrawn from him by the American Consulate in Paris. In May 1953 a summons to appear before the Federal Grand Jury in New York was notified to him, ordering him to appear on 21 May 1953 'to testify and give evidence' concerning possible violation of section 371, title 18, United States code: 'Conspiracy to commit offence or to defraud the United States'. He refused to go, for reasons of conscience, in spite of an express order from the director-general, Luther H. Evans. He was then suspended, and later reinstated with the proposal that he should agree to a transfer to New York, against which he and the Staff Association protested. In July 1954 the director-general received communication of the report of the Loyalty Board, stating 'that there is reasonable doubt as to the loyalty of David Neal Leff to the Government of the United States' and that this determination was submitted to the director-general 'for your use in exercising your rights and duties with respect to the integrity of the personnel of UNESCO'. In August 1954 the director-general informed Leff that his appointment would not be extended beyond its expiry date (31 July 1954), as he 'cannot accept your conduct as being consistent with the standards of integrity which are required of those employed by the Organization'.

Leff appealed twice to the ILOAT. The Tribunal subscribed to the opinion of the UNESCO Appeals Board, to which a recourse had previously been submitted, regarding the director-general's instruction to Leff to proceed to New York for the purpose of responding to the Grand Jury's subpoena. The Tribunal considered that 'this order obviously does not concern the actual service of the international organization'. However, the conduct of an official with regard to the government of his country, although outside the actual service of the international organisation, is not entirely outside the control of the disciplinary authority of the organization. This would be the case when that conduct was judged to be seriously likely to affect the dignity of the official and the prestige of the organization — a fact which was not established in Leff's case. The director-general's order was rescinded by the Tribunal in a first judgment. In a second judgment,[28] the Tribunal gave a clear rebuff as well as stern guidance to the executive head on the principles of an independent international civil service, censuring both his decisions and, indirectly, the American interference.[29] It considered that the director-general of an international organization cannot associate himself with the execution of the policy of the government's authorities of any member state without disregarding the obligations imposed on all international officials without distinction and, in consequence, without misusing the authority which has been conferred on him solely for the purpose of directing that organization towards the achievement of its own, exclusively international objectives.

What would the director-general do if all other member states of the organization acted like the United States in similar circumstances? For the Tribunal,

> It will suffice to realize that if any of the seventy-two States and governments ... brought against an official, one of its citizens, an accusation of disloyalty and claimed to subject him to a similar enquiry, the attitude adopted by the Director-General would constitute a precedent obliging him to lend his assistance to such an enquiry and, moreover, to invoke the same disciplinary or statutory consequences, the same withdrawal of confidence, on the basis of any opposal by the person concerned to the action of his national Government. If this were the case, there would result for all international officials, in matters touching on conscience, a state of uncertainty and insecurity prejudicial to the performance of their duties and liable to provoke disturbances in the international administration such as cannot be imagined to have been in the intention of those who drew up the Constitution of the ... Organization.

The Tribunal also rejected the confusion as to the meaning of the expression 'loyalty towards a State', which is entirely different from the idea of 'integrity' as embodied in the Staff Regulations and Rules. In an attempt to clarify the standards of conduct required of international civil servants, the Tribunal considered that in clearly establishing the complete freedom of conscience of international officials in respect of both their philosophical convictions and their political opinions, the Regulations impose on them the duty to abstain from all acts capable of being interpreted as associating them with propaganda or militant proselytism in any sense whatever and that 'this abstention is rigorously imposed on them by the overriding interest of the international organization to which they owe their loyalty and devotion'.

The Tribunal ordered the director-general's decision not to renew Leff's appointment to be rescinded and declared in law that it constituted the wrongful exercise of power and an abuse of rights causing prejudice to the complainant. Leff received two years' salary as compensation, in the absence of reinstatement.

All the UNESCO officials who had appealed to the ILOAT won their cases and were granted financial compensation.[30]

Dissatisfied with the Tribunal's decisions, the Executive Board of UNESCO appealed to the International Court of Justice, alleging that the Tribunal had committed an excess of jurisdiction in pronouncing on the constitutional obligations of the head of the secretariat and on his relations with a state member of the organization. In its advisory opinion of 23 October 1956, the Court accepted the decisions of the Tribunal and rejected UNESCO's allegations.[31]

The FAO Case

American loyalty investigations were also carried out in FAO in Rome. Here the *cause célèbre* was that of Gordon McIntire, which illustrates the continuing crisis.

McIntire had been employed by the FAO since June 1952 in the Budget and Administrative Planning Branch with a five-year contract. His contract was changed to a permanent contract, with many others, on 1 July 1952 with a probationary period due to expire on 4 June 1953. After some initial performance difficulties, his work improved and he was given the title of Chief of the Policy and Procedures Section on 30 March 1953.

On 8 April the FAO administration informed him that his appointment would not be confirmed but terminated on 31 May 1953, for unsatisfactory performance. McIntire appealed to the ILOAT against this decision. In its judgment,[32] the Tribunal revealed that between 30 March and 8 April the director-general had received a letter from the United States' Assistant Secretary of State concerning the appellant. The FAO representative had recognized this fact and stated that the letter confirmed officially information given verbally to the director-general during his visit to Washington one month previously, without the complainant having been informed at the time. The FAO had refused to communicate this document, as this 'confidential' letter came from the government of a sovereign state and could not be produced without the authorization of the government concerned.

The Tribunal found inadmissible that these considerations could in any way prejudice the legitimate interests of the complainant—that the existence of a secret document concerning the complainant, the content of which was unknown to him and against which he was consequently powerless to defend himself, obviously vitiated the just application of the Regulations to the complainant and affected not only the interests of the staff as a whole but also the interests of justice itself. The wrath of the Tribunal was well justified: the organization had attempted to terminate McIntire's contract on the grounds of unsatisfactory service, while the real grounds were 'personal considerations extraneous to such grounds'.

The Tribunal decided to rescind the termination decision as constituting an act of misuse of power and awarded him financial compensation for the shortened employment and for having been subjected for a long time to conditions of material and moral insecurity causing him 'serious suffering'.

The case had caused unrest in the FAO secretariat, where the staff association and part of the staff (particularly among staff members from European countries) gave McIntire strong moral support.[33] The Tribunal judgment was acclaimed by these groups and international circles as a victory for justice.

The situation in WHO

The Swiss government had refused to allow US officials to carry out loyalty investigations in Switzerland, regarding them as incompatible with its national sovereignty.[34]

In the case of WHO in Geneva, the director-general, Dr Brock Chisholm from Canada, and his successor, Dr Marcolino G. Candau from Brazil, refused to allow WHO officials to appear before the American Loyalty Board in Europe. Both directors took a very firm attitude against any pressure considered as violating Article 37 of the WHO constitution. While agreeing to transmit to members of their staff any communications from their national authorities, both directors maintained that the observance of the provisions of national legislation was a question between each individual and his government, and that the disciplinary powers possessed by international organizations in relation to their staff could be exercised only in connection with a staff member's conduct as an international official.

As noted by Langrod, this courageous and resolute defence of the international character of the international secretariats made a profound impression at the time in international circles; other organizations subsequently adopted the same attitude, which certainly helped to influence the views of the US government in the long run.[35]

The crisis finally abated in UN organizations as it did in the United States. It had shown the relative fragility of the international civil service, a tender plant which must be nursed carefully if it is not to wither before it has a chance to grow,[36] when confronted with the blunt attack of a powerful member state. It has also shown its resilience and its capacity to overcome temporary stresses. Thanks to the courageous stance of secretariat heads, the support of staff associations and the clear formulation of international principles by the two administrative tribunals, the international civil service can be said to have been fortified by this crisis. However, it also showed how difficult it was for a great power, in spite of the democratic nature of its political regime, to exert restraint in its interventions and to show respect for international law and for its international obligations.

The end of the US loyalty clearance

For thirty-three years UN organizations had to secure loyalty clearance from the American authorities before being allowed to employ any US citizen, for whatever duration. Such an employment precondition was only required by the United States (the only democracy to do so) and by socialist countries.[37]

In May 1986 the United States government informed UN organisations that 'the investigative program for US citizens being considered for either long-term employment with international organizations has been suspended as a result of a judicial decision concerning the constitutionality of Executive Order 10422'.[38]

The judicial decision was that of the United States district court for the Eastern District of Pennsylvania taken on 8 April 1986 in the case of *Hinton* v. *Devine* (Civ. No. 84-1130). The court held that Executive Order No. 14422 of 9 January 1953, as amended, under which the International Organizations Employees Loyalty Program had been instituted, was unconstitutional in that it violated the First Amendment rights of American citizens. The United States government decided not to appeal against this landmark judgment. William H. Hinton, a former FAO staff member, was the second appellant to challenge the constitutionality of the Executive Order.

The first test case, *Ozonoff* v. *Berzak* (Civ. No. 71-1046-MC), was brought before the United States district court for the District of Massachussetts in 1971 on behalf of Dr David Ozonoff, a former WHO employee. Both the district court and the US Court of Appeals for the First Circuit (No. 83-1850) rendered judgments in favour of Ozonoff.[39]

After thirty-three years, McCarthyism in UN organizations had finally died: liberalism and good sense had prevailed.

The second US attack against the UN

In 1986 the United States withheld a sizable part of its assessed contributions to the budgets of the UN organizations and made additional cuts in 1987. The decrease in revenues due to the witholdings of the major contributor caused financial crises and resulted in budget, programme and staffing reductions in the organizations.

While the McCarthy crisis affected American citizens in the UN secretariats and challenged the independence of the international civil service, the second crisis was an expression of distrust in the UN organizations on the part of the American administration and Congress, which challenged the objectives, programmes and activities of these organizations, their relevance to basic US interests and values, and therefore their very existence. The American withdrawal from UNESCO in 1985 and that of the United Kingdom in 1986 served in part as a leverage for reform, but mainly as a warning to the other UN organizations to 'mend their ways or else', and a warning to other member states to be more sensitive to US concerns, or else to do without the United States. Would global organizations survive in the absence of the United States, when universality is one of their basic tenets ?

The American legislation

The American withholdings are a consequence of several legislative acts:

(1)   The 'Kassebaum Amendment',[40] which mandates a reduction of the

American share of the assessed contributions to the budgets of the UN organizations from 25 to 20 per cent unless those organizations adopt weighted voting—based on the amount of a member's contribution—on budgetary questions. The share reduction would start with fiscal year 1987 contributions. This action was taken in order to 'foster greater financial responsibility by the organizations'.

The adoption of weighted voting by the General Assembly would require amendment of Article 18 of the Charter, which gives each country one vote without regard to any other criteria. Such an amendment is deemed impossible in view of other Charter requirements.[41] As a second best, the General Assembly agreed in December 1986 to give to the Committee for Programme and Coordination (CPC) a decision role, by consensus, in controlling the level of the proposed biennial budget.[42]

By the end of 1987 there was no sign that this compromise would make the US Congress withdraw the Kassebaum Amendment, which, in the meantime, continues to be applied by the US Administration.

(2)   The 'Sundquist Amendment' is a protest against the alleged practice of socialist countries requiring their nationals in UN organizations to relinquish part of their salaries to their governments. In the absence of 'substantial progress in correcting this practice', the amendment would require withholding the American proportionate share of the UN salaries of such officials. In fact, it would be next to impossible to identify precisely the extent of these practices, which are carried out discreetly (see Ch. 4 below).

(3)   Another potential witholding specified that 'if Israel is illegally expelled, suspended, denied its credentials, or in any other manner denied its rights to participate' in UN organizations, the United States would suspend its own participation and 'reduce its annual assessed contribution ... by 8.34 per cent for each month' of American suspended participation.[43]

(4)   The Gramm-Rudman-Hollings Act: additional reductions of American contributions to UN organizations may result from overall US budget reductions decided by the Congress in an effort to balance the federal budget. Approximately $20 million were withheld on that account in December 1985, or 10 per cent of the American contribution; $38 million are to be cut in 1987.

(5)   In recent years the United States has withheld certain amounts from the costs of specific UN activities which were politically disapproved by the Congress—for example, funds for the Palestine Liberation Organization (PLO), the South-West African People's Organization (SWAPO) and for the Preparatory Commission implementing the 1982 Law of the Sea Convention.

The American unilateral withholdings of their assessed contribution are a breach of their Charter obligations. The withholdings are in conflict with Article 17.2 of the Charter, which states that 'The expenses of the Organization shall be borne by the Members as apportioned by the General Assembly'. The advisory opinion of the International Court of Justice of 20

July 1962[44] included in these expenses all costs related to the purposes of the United Nations. This opinion was endorsed by the General Assembly[45] and then supported by the US Congress.[46]

To be fair, the United States is not the only, nor the first, UN member to withold assessed contributions. Many other member states are also doing it with different justifications.[47]

Other reasons for the American Withholdings

Besides the reasons stated in the Acts themselves—that is, essentially better budget control in the UN, US budget-balancing efforts and the protection of Israel—the legislative decisions seem directly related to an insistent anti-UN campaign launched by US conservative circles in recent years. As noted by Ruggie, Heritage Foundation, a conservative think-tank in Washington, DC, has been most effective in shaping official attitudes towards the UN during the early phases of the first Reagan administration.[48] Its recurrent criticisms received extensive coverage by the American press. The Foundation's main criticisms of the UN can be summarized from its 1984 'Report on the US and the UN: A Balance Sheet', a pamphlet prepared to assist the American administration to report to the Congress on the US contribution to the UN, the importance of the UN in fulfilling the policies and objectives of the United States and the benefits derived by the United States from participation in the UN:[49]

(1) The General Assembly voting pattern reveals the UN's anti-United States sentiment.[50]
(2) Americans hold a disproportionately low number of positions compared to their budgetary contribution.[51]
(3) Israel is excluded from the Economic Commission of Western Asia, while the PLO and SWAPO have been admitted as permanent official observers at the UN.
(4) South Africa has been illegally denied participation in the General Assembly since 1974.
(5) UN employees from Soviet-bloc countries receive instructions from their governments: one-third of them are spies.
(6) The UN has failed to maintain international peace or to encourage respect for human rights.
(7) The United States and its allies have been ineffectual in curbing overall UN spending, although they pay 74.3 per cent of the UN budget.[52]
(8) There is no control of the budgets of the UN specialized agencies.[53]
(9) The UN is waging a war against the liberal economic order and the Western companies (transnational corporations).
(10) The few benefits accruing to the United States from its participation in the UN are almost always offset by significant drawbacks, particularly in view of politicization, mismanagement and corruption within the bodies and programmes of the organizations.

The motivation behind this campaign has been diagnosed by Marc Nerfin[54] as due to external and internal determinants. External determinants include the declining hegemony of the United States (and the west) through the loss of control in the deliberative organs of the UN system and a receding control over the execution of decisions, through key staff and the power of the purse; resistance to attempts at regulating or restructuring world economic relations or their embryonic regulation and the concomitant emergence of development accountability, all of which somewhat reduce the omnipotence of free enterprise; the role of ideology, that is new self-assertiveness of the United States; and a decline in the interest of multilateralism, shared by the West Europeans. For Nerfin, the UN crisis is largely a Northern expression of a felt challenge to the old order and a reflection of the North's unwillingness to accept that change is necessary. Internal determinants include the proliferation of agencies, programmes, funds, diplomatic meetings, bureaucratic reports, problems of the secretariat's staffing, its efficiency and independence, the effectiveness of the operation in terms of cost-benefits, the deployment of resources and its financing.

Heritage Foundation recommended that Congress should curb UN spending by reducing sharply the American contribution to the UN: the US Congress is now implementing this recommendation.

American criticisms of poor management and of a bloated and inefficient bureaucracy have been taken seriously by the UN secretary-general, Javier Perez de Cuellar, and by the Group of 18. The secretary-general decided in 1986 to apply various economy measures to the internal management of the UN, to limit or reduce meetings, travel and documentation costs. The Group of 18 has recommended restructuring the intergovernmental machinery dealing with political economic and social problems, as well as the economic and social departments in the UN secretariats.[55]

A more realistic and moderate American attitude towards the UN has been proposed by some authors, while others ask that 'Unnecessary UN Bashing should stop'.[56]

Still, it appears that the US administration has not yet been able to convince Congress that the American contributions should now be paid in full. In 1986 the United States paid only $100 million out of their $220 million assessed contribution to the UN budget. In September 1987 it was expected that the United States would probably pay only $120 million for 1987. The United States has withheld most of its 1986 contributions to WHO—by September 1987, it had paid only $7 million out of its $62 million assessment—and had paid none of its 1987 assessment.[57] Such major financial cuts and the continuing uncertainty can but severely impair the implementation of the organizations' programmes.

An assessment

The McCarthy episode was damaging and could have been destructive; it was addressed specifically to the dogma of an independent international civil service, a notion which needs protection. The international civil service survived these attacks, which however destroyed some lives and affected the morale of the staff. The determination of staff members and associations, executive heads and judges finally reinforced the internationalist concept of the international civil service.

The current American attacks are broader and more pernicious. In a renewed isolationism and unilateralism, the present American policy shows a basic ideological distrust of internationalism, of multilateral negotiations, of international organization and a shying away from international obligations. The United States is trying to impose its own solutions in the international debates: when they fail, it withholds funds and threatens to withdraw from international fora and institutions where it has lost, since the 1960's its previous, comfortable, 'automatic majority'. Will the United States proceed from fund-cutting to a progressive disengagement from global organizations? The US administration seems to have realized belatedly that there are more benefits than costs to American participation in the UN organizations.

At the same time the political and financial pressures on the UN organizations on the part of the United States and also on the part of other Western democracies, have not had only negative effects, providing they find their limits. Efforts towards structural and administrative reforms have been initiated at the UN, and the senior managers of the specialized agencies are deeply conscious that their organizations need to show results in programme and management areas.

The withdrawal of the United States from the UN system of organizations, probably followed by other democracies, as in UNESCO, would destroy the universality and credibility of these organizations, as well as their inner political balance and their financial credit. It would also isolate these countries from world fora, events and trends. No one would benefit from such decisions.

Let us hope that the United States can, again, play a dynamic role in the organizations' programmes, respect its financial obligations and contribute to the effectiveness of the secretariats by associating its nationals' efforts with those of many other countries.[58]

Notes

1. The Baruch Plan. See Daniel P. Moynihan, *Loyalties*, Harcourt Brace Jovanovich, New York, 1984, pp. 61, 96.
2. See Francis Anthony Boyle, *World Politics and International Law*, Duke University Press, Durham, NC, 1985, pp. 11, 12, 70, 71, 293, 295: Hans Morganthau and his colleagues founded the 'realist' or power-politics school of international political science, which essentially denies the relevance of international law and organizations to matters of 'vital national interest' or of 'high international politics'. According to Boyle, Morgenthau made a total volte-

face in May 1978, saying that it was vital for the future of mankind to create a world government through the progressive development of international organizations, requiring a central role for international law.

3. Richard E. Bissell, 'US Participation in the UN System', Tony Trister Gati (ed.), in *The US, the UN and the Management of Total Change'*, New York University Press, New York, 1983, pp. 82-3.

4. See Yves Beigbeder, 'The US Withdrawal from the ILO', *Industrial Relations*, Quebec, vol. 34, no. 2, 1979, p. 233. The United States is not alone in applying these tactics: the Soviet Union and France were first in refusing to contribute to the costs of the UN peacekeeping forces in Suez and in the Congo. See Yves Beigbeder, *Management Problems in UN Organizations,* Frances Pinter, London, 1987, pp. 147-8.

5. Eastern European countries also withdrew from UN organizations during the War. See Beigbeder, 'The US Withdrawal from the ILO', p. 231.

6. Professor Yuri Kashlev, 'Humanitarian Aspects of International Cooperation', *International Affairs,* Moscow, December 1986, p. 90.

7. The US has not ratified the International Convention on the Prevention and Punishment of the Crime of Genocide (1948), the International Covenant on Civil and Political Rights (1966), the International Covenant on Economic, Social and Cultural Rights (1966). As from January 1987 the United States had ratified 7 of the 162 ILO International Labour Conventions; Canada, 26; the Soviet Union, 43; the UK, 79; France, 110. See ILO Document on Ratifications of the Conventions.

8. J. W. Skelton Jr, 'The US Approach to Ratification of the International Covenants on Human Rights', *Houston Journal of International Law,* vol. 103, 1979, pp. 114-16.

9. The Court found on 27 June 1986 that the United States had broken customary international law and was obliged to make reparations to Nicaragua: Communiqué No. 86/8, ICJ Reports 1986. However, the United States pledged to continue to use the Court on a voluntary basis, through the practice of 'special chambers'. See *Issues/41,* UN Association of the USA, p. 137.

10. In a recent case a senior IMF official, C. David Finch, resigned to protest against 'undue pressure' brought by the United States on the Fund to approve loans for Zaire and for Egypt: see *International Herald Tribune,* 21-2 March 1987.

11. The United States considers disarmament and development as separate issues and rejects any suggestion that developing nations have a claim on money that might be freed by cuts in Western military spending. In the absence of the United States, the European Common Market countries played a leading role in promoting the Western viewpoints: See *International Herald Tribune,* 24 August 1987; *Le Monde,* 25 August 1987.

12. John Gerard Ruggie, 'The US and the UN: Toward a new Realism', *International Organization,* Vol. 39, no. 2, spring 1985, p. 344, note 6. Also quoted by Y. Yakovenko, 'The UN and the US Obstructionist Stand', *Internatiomal Affairs*, September 1984, p. 117.

13. Quoted by Paul D. Martin, 'US Public Opinion and the UN', in Gati, p. 287.

14. John Gerard Ruggie, 'The US and the UN', in *International Organization* vol. 39, no. 2, Spring 1985, p. 355.

15. Article 99 states, 'The Secretary-General may bring to the attention of the Security Council any matter which in his opinion may threaten the maintenance of international peace and security'.

16. 'The Personnel Policy of the UN', *UN Bulletin*, vol. XIV, no. 6, March 15, 1953.

17. Among them, UNESCO and ITU. Our description of the loyalty crisis is summarized essentially from Georges Langrod, *The International Civil Service*, A.W. Sijthoff-Leyden; Oceana Publications, Dobbs Ferry, NY, 1968, pp. 212-32 and from the judgments of the Administrative Tribunals of the UN and of the

ILO. Comments and assessments are those of the author. See also Arthur W. Rovine, *The First Fifty Years: The Secretary-General in World Politics*, A.W. Sijthoff-Leyden, 1970, pp. 251-6; Inis L. Claude, *Swords into Plowshares*, Random House, New York, 1971, pp. 185-9.

18. Statement by H. Wood, *The Nation*, 20 September 1952.
19. Rovine, p. 254.
20. 'The Personnel Policy of the UN', pp. 6 and 10. Trygve Lie also said that he had resisted strong pressures to appoint or replace secretariat officials. For example, he had refused to replace competent personnel simply because revolutions, coups d'état or elections have brought about a change of government in a country (ibid., p. 3).
21. Trygve Lie's resignation was caused by the Soviet refusal to recognise him as secretary-general after his first term expired in February 1951. His second term had been vetoed by the Soviet Union in the Security Council and approved, in contradiction with Article 97 of the Charter, by the General Assembly. In substance, the Soviet attitude resulted from Lie's strong and public support for the UN/US military intervention in Korea, in response to North Korea's aggression against South Korea.
22. Rovine, p. 255.
23. Wilder Foote (ed.), *Dag Hammarskjold: Servant of Peace*, Harper & Row, New York, 1962, p. 340, quoted by Rovine, p. 256.
24. In Judgment No. 18, Ruth E. Crawford had informed the US government that she had been a member of the Communist Party in 1935 for just over a year. She refused to answer the question of the Internal Security Sub-Committee of the US Senate on 15 October 1952 as to who in 1935 had asked her to join the Communist Party. It was not clear to the Tribunal 'in what way the services of a staff member can be of less value in her employment with the UN, by reason of declining to name some one person who invited her, many years before the creation of the UN to join the Communist Party, a membership which she had terminated within just over one year, particularly in the light of the fact that her previous refusal to give such information to the FBI had not precluded her employment by the US Government'. Even though she had held a temporary/indefinite appointment and not a permanent one, the Tribunal decided that the termination of her appointment was *ultra vires* and illegal. The complaints of other complainants holding temporary appointments were rejected, as no evidence had established improper motivation on the part of the UN administration—for instance, Judgment No. 19, *in re* Kaplan, 21 August 1953. The 'permanent' appointees (Judgments No. 28-38) were granted full salary from termination date to the date of the judgment, plus indemnities ranging ranging from $6,000 to $10,000.
25. Langrod, p. 220.
26. UN General Assembly Resol. 785(VIII) of 9 December 1953, and International Court of Justice Reports, 'Effects of Awards of Compensation made by the UNAT' (ICJ, 1954, pp. 47-87). General Assembly Resol. 888(IX) of 17 December 1954 decided to pay the compensation, in spite of the opposition of the US House of Representatives.
27. Langrod, p. 236, note 23.
28. Judgments No. 15 of 6 September 1954 and No. 18 of 26 April 1955.
29. US pressures were continuing. In the autumn of 1954, Ambassador Lodge denounced the director-general of UNESCO for having failed promptly and unquestioningly to dismiss all Americans on his staff who had received unfavourable loyalty reports. Moreover, Lodge entered public objections to the Report of ICSAB on 'Standards of Conduct', in which the basic principles of international loyalty of Secretariat officials prescribed in Article 100 of the

Charter was restated and declared his intention 'to do something about it': see Claude, p. 188.

30. Judgments No. 17, *in re* Duberg; No. 19, *in re* Wilcox; No. 21, *in re* Bernstein; No. 22, *in re* Froma; No. 23, *in re* Pankey; No. 24, *in re* Van Gelder.

31. ICJ Reports, 1956, pp. 77-168. Julian Behrstock, a former UNESCO staff member involved in the US loyalty investigations has related his experience in *The Eighth Case: Troubled Times at the UN*, University Press of America, Lanham, Md and London, 1987.

32. Judgment No. 13 rendered on 3 September 1953.

33. At the time of the case, the director-general of FAO, the director of administration, the chief of personnel and McIntire's chief were all US citizens, which may have influenced their attitude and decisions in response to US pressures. Such a lack of 'equitable geographical distributions' has been corrected since then.

34. Langrod, p. 225.

35. Ibid., pp. 225-6.

36. F. Honig, 'International Civil Service: Basic Problems and Contemporary difficulties', *International Affairs*, London, no. 30, 1954, p. 175.

37. See Peter Ozorio, 'McCarthyism Is Alive and Living in the UN', *UN Special*, Geneva, March 1984.

38. See Letter from US Mission to International Organizations, Geneva, Switzerland, dated 30 May 1986 to the director-general of WHO. Seconded US federal employees still require the agreement of their releasing organization, in accordance with the established practice of all countries.

39. Mark A. Roy, 'US Loyalty Program for Certain UN Employees Declared Unconstitutional', *The American Journal of International Law*, vol. 80, no. 4, October 1986, pp. 984-5.

40. See Richard W. Nelson, 'International Law and US Withholding of Payments to International Organizations', *American Journal of International Law*, vol. 80, no. 4, October 1986, pp. 973-83.

41. Charter amendments require a two-thirds vote in the General Assembly, plus ratification by two-thirds of member states including all five permanent members of the Security Council: Article 108. Most Third World countries are likely to reject weighted voting. Weighted voting is applied in the World Bank Group and the International Monetary Fund.

42. Beigbeder, *Management Problems in UN Organizations,* pp. 168-9.

43. *Nelson,* p. 976.

44. *'Certain Expenses of the UN: Art. 17, Paragraph 2, of the Charter'*, ICJ Reports, 151, 1962.

45. General Assembly Resol. 1854 of 19 December 1962.

46. Nelson, p. 979.

47. Beigbeder, *Management Problems in UN Organizations*, Pinter Publishers, London 1987, pp. 147-8. In July 1986 the eight largest outstanding contributions were, in millions of US dollars as follows: United States, 247; Soviet Union, 76.7; Ukraine, 10; Brazil, 8.1; Iran, 7.9; German Democratic Republic, 6.9; Saudi Arabia, 6.7; Poland, 6.4. See UN Doc. A/40/1102/ ADD.5—excluding South Africa's debt to the UN.

48. Ruggie, p. 344 and note 7.

49. US Public Law 98-164, 98th Congress, Section 116.

50. According to a reporttof the US Mission to the UN, New York, the average member nations voted with the US 23.7 per cent of the time in the General Assembly session of September-December 1986, an increase of 1 percentage point from 1985. The report did not take into account that 159 out of 314 resolutions considered by the General Assembly were adopted by consensus with

American approval. Diplomats from other countries say that votes against an American stand do not necessarily reflect anti-American feelings, but only show that the US is in the minority on many UN issues: *New York Times*, 15 July 1987.

51. In December 1983, the percentage of US staff in relation to all staff was 15.85 in the UN, and less in the major UN specialized agencies, for a budgetary contribution of 25 per cent: see the *Heritage Foundation* 'Report on the US and the UN: A Balance Sheet', 18 June 1984, p. 3. At 31 December 1986 the percentage was 7 per cent for all UN organizations: 3,621 US staff in relation to a total of 51,654: see UN Doc. ACC/1987/PER/R.35/Rev.1 of 14 September 1987. This is, however, not due to a deliberate practice on the part of the UN administrations but more to the recruitment difficulties of attracting US candidates to mostly expatriated UN jobs and relatively uncompetitive UN salaries.

52. The UN budget rose from $19,390,000 in 1946 to $872,130,450 for 1987 (General Assembly Resol. 41/211 C of 11 December 1986).

53. Wrong: these budgets are approved and controlled by the organizations' governing bodies. Further control is exercised by the Internal and External Auditors and by the Joint Inspection Unit.

54. See Beigbeder, *Management Problems in UN Organizations*, Pinter Publishers, London, 1987, pp. 17-18.

55. Beigbeder, ibid, pp. 153-6, 168-9. The 'Group of 18' intergovernmental experts was set up in 1986 'to conduct a thorough review of the administrative and financial functioning of the UN, which would contribute to strengthening the effectiveness of the UN in dealing with political, economic and social issues'. The Group's report is in UN Doc. A/41/49 of 15 August 1986.

56. Ruggie; Thomas M. Franck, 'Unnecessary UN-Bashing Should Stop', *The American Journal of International Law*, Washington, DC, vol. 80, no. 2, April 1986, pp. 336-7.

57. See UN Press Release SG/SM/786, 19 June 1987; *International Herald Tribune*, 1 July 1987, *Le Monde*, 16 September 1987. In the summer of 1987 the Heritage Foundation announced that it was organizing an 80-million letter campaign in an attempt to prevent the payment of the US contributions to the UN, by persuading voters to get Congress to block pending appropriation bills. General Vernon Walters, US ambassador to the UN had expressed, on behalf of the US government, satisfaction with the budgetary and financial changes agreed by the UN and advised that the administration would seek supplementary funding from Congress to pay all dues owing: see *WHO Dialogue*, Geneva, June 1987.

58. Many US nationals, as seconded officials or free agents, have played or are playing significant roles in the UN secretariats. In WHO alone, one may quote among others Milton P. Siegel as a long-term assistant-director-general for administration and finance, Dr Donald Henderson as the WHO manager for the successful Smallpox Eradication Campaign and Dr Jonathan Mann as director of the WHO Global Programme for AIDS.

Chapter 4

The socialist countries' minority view:
Marx or Perez de Cuellar?

> There should be no distinction among staff members based on nationality[1]

This exhortation of the UN secretary-general is addressed to member states as well as to the UN administrations: once recruited, all international staff should be treated alike, subject as they are to common rules and obligations. However, member states do not always respect this obligation.

The present secretary-general, J. Perez de Cuellar revealed in 1983 that his administrative task was made complex and sometimes exasperating as, 'while all member states profess their dedication to the principles of independent and objective international administration, few refrain from trying to bring pressure to bear in favour of their own particular interests. This is especially so on the personnel side'.[2]

The United States applied such pressures in the personnel field in the 1950s and is now applying financial pressures on the organizations, with an impact on their staffing.

Many states interfere with the personnel prerogatives of the executive heads of the UN secretariats in order to encourage the recruitment of their nationals and to promote the career of their citizens already employed in the organizations. They do so with a bad conscience, knowing that they contravene the spirit and letter of the UN Charter regarding the independence of the international civil service. Their occasional interventions are exceptions to the legitimate and acceptable conduct of member states which formally and sincerely respect their international obligations and support the internationalist concept of the international civil service.

The position of the socialist states of Eastern Europe is different.[3] Their concept of an international civil service is in total contradiction with the principles of the Charter. For these states, 'their' international staff does not acquire a real international, independent, status: they remain primarily dependent on their socialist state.

Following a review of the socialist conception of international organizations and of the international civil service, we will give a few examples of the attitudes and practices of the socialist countries' authorities in such domains as the independence of international staff, their employment tenure, recruitment, geographical distribution, non-renewal of secondments, withholdings of salaries, and espionage. We will then examine the consequences of these practices for the organizations and for the states concerned, and we will consider what attitude and measures could be adopted by the UN secretariats heads in order to limit these practices or decrease their negative effects.

The socialist concept of international organizations

According to Morozov, the socialist doctrine emphasizes conflict within international organizations and rejects supranationality or world government:

> Particular attention must be paid to the Leninist principle that, in foreign policy, it is essential to take into account not only the aggressive schemes of capitalist circles but also the attitudes of sane-thinking bourgeois politicians and opportunities for agreement with the Capitalist States. The activity of these intergovernmental organizations is therefore marked not only by cooperation but also by bitter contention, because peaceful coexistence in no way implies compromise in ideological matters.[4]

For the socialist countries, intergovernmental organizations are, on the whole, second-class members of the international system. They are not self-sufficient, and they cannot determine the course of world development.[5] Questions of war and peace and fundamental social problems can be solved only as a result of action by states and of interaction and cooperation between the major political forces. The wills of states with different social systems cannot be fused together to form some kind of single 'general' or 'supreme' will. Clashing class interests cannot produce a synthesis of wills.

For L.I. Brezhnev the UN actions and positions 'merely reflect the existing balance of forces between the States of the world'. The role of the secretary-general is limited; for instance, the Charter does not give him independent and personal powers to conduct peacekeeping operations.

A Polish view confirms the Socialist position that international organizations should be limited to the lowest level of institutional control.[6] This cautious attitude reflects the socialist countries' fear that since they are a numerical minority, they are exposed to high risks, as proved by their past experience (e.g. the UN interventions in Korea and in the ex-Belgian Congo). The Soviet Union views international law as a body of rules and principles through which powerful classes in several societies undertake jointly to promote 'class exploitation' in the international system.[7]

Socialist states demand limitations to the budgetary powers of the international organizations. They have proposed budgetary ceilings and argue that only administrative expenses should be included in the organizations' regular budget. They support a system of voluntary contributions for the expenditures for economic, social and military operations. They oppose a weighted voting system for the UN organizations as in the World Bank and in the International Monetary Fund.

Regarding the secretariats, socialist countries ask, as an institutional precaution, that a strict politico-geographical distribution of staff posts and an appropriate formula for collective leadership be applied. This would eliminate the risk that the organization could be transformed into a hostile instrument capable of being used against some of its members.

For Western observers the UN is perceived by the Soviet Union primarily as a threat and secondly as a means of extending its influence in the Third World, as a forum for embarrassing the West. They give verbal support to the New International Economic Order while arguing that since global poverty is the result of colonialism and exploitation, the bill should be presented to the west.[8]

In the UN organizations, the Soviet Union wants to cast the image of a peace-loving country working for general and complete disarmament, a lessening of international tensions, freedom for all colonial areas—everywhere opposed by the reactionary Western powers who dominate the Security Council and the secretariat.[9]

The general Soviet view is therefore to see the UN as a place of conflicts between the two world systems (rather than a centre of cooperation) where the socialist group, still in the minority, is trying to preach its gospel, convert the non-aligned and blame the aggressive, exploitative West. The presence of a superpower with a deeply engrained 'two-camp' view in a 'one world' organization, presents a continuing problem for the global organizations.[10]

The socialist concept of the international civil service

The fundamental socialist-capitalist conflict extends to the UN organizations' staff. The socialist concept rejects the internationalist view of the international civil service.

For Khilchevsky, international civil service activities have always borne the imprint of the struggle of the main forces operating on the international scene.[11] Initially (in the nineteenth and twentieth centuries' intergovernmental organizations, until 1917) the international civil service included representatives of politically homogeneous groups and reflected only the inter-imperialist contradictions. After the October Revolution, the international service became characterized by processes conditioned by the confrontation of the two opposing social systems. Recreated in the UN system, the international civil service immediately became the focus of acute ideological and political struggle. The struggle by states for fair staffing positions in the secretariats is in effect a political struggle, reflecting the alignment of forces both in the organizations and on the international scene. The international universality of the staff is the key condition of the organizations' viability. The two sets of recruitment criteria of efficiency, competence and integrity on one hand, and a wide geographical basis on the other, are interconnected.

However, the principle of fair geographical distribution of posts is not applied properly; in particular, Eastern Europeans continue to be underrepresented in the secretariats. Obstacles prevent the growth of influence of the representatives of the socialist and developing countries, maintaining the unjustified monopoly, especially in the top echelons, enjoyed by Western states.[12] One such obstacle is the practice of granting permanent appointments, which become the 'exclusive property of the states whose nationals fill them.

The functions of the secretariats should be static and limited: for the Soviet Union, their task is not to interpret the positions of the member states but rather to provide a basis for comparing different viewpoints on particular problems.

Independence and neutrality

Soviet Foreign Minister Litvinov said that only an angel could be neutral in issues between the communist and non-communist countries.[13] Chairman Khrushchev stated that 'while there are neutral countries, there are no neutral men'....'There can be no such thing as an impartial civil servant in this deeply divided world'....'The kind of political celibacy which the British theory of the civil servant calls for, is in international affairs a fiction'.[14]

Rubinstein has noted that Moscow's interpretation of the functions of the secretariat are diametrically opposed to that of the West: it does not see the secretariat as the administrative arm of the General Assembly or the Security Council, operating to fulfil the mandates of the political organs, independent of control by any particular government. Rather, it conceives of the secretariat as a body openly constituted on an ideological and political basis, devoid of impartiality and independence. For him, the Soviets seek to discredit, weaken and destroy the concept and structure of the international civil service: they do not believe that individuals will make decisions which contravene their class or political interest.[15]

This is confirmed by Khilchevsky, who rejects the Western 'traditional ideal' of a neutral international civil servant, devoid of any political sympathies or national allegiances, and denounces the 'oft-repeated ploy about the "unbiased, apolitical and ideal" international civil servant employed on a permanent basis'.[16]

The Gubishchev affair illustrates the initial difficulties of the Soviet Union in separating the status of a national civil servant from that of an international civil servant.[17] Gubishchev was employed by the UN in New York from July 1946 until his arrest by the American authorities for espionage, in March 1949. The Soviet Embassy claimed that he was employed by the UN secretariat as a member of the diplomatic service of the Soviet Union, with the permission of the Soviet government. The Soviet government did not revoke Gubishchev's diplomatic status, who thus remained a civil servant of the Soviet Ministry of Foreign Affairs, at the same time as he had become an international civil servant. This position is in contradiction with the very notion of the international civil service.

In 1953 UN Secretary-General Trygve Lie denounced the actions of the Soviet government and its allies as a 'policy of the crudest form of pressure, not only against me, but against any future Secretary-General who may incur the displeasure of the Soviet Union for doing his duty as he sees it under the Charter'.[18] Lie was being punished for having supported the UN action against armed agression in Korea. The central theme of the Soviet abuse and 'vilifications' was the charge that the secretariat was dominated by the Americans, as an obedient tool of Wall Street and Washington. Lie observed that it was ironic that at the same time the secretariat was being subjected to attacks in the United States for exactly opposite reasons.

Hammarskjold was also subjected to Soviet attacks, as a result of his conduct of the UN operations in the ex-Belgian Congo. His conduct was considered too independent from Security Council control and detrimental to Soviet interests. On 23 September 1960, in the UN General Assembly, Khrushchev launched a frontal attack on the Office of the Secretary-General and on the concept of an impartial and independent international civil service: in his famous troika proposal, the secretary-general was to be replaced by three persons representing the major groups, that is the military bloc of the Western powers, socialist states and neutralist countries. Khrushchev said, to explain his proposal:

We consider it advisable to set up, in the place of a Secretary-General who is at present the interpreter and executor of the decisions of the General Assembly and the Security Council, a collective executive organ of the UN consisting of three persons, each of whom would represent a certain group of States. That would provide a definite guarantee that the work of the UN executive organ would not be carried on to the detriment of any one of these groups of States. The UN executive organ would then be a genuinely democratic organ: it would really guard the interests of all States members of the UN.[19]

The troika was to apply to all UN organizations and to all hierarchical levels in these organizations: it would have effectively transformed the international secretariats into intergovernmental bodies, thus reversing to the political and administrative position of international institutions prior to the League of Nations. It would also, most probably, have paralysed the management of the organizations, by the insertion of a conflictual debating group at all decision-making levels.

The Eastern European group did not find a majority in the General Assembly to endorse its proposal. However, it constituted a visible and symbolic rejection by the Soviet authorities of the concept of an independent, impartial, international civil service, a position which has been firmly maintained up to the present. It also appeared as an attempt to weaken the role and effectiveness of the UN organizations by weakening their executive heads. The Soviet rejection of a strong secretary-general had been formulated during the San Francisco Conference in 1945: the Soviet Union then proposed that the secretary-general should be elected for two years and not be re-eligible. Four assistant-secretaries-general would be elected, in order to control the secretary-general and reinforce the privileged position of the Four Big Powers.[20] The troika was designed to give the Soviet bloc a veto in the running of the secretariat and to exercise a greater influence over decisions made in the secretariat.

As they do not believe that non-socialist UN staff can be impartial, the socialist countries do not want nor expect their own citizens to become true international civil servants nor to respect their international obligations.

Gromyko told Shevchenko, when the latter was appointed UN under-secretary-general, 'Never forget, Shevchenko, you are a Soviet ambassador first, not an international bureaucrat'.[21] He also asked him to seek international information useful to the Soviet Union. According to Shevchenko, every Soviet national who takes the organization's international oath must commit perjury. Before an individual's candidature is submitted by the Soviet Union to the UN Office of Personnel Services, that individual undertakes an obligation to do his best in the interests of the Soviet Union and to use his prospective job to achieve this purpose.

Duties and rules governing the conduct of Soviet nationals in the UN secretariat are defined in detail in a 'Statute on Soviet Employees of International Organizations'. The Soviet Mission in New York, and in other headquarters stations, maintains full control over the daily work of Soviet nationals in the UN organizations. All these staff members are part of the 'United Sections' of the Soviet Mission, where they receive direct instructions about how they should do their jobs in the secretariat and what their specific contributions to the work of the Mission itself should be. Soviet employees of the UN secretariat attend regularly meetings of the Communist Party section (functioning in New York in the guise of a trade-union organization): Party decisions are mandatory instructions for them, whether they are consonant or not with their international functions. Shevchenko gives several examples of activities pursued at the request and in the interest of Soviet authorities which clearly violated his international obligations.

Although the behaviour of the authorities of other socialist countries may, in some cases, be more flexible than that of the Soviet Union, it is clear that their position of principle is the same.[22]

In 1986 the Soviet Union pressed for the dismissal of American and British staff members by the UNESCO secretariat, after the withdrawal of their governments from the organization. This was a logical consequence of the socialist contention that international staff members represent their country: when their country ceases to be a member state, its 'representatives' should leave the organization. The UNESCO General Conference at its twenty-third session requested the director-general to take into account the necessity of ensuring an equitable geographical distribution of staff in any decision he will take on the renewal of fixed-term appointments and on reduction of staff.

The Federation of International Civil Servants' Associations (FICSA) opposed this resolution. It recalled that while nationality is a criterion which is taken into account in the recruitment to posts subject to geographical distribution, international civil servants, once appointed, are in the service of the international community as a whole. Any discrimination based on nationality would pose a direct threat to the integrity and independence of the international civil service.[23]

Career officials or temporary and seconded staff?

Soviet representatives have constantly expressed their opposition to a career international civil service.[24] They would like their own practice, and that of most other socialist countries, of seconding their civil servants to UN organizations for temporary periods, to become the norm, rather than the exception.[25]

Khilchevsky summarizes the socialist position in this respect by asking that the 'harmful' practice of permanent contracts should be discarded.[26] In his view, these contracts often shield mediocre or substandard officials, since their status gives them a maximum of safeguards against dismissal. The UN is practically powerless to get rid of a mediocre civil servant, who upon receipt of a permanent contract loses zeal for his work, limiting himself to fulfilling only a minimum of the requirements he has to cope with. The system of permanent contracts leads to the gradual formation of a closely-knit 'cosmopolitan caste' of international officials divorced from the topical problems of their own countries. Permanent contracts are also the main obstacles to an equitable geographical distribution of staff. On the other hand, the temporary secondment of officials from national institutions to the international organization is much to be preferred as it provides a useful exchange of experience. It would also assist developing countries, who would not lose their rare specialists to an international organization.

In fact, only a minority of UN staff on fixed-term appointments are also on secondment from their national civil service.[27] The two notions are made one only for socialist countries, because their candidates to UN employment are practically all employed by state organizations and therefore need to be formally seconded to the UN organization: there are no 'free' candidates from socialist countries. They are not normally allowed by their government authorities to accept a permanent contract, in the probable fear that a too long exposure to capitalist delights might erode their socialist virtues and faith.[28]

The socialist anti-career position has not gained ground over the years since the UN organizations were created. The UN career model was inherited from the League of Nations, which had taken the pattern from the British and French civil services. It has been repeatedly confirmed by the International Civil Service Commission (ICSC) and by the General Assembly,[29] who have emphasized the need for human resources planning and career development.

In opposition to the socialist arguments, promoters of the career concept submit that by ensuring security of employment, permanent contracts guarantee the independence of the staff; security of tenure enables employees to concentrate on their functions rather than worrying about a possible non-extension of contract and ensuing unemployment; permanent officials can participate fully and devote themselves entirely to their organization and their work; career prospects will attract qualified candidates; the experience acquired in the organization will increase progressively the qualifications and usefulness of the staff; long-term employees will be a lesser cost for the organization by avoiding recurrent recruitment costs, and for the individual, who will benefit from more individual and family stability; and permanent contracts facilitate the necessary continuity in the organization.

Opponents of the career concept denounce the possible bureaucratization, the lack of 'new blood' and innovation, the lesser dynamism due to an excessive security of tenure. Some managers favour fixed-term contracts as a means to maintain closer control on their staff. Other arguments in favour of fixed-term contracts include those points: these contracts help to ensure the exchange or rotation of staff between the UN organizations and national governments or institutions, thus providing a constant exchange of knowledge, updated technology and skills; they give greater flexibility to the organization and facilitate the attainment of equitable geographical distribution of staff; they facilitate the removal of staff members whose performance has ceased to be of high quality; on the other hand, fixed-term contracts may be renewed repeatedly if service is satisfactory.[30] In practice, there is need for the two types of contracts and the career dogma is not uniformly applied in all UN organizations.[31] Some of the specialized agencies, like WHO, have argued that they need fixed-term staff in varying proportions, in addition to permanent staff, because they require flexibility in the composition of their secretariat, and because temporary specialists are needed for technical work and in operational activities.

Is the Soviet policy of temporary secondments successful? A 1964 study gave a negative reply.[32] The study found that in general Soviet nationals had had little impact on international secretariats. In no secretariat had they become a power in the decision-making hierarchy. Reasons for this marginal influence were quoted as their short stay; the run-of-the-mill quality of most of the Soviets assigned; the language barrier; and the self-imposed isolation of the great majority of the Soviet staff. The most significant factor was the brevity of their assignments. The Soviet staff members hardly have time to familiarize themselves with the complexity of international administration before they are sent back home. They cannot accrue the source of authority derived from seniority.[33]

The reasons given for Moscow's policy of short-term appointments included an initial, fundamental lack of interest by the Soviet government in the UN secretariats; the initial lack of appreciation that the Soviet Union would gain by having Soviet nationals made an integral and continuing part of the secretariats; the individual Soviet nationals' reluctance to be seconded to UN organizations for more than a few years, because of their fear that it would jeopardize their promotion prospects at home; as already mentioned, the fear of the authorities that exposure to life in non-socialist countries might result in more critical attitudes toward the official ideology and policy, or even in outright defections.

While retaining their 'short-term secondments' policy, the Soviet authorities seem to have changed, to some extent, their attitude towards the presence of Soviet nationals in the secretariats. They have extended the periods of secondment from three or four years to seven or eight years.[34] They also allow some of those seconded to UN organizations to be re-employed by the organizations after a period in the Soviet Union, a practice which has proved beneficial to all parties concerned.

Recruitment

In 1953 secretary-general Trygve Lie stated that the procedures for the international recruitment of staff were now working fairly well in most member countries, with the notable exception of the Soviet Union. Soviet recruitment practices did not uphold his exclusive and independent authority for the selection of personnel.[35] This state of affairs has not changed.

The well-established position of the Soviet Union and other socialist states is that the recruitment of all its nationals is done exclusively on the recommendation of their Ministry of Foreign Affairs. The difference with non-socialist governments is that all socialist candidates are official government candidates, while the great majority of non-socialist candidates are 'free agents', whose applications need not be endorsed by their governments.[36] The other difference is that the Soviet Union usually recommends only one Soviet candidate for one specified post, thus leaving no choice to the secretariat head. The obvious answer to this practice would be to ask the Soviet authorities to submit lists of candidates for numerous vacancies, in order to allow candidates of other nationalities to compete, and to preserve the selection and appointment authority of the secretary-general.

In re Levcik the UN Counsel recognized that 'With respect to the nationals from some states, the applications are almost always received from the national missions of their governments. This is the case with respect to most Eastern European countries'.[37] The UN director of personnel assured the permanent representative of Czechoslovakia that the UN policy of 'close consultation with the Czechoslovak authorities will continue to be our rule'.

In re Rosescu the International Atomic Energy Agency (IAEA) argued that because of the need for geographical distribution of posts, it has to consult member states before making appointments:[38] such consultations are long-established practices.[39] The IAEA may recruit Romanian citizens only through or with the consent of the Romanian government since all citizens who are qualified for a professional post in the agency are government employees and have to be released from a government department before they can take up employment in the agency.

Regarding the UN and the Soviet Union, the practice of submitting only one candidate for a specific post has been demonstrated *in re* Yakimetz.[40] On 20 July 1977 the deputy permanent representative of the Soviet Union to the UN recommended Yakimetz for a post of reviser, grade P.4, in the Russian Translation Service of the UN in New York. On 31 October the UN Appointment and Promotion Board recommended the appointment of the applicant 'as a Russian reviser at the First Officer (P.4) level on a fixed-term secondment basis for a period of five years'. The UN Office of Personnel Services approved this recommendation and on 23 November offered the appointment to the applicant, informing the Soviet Mission by *note verbale*. In the same judgement, evidence is available that the Soviet authorities were contemplating replacing the applicant by another person whom they had already selected and whom they wished to be trained further by the applicant.

According to Shevchenko, every Soviet national has a duty to help recruit his countrymen to fill posts in the secretariat, often regardless of qualifications. 'The operative rule was: the more, the better'.[41] He was constantly pressurized by the Soviet Mission to use his position and influence to expand the Soviet presence. There was similarly persistent 'wheedling' from representatives of Soviet-bloc countries for expansion of their footholds in the secretariat.

Yakimetz had been a member of the UN Appointment and Promotion Board for two years. In his statement to the *New York Times* on 17 July 1984, he said that he was responsible for ensuring that all Soviet candidates proposed by his government be appointed.

In 1983 the president of FICSA called the attention of the International Civil Service Commision (ICSC) to the question of political influence in the recruitment process and its serious repercussions on the independence and integrity of the international civil service.[42] He was not limiting his remarks to the director's level, but was presumably referring to all professional levels and higher categories.

Non-socialist countries also submit official applications; however, these are reviewed together with applications from non-sponsored candidates of the same country, and with sponsored or free applications from other countries. Specific individualized recommendations may, from time to time, be submitted formally, or more discreetly, by non-socialist countries for specific high functions at director or higher level; these are normally the object of consultations with the secretariats' senior officials.

The socialist countries practice of presenting one and only one candidate for a specific post is an exorbitant privilege, not shared by other countries. Furthermore, the selection by the member states, rather than by the Personnel Services of the UN organization, does not necessarily guarantee that the person so appointed will be the best available candidate for the job.

Geographical distribution

Socialist countries justify their recruitment practices and pressures on UN organizations partly on the grounds that the composition of the secretariats does not reflect fairly and equitably the level of their participation in the organizations.[43] This argument is well founded.

Westerners dominated the UN secretariats from the start. Their numerical domination was due to the ease of recruitment at the locations of the organizations, in non-socialist states and the fact that training, experience, professional and linguistic requirements for the posts were better adapted to those countries than to socialist countries. Another reason was the initial Soviet concern about the security functions of the UN, and a consequent initial lack of interest in the specialized agencies. As previously noted, there was also a lack of appreciation of the importance of having more socialist countries nationals in the secretariats, a neglect which ceased in the 1960s.

Roshchin felt that this situation had a negative impact on the functioning of the UN;[44] throughout the subsequent years, Western countries, above all the United States, tried to use the numerical preponderance of their citizens in the UN system to control the organizations. The following figures confirm the persistent underrepresentation of the group of Eastern European countries in the UN secretariat, in relation to the impressive representation of Western Europe and North America. These figures in table 4.1 show that immediately following the creation of the UN, over 80 per cent of the posts were occupied by nationals from two regions, North America and Western Europe; in effect, two-thirds of the posts were filled by American, British and French nationals.

Table 4.1 Percentage of total number of UN secretariat posts, filled by nationals of different regions

Regions	1946	1963	1980
Africa	0.6	7.6	13.8
Asia and Pacific	6.6	17.4	15.5
Eastern Europe	6.6	11.8	10.2
Western Europe	31.3	25.1	23.5
Latin America	4.4	10.1	8.5
Middle East	0.5	4.3	4.9
North America	48.4	21.5	22.5
Non-members	1.6	2.2	1.2

Source: UN Doc. JIU/REP/81/10, July 1981, Tables 1, 2 and 3.

In 1963 the percentage of Western Europe and North America had decreased to 46.6 per cent, while Eastern Europe had risen from 6.6 to 11.8 per cent. Two Joint Inspection Unit (JIU) reports noted in 1981 and 1982 that a most serious situation concerning geographical distribution of the staff persisted in respect of Eastern European countries, a group which had always been underrepresented.[45] Their percentage of total posts even decreased from 1963 to 1980 from 11.8 to 10.2 per cent. The reports identified the following most important factors in this failure to attain an equitable geographical distribution: insufficient efforts made in many divisions of the secretariat to appoint candidates from unrepresented or underrepresented countries to vacant geographical posts, the extensive use of permanent contracts and the practice of filling vacancies by giving preference to internal over external candidates.

To these traditional, official arguments one should add reasons specific to recruitment from socialist countries: the slow bureaucratic formalities required to process at the national level the selection, clearance and secondment of a candidate from a socialist country; the short-term duration of their secondment with a consequent need to constantly (every five to eight years) recruit new candidates, only to maintain their level in the UN secretariats;[46] the difficulties of the authorities to find well-qualified candidates, professionally and linguistically, and the reluctance of candidates already mentioned above.

In 1982 the budgetary contribution of the Eastern European countries to the UN amounted to 17.5 per cent of the total, the number of their UN-determined 'desirable range' was 374 to 504 posts, the number of employed staff from that region was 312, or a percentage of 10.54 of total staff. The position of the Soviet budget contributions and staffing representation in December 1981 in UN organizations is shown in Table 4.2.

Table 4.2 Percentage of Soviet professional staff employed in UN organizations in relation to the percentage of the Soviet contributions to their respective budgets December 1981

Organization	Percentage of Soviet budgetary contribution	Percentage of Soviet staff employed
UN	11.01	6.04
ICAO	10.64	1.76
IAEA	11.59	9.16
ILO	11.02	3.87
IMO	5.61	3.57
ITU	7.00	3.73
UNESCO	10.98	3.05
UPU	2.35	-
WHO	10.91	3.15
WIPO	7.65	4.49
WMO	10.36	10.42

Source: 'Americans at the UN: An Endangered Species', **Heritage Foundation Backgrounder,** 14 February 1983.

The situation is unsatisfactory in all the organizations. UNESCO is accused by American conservatives of being a Soviet bastion; in reality, between 1979 and 1982 the representation of Eastern European countries decreased. The number of posts subject to geographical distribution held by these countries declined from sixty-nine in 1979 (8.8 per cent of the total) to fifty-five in 1982 (6.9 per cent of the total). This group has always been underrepresented in

UNESCO.[47]

A similar pattern is found at senior and policy-formulating levels (grades D.1 and above). In the UN secretariat, in the period 1978-81, the position of developing countries has improved, that of Western countries has decreased, and Eastern European countries have continued to be underrepresented.[48]

In ILO, out of eighty-two positions held at the D.1 and D.2 levels, Africa held fourteen; Americas, thirteen; Asia, seventeen; East Europe, three; West Europe, thirty-four; Middle East, one. At the directorate level, one assistant-director-general is Soviet. Altogether the number of Soviet nationals on the ILO staff is lower than its budgetary contributions would entitle it to be.[49]

Rather than blaming the UN secretariats for their chronic underrepresentation, the socialist countries could analyse and improve their own selection methods, expand their search for candidates, initiate training sessions for candidates in cooperation with the organizations and UNITAR (in particular language training), extend the periods of secondments to at least two terms of five years, with possible re-employment after a period at home.

Non-renewals of appointments

The secondment process gives the seconding member state the power to authorize the organization to renew the contract between the staff member and the organization, or to refuse the extension. Appointments, extensions and terminations of appointments are the statutory prerogatives of the executive heads: secondments therefore restrict those prerogatives.

In re Levcik, the UN Administrative Tribunal (UNAT), on the basis of the Higgins case (Judgment No. 92) recalled that any subsequent change in the terms of a secondment initially agreed on, for example its extension, 'obviously requires the agreement of the three parties concerned', that is the seconding government, the organization and the seconded staff member.[50] The Tribunal concluded that when a government which has seconded an official to the UN secretariat refuses to extend the secondment, the secretary-general is obliged to take into account the decision of the government. As a consequence, the seconded official whose secondment ends, cannot expect that his UN appointment will be renewed.

The Yakimetz case

In this case the UNAT considered that

> Insofar as he was on secondment from the USSR government, none of the actions he took could bring about any legal expectancy of renewal of his appointment. If his fixed-term appointment were not based on secondment, he could, in the jurisprudence of the Tribunal, have in certain circumstances expectation of one kind or another for an extension, but such a situation did not arise.[51]

Appointed for five years as from 27 December 1977, Yakimetz's UN appointment was extended from 27 December 1982 to 26 December 1983, his secondment having been extended for the same duration. On 9 February 1983 he applied for asylum in the United States. On 10 February he informed the permanent representative of the Soviet Union to the UN that he was resigning from his position with the Ministry of Foreign Affairs of the Soviet Union and from all other official functions he held in the Soviet government. On 1 March the UN secretary-general placed Yakimetz on special leave with full pay in accordance with Staff Rule 105.2(a), that is 'for other important reasons, for such period as the Secretary-General may prescribe'. On 11 March he was informed that he should not enter the premises of the UN until further notice. On 29 June he was promoted to grade P.5. with effect from 1 April 1983.

On 23 November Yakimetz was informed that 'upon instruction of the Secretary-General', it was not the intention of the organization to extend his fixed-term appointment beyond its expiry date, that is 26 December 1983. On 21 December he was reminded that his current one-year contract had been concluded on the basis of a secondment from his national civil service. The UN administration wrote:

At the time your present appointment was made, your government agreed to release you for service under a one-year contract, the organization agreed so to limit the duration of your UN service, and you yourself were aware of that arrangement which, therefore, cannot give you any expectancy of renewal without the involvement of all the parties originally concerned.

On 6 January 1984 Yakimetz filed an application to the UNAT in which he requested the Tribunal, among other claims, to order the rescission of the administrative decision not to consider an extension to his UN service.

In its judgment the Tribunal acknowledged that the legal issues involved were interspersed with political considerations. On legal grounds the Tribunal concluded that during his UN service Yakimetz was under secondment which could not be modified except with the consent of all three parties and that no tacit agreement existed between the applicant and the organization between 10 February and 26 December 1983 changing the character of their relationship.[52] The Tribunal therefore approved the position of the organization according to which the end of the secondment resulted in the expiry of the UN appointment.

The judgment also raised the question of Yakimetz's suitability as an international civil servant. In Judgment No.326 (Fischman), the Tribunal had referred to the widely held belief mentioned in a report of the Fifth Committee of the General Assembly that 'International officials should be true representatives of the cultures and personality of the country of which they were nationals, and that those who elected to break their ties with that country could no longer claim to fulfill the conditions governing employment in the UN.'

In the same judgment the Tribunal also recalled an Information Circular which stated, 'The decision of a staff member to remain or to acquire permanent residence status in the country of his duty station in no way represents an interest of the UN. On the contrary, this decision may adversely affect the interests of the UN in the case of internationally recruited staff members in the professional category'.[53]

The Yakimetz judgement therefore implies that the non-renewal of appointment was justified not only by the end of the secondment but also because his decision to apply for asylum and to change his nationality made him unsuitable as an international civil servant. Should one conclude that, according to the Tribunal, changing one's nationality constitutes serious misconduct which should be sanctioned by a dismissal (or non-renewal of appointment)? The staff Regulations and Rules of the UN organizations do not support such an interpretation.[54]

In his dissenting opinion Mr Arnold Kean rejected these findings. For him, 'it cannot be believed that the UN would ever have been a party to so unreasonable an agreement', that is to prevent the applicant from being employed by the UN then, or at any future time, however valuable or necessary his services may be.[55]

In the final analysis the interest of the organization, in continuing to benefit from the services of a competent and efficient staff member, and the staff member's individual rights should not be prejudiced: the interests of member states should be considered, but they should not necessarily and blindly prevail over these other interests.

On 23 August 1984 the UN Committee on Applications for Review of Administrative Tribunal Judgments decided that there was a substantial basis for review of the UNTA judgment and requested an advisory opinion from the International Court of Justice. On 27 May 1987 the Court confirmed the Tribunal's Judgment.[56]

In summary, it appears that the UN administration has refused to extend Yakimetz's appointment after his application for asylum under the pressure of the Soviet authorities,[57] in spite of the repeated requests of his supervisors. If a French (or Indian, or Peruvian) civil servant on secondment to the UN applied for US citizenship and resigned from his national civil service, would the French government apply pressure on the UN to prevent his contract from being extended? Would the UN bend to such pressures?

In view of the political nature of its activities, the UN is perhaps more exposed to such pressures than the specialized agencies. Besides, all the organizations are more sensitive to the pressures emanating from the Big Powers, which finance a large part of the organizations' budgets than to those of medium or small powers.

Other causes célèbres

In re Ballo the director-general of UNESCO had decided not to extend the appellant's appointment, as a matter within his entire discretion and solely on account of the official's merits or qualifications and his usefulness to the organization.[58] The Czechoslovak Permanent Delegation to UNESCO had in fact informed the director-general that it could not agree to the extension of Ballo's contract. The administrative Tribunal of the ILO (ILOAT) agreed that the director-general's decision not to renew a fixed-term appointment lay within the discretionary authority enjoyed by the secretariat head as the person responsible for its smooth running. Accordingly, the complainant could not claim any right to have his appointment renewed and, so as not to impair the director-general's authority, the Tribunal's power of review was limited.

Discretionary power must not, however, be confused with arbitrary power. In refusing to extend Ballo's appointment contrary to the unanimous recommendations of the high-ranking officials who were the complainant's supervisors and to the equally unanimous recommendation of the Senior Personnel Advisory Board, the director-general based his decision on an opinion which took account merely of a very small part of his work. The tribunal decided in favour of Ballo, not on the political grounds of the Czechoslovak government pressures, but on the administrative grounds that the director-general had ignored most of the facts in favour of the appellant's claim for extension, and had thus shown partiality. However, the political pressures of the Czechoslovak authorities were very apparent in the text of the judgment.[59]

In re Rosescu, the ILOAT added an important qualification to the obligation of the organization to accept without discussion the government decision not to renew the secondment, which normally causes the end of the seconded person's appointment with the UN organization.[60]

The tribunal considered that if a director-general intends to appoint a government official to the organization's staff, he will normally consult the member state, which may wish to keep the official in its service. Such consultation would also take place in the case of a proposed extension of the appointment. However, this does not mean that a director-general 'must bow unquestioningly to the wishes of the government he consults'. The director-general should retain his discretionary right of personal judgement to decide one way or another; he will be right to accede where sound reasons for opposition are expressed or implied. But he may not forgo taking a decision in the organization's interests 'for the sole purpose of satisfying a member State. The organization had an interest in being on good terms with all member States, but that is no valid ground for a Director-General to fall in with the wishes of every one of them'.

In the Rosescu case, if the Romanian authorities had explained that they were opposed to the five-year extension because they wanted the complainant back again, this might have been a sound reason, subject to the individual's consent. However, this reason was not valid, as Rosescu was unwilling to go back to his own country.

In taking the impugned decision (non-renewal of appointment) for no valid reason, the director general had let the interests of a member state prevail over the interests of the IAEA: according to the Tribunal, he had committed a misuse of authority which tainted his decision.[61] The complainant was granted

$50,000 as compensation plus costs.

Neither the UNAT nor the International Court of Justice has followed this jurisprudence in the Yakimetz case.

Salary withholdings

Some Eastern European countries require their nationals employed by UN organizations to repay to their government part of their international remuneration, presumably on the grounds that these emoluments are excessive (they provide a remuneration in excess of the normal satisfaction of basic needs for expatriated socialist personnel) and that the resulting financial surplus should benefit the socialist community, that is the state.

Shevchenko states that at the end of each month, Soviet employees of the Soviet secretariat in New York have to hand over all their UN emoluments to the Soviet Mission.[62] They are then paid a salary according to a Soviet-established scale, which deducts a large amount of the UN salary. For example a P.5 officer would only receive approximately $800 (the amount paid to a Soviet Mission counsellor) out of a monthly UN pay of $2,000. All those concerned had to comply without discussion, under the threat of a public accusation and under pressure of the Soviet ambassador.[63] In part compensation, the Soviet staff members in New York and Geneva are lodged by the Mission, which rents the appartments and pays for their maintence.

Polish staff in UN organizations have to repay about 15 per cent of their net UN emoluments, after deduction of their lodging expenses and contributions to insurance and pension. They receive no receipt of their payments. Hungarian staff members are apparently not required to pay such contributions to their government.[64]

The Dumitrescu case in UNESCO[65] has revealed the existence of Decree No. 233/1974, which requires Romanian employees of UN organizations to repay to their state a significant part of their UN emoluments: in the case of Rosescu, a UN director, this contribution amounted to more than two-thirds of his net emoluments. In the Rosescu case, his lawyers stated that a major reason for the Romanian refusal to approve a contract extension was a 'financial contribution' demanded by the Romanian Mission. It appears that Rosescu was willing to pay his government the percentage of his emoluments that it demanded, but only with respect to his base salary, and not with respect to his post (cost-of-living) adjustment.[66]

The Romanian decree and similar practices from other socialist countries are contrary to Section 18b of the Convention on Privileges and Immunities of the UN and to Section 19b of the similar conventions of the specialized agencies, which exempt UN staff from taxation in respect of their UN salary and other emoluments.

On the recommendation of ICSC, the General Assembly in 1982 called to the attention of member states the fact that 'the practice of ... deductions is inconsistent with the provisions of the Staff Regulations of the UN and, therefore, inappropriate'.[67]

The salary-witholding practice of most socialist countries is contrary to the undertaking of UN member states to respect the exclusively international character of the responsibilities of UN staff (Article 100.2 of the Charter). It is contrary to UN Staff Regulation 3.3 which determines the assessment rates on UN salaries. It is contrary to the fair labour principle of 'equal pay for equal work' and to the principle of equality of treatment of all UN staff members irrespective of their nationality.

Up to now, the concerned socialist countries have ignored these considerations and the General Assembly appeal.

Socialist spies in UN organizations

Placed under the authority of the secretariat head, international civil servants must neither seek nor accept instructions from their government. Their whole time should be given to their official functions. They cannot assume any other activities without the authorization of the executive head. They have an obligation of reserve and cannot engage in any political activity which would be inconsistent with or might reflect upon the independence and impartiality required by their status as international civil servants.[68] They must also avoid any action which would impair good relations with governments or destroy confidence in the secretariat. They must comply scrupulously with the laws of the host country.[69]

All these obligations are flouted by spies using and abusing the status of international civil servants. A number of staff members of UN organizations, Soviet citizens, have been suspected, accused or convicted of espionage since the creation of the UN organizations.

According to some sources,[70] the largest spy operation in New York is run by the Soviet Union. It is estimated that the Soviet network, including KGB (Soviet State Security) and GRU (Soviet Military Intelligence) officers and helpful Soviet officials employed by the UN secretariats, and informants, total about 1,000 persons. According to Heritage Foundation,[71] at least one in three of all Soviet, Eastern-bloc and client-state diplomats posted to the United States engages in espionage. According to Shevchenko, at least half the Soviet nationals working in the UN are not diplomats but KGB or GRU professionals.[72] In his post as chief of the Security Council and Political Affairs Division of the Soviet Mission to the UN, he discovered that seventeen members of his staff were KGB or GRU agents. In his own UN department, nine of the twelve Soviet employees were information agents, as well as one Czechoslovak, one Hungarian, one East German and one Bulgarian official. For them, intelligence was top priority in New York—the UN did not matter. According to de Borchgrave,[73] seventy-eight of the 300 Soviet employees serving the various UN organizations in Geneva are KGB or GRU agents. Espionage is rarely directed against the organizations themselves, as their activities are generally not confidential and are rarely valued as spy material.

Espionage usually applies to the host country or as a base for neighbouring countries.

Examples are many: for example, Gubishchev was arrested for espionage by the American authorities in New York, in March 1949.[74] On 24 February 1967 Nicolas Petrov, elected official of the ITU was expelled from Switzerland for espionage: he had tried to corrupt a high Swiss official in order to obtain information concerning Switzerland and another country.[75]

Shevchenko's defection on 10 April 1978 was followed by the discovery of several espionage cases. On 20 May 1978 two other UN officials in New York, R.P. Tchernyayev and V.A. Enger, were arrested while attempting to obtain secret US military documents. They were suspended from their UN functions the same day, without salary, and dismissed on 30 September. On 30 October 1978 they were condemned by a United States court to fifty years' imprisonment. They were exchanged on 27 April 1979 against five dissidents detained in the Soviet Union.[76] On 6 June 1978 V. Boukreev, an ILO director, left his post for 'family reasons'.[77] On 31 July 1978 ILO terminated the contract of G. Miagkov, at the request of Switzerland.

Informed of allegations according to which several senior UN officials of Soviet nationality were 'KGB colonels',[78] secretary-general Kurt Waldheim replied that he had only been informed of press reports, but he had no formal evidence of these allegations.[79]

In April 1980 a Soviet WHO Public Information employee, Ilya Dzhirkvelov, defected to Britain: he revealed that he had been a KGB agent until 1956, then a Tass correspondent. He had continued to work for the Soviet information services during his WHO employment.[80] In April 1983 the French government expelled forty-seven Soviet citizens, including Soviet diplomatic personnel and five UNESCO staff members. The latter resigned from their UNESCO employment from Moscow.[81]

A more recent, documented spy case is that of Gennadi F. Zacharov, another Soviet national employed by the UN at the center for Science and Technology for Development. He was arrested on 23 August 1986 in New York and charged with espionage.[82]

In October 1986 the United States Senate Select Committee on Intelligence charged that a Soviet intelligence officer was holding the position of assistant-secretary-general at the UN, confirming the Reagan administration's assertion that the Soviet Union is using the UN as a platform for spying.[83]

In an attempt to counter espionage activities based in the UN, in December 1985 the US administration required specific authorization for travel outside New York by several communist countries' and other countries' nationals employed by the UN and mandated that their travel arrangements be notified to and booked by the United States governement. The secretary-general responded by making the controls applicable equally to all staff.[84]

In March 1986 the US administration ordered a 38 per cent reduction in the Soviet, Ukrainian and Byelorussian delegations, accusing them of espionage and calling the size of the missions 'a threat to national security'. The delegations' permanent staff would be cut from a total of 275 to 170 by 1 April 1988.[85]

What can be done ?

The practices of East European socialist countries described above conflict with the principles of the international civil service defined in the UN Charter and in the constitutions of the specialized agencies, in the Staff Rules and Regulations and in the conventions on the privileges and immunities of the UN organizations.

Secretariat heads have had to accept most of these practices (espionage excluded) which, for the states concerned, are not negotiable: they are part and parcel of the rigid and authoritarian framework of relations between the socialist state and its citizens, within the context of the socialist concept of international organizations, second-rate, non-autonomous actors on the international stage. The participation of socialist states to the UN organizations seems to be dependent on the acceptance of these practices by the international administrations.

The consequences of these practices are generally unfavourable for the organizations and for the states concerned.

For the organizations, these practices divide the secretariat into an international sector placed under the authority of the executive head, and an intergovernmental sector which remains under the control of a few member states. They destroy the unity of the secretariat in creating national or ideological enclaves, and they challenge the impartiality of the international civil service and therefore the credibility of the international secretariats.

The exclusive practice of official applications for employment, if they are not submitted to a critical review and selection, may result in the recruitment of unqualified, or insufficiently qualified, personnel, on professional and/or linguistic grounds

Contracts restricted to five or eight years limit the efficiency of staff of those nationalities: the orientation and adjustment of new employees to the very specific constraints and characteristics of the international secretariat may require at least twelve months as an apprenticeship. The exclusive practice of temporary contracts, not renewable beyond a set duration, is prejudicial to the continuity and memory of the secretariats, and therefore to their effectiveness. The activities of some seconded officials to the exclusive, or priority, benefit of their government make a mockery of their official, professional obligations.

By a reaction of defence, some of the organizations or departments only assign secondary or temporary tasks to seconded officials from socialist countries, or isolate them in positions without substance or responsibilities, secluded from the mainstream of the organization's life. This unfortunate attitude may be explained by the knowledge that these officials will only spend a few years in the organization, and by the suspicion that some of them will use their position in the UN for the exclusive benefit of their country.

These practices have had negative consequences for the socialist countries, which do not always allow their nationals to demonstrate their abilities, their competence, their interest, if not their devotion, in the international service.

Socialist countries also lose a potential influence in the secretariats by lack of continuity, the constant turnover of their nationals.

Their recurring spying activities contribute significantly to the deterioration of their public image and to distrust of many of their colleagues in the secretariats. The recurrent discovery of 'espionage in the UN' makes the organizations easy targets for media criticisms of the organizations themselves, although they have no possible responsibility in such activities. The effective benefits of the socialist personnel practices to those countries are questionable in relation to their very substantial costs.

Executive heads cannot stop member states from submitting official applications, nor make them authorize longer-term secondments. However, the organizations may and must apply to the staff members of socialist countries the same rules as to international staff of other nationalities in order to avoid any injustice and to preserve the integrity of the organizations' personnel policies.

With the full support of the secretariat head, the Personnel Services should ensure that the applications submitted by those states fulfil the education, training, experience and linguistic qualifications of the posts to be filled. Competitive selection should apply in all cases, by taking into account internal and external candidates of all nationalities, in order to avoid the creation of national fiefdoms.

On appointment the new UN employee should not only sign the oath of office (Article 1.9 of the UN Staff Regulations) but also participate in group briefing sessions during which their obligations of independence would be stressed. The functions and responsibilities of positions offered to East European countries' candidates should be clearly related to the grading of the posts. Their supervisors should be encouraged to control carefully their initial orientation, their performance and conduct, like those of their other subordinates. They should not hesitate to sanction, after a warning, any negligence, unsatisfactory performance, unexplained absence, indiscretion, partiality or violation of the standards of conduct of international civil servants.

All member states contribute to the budgets of the organizations, three quarters of which are spent on personnel costs. All member states, including the socialist countries, should be equally insistent that all staff members work hard, be devoted and loyal and respect the Rules and Regulations.

Morozov stated that the 'functional efficiency of the machinery of an intergovernmental organization, i.e. the quality of the international civil service, is naturally also of considerable importance'.[86] Should not the socialist nationals employed by UN organizations *also* show this quality?

Finally, the protection of the independence of the international civil service against governmental interventions relies to a large extent on the firm determination of the executive head, himself relying on the statutory texts and regulations. In so doing, he can also rely on the support of a majority of member states and on that of the staff associations and unions.

Notes

1. 'Report of the Secretary-General on the Work of the Organization', UN Doc. A/41/1, 9 September 1986.
2. 'Report of the Secretary-General on the Work of the Organization', UN Doc. A/38/1, 1983.
3. Albania, Bulgaria, Hungary, Poland, the German Democratic Republic, Byelorussia, Ukraine, Romania, Czechoslovakia, the Soviet Union and Yugoslavia constitute the Eastern European Group. In the context of this chapter, Albania may be excluded, as no Albanian citizen has been employed by the UN since its creation. No reference will be made to Yugoslavia, as its personnel practices are very similar to those of non-socialist countries.
4. Grigorii Morozov, 'The Socialist Conception of International Organization', in Georges Abi-Saab (ed.), *The Concept of International Organization*, UNESCO, Paris, 1981, pp. 173-92.
5. Socialist countries do not support economic reform, their objective being the revolutionary conversion of developing countries to socialism. While in 1984 Western industrialized countries provided approximately 86 per cent of the voluntary contributions to the UN system for operational activities for development, developing countries provided 13 per cent and East European countries only 1 per cent. See UN Doc. A/41/461, E/1986/119 of 16 July 1986, Annex. See also Yves Beigbeder, 'Views of Socialist States', in *Management Problems in UN Organizations*, Frances Pinter, London, 1987, pp. 19-20
6. Wojciech Morawiecki, 'Institutional and Political Conditions of Participation of Socialist States in International Organizations: A Polish View', *International Organization*, vol. XXII, no. 2, spring 1968, pp. 494-507.
7. Watter S. Jones and Steven J. Rosen, *The Logic of International Relations* Winthrop, Cambridge, Mass., 1974, p. 465.
8. Ivor Richard (UN permanent representative to the UN between 1974 and 1979) detected no sign whatsoever during his time at the UN that the Russains were prepared to participate in the establishment of a system of world order that might inhibit their national freedom of action. The Soviet Union was often extremely difficult to deal with: narrow, introverted, suspicious, with a slow bureaucracy and a pervading security service: Ivor Richard, 'Major Objectives and Functions of the UN: The View from Abroad', in Toby Trister Gati, (ed.), *The US., the UN and the Management of Global Change*, New York University Press, New York, 1983, pp. 58-60.
9. Alvin Z. Rubinstein, *The Soviets in International organizations*, Princeton University Press, Princeton, NJ, 1964, p. 258. According to Arkady N. Shevchenko, *Breaking with Moscow* (Alfred A. Knopf, New York, 1985), Gromyko, one of the UN's founding fathers, regarded the organization 'as no more than a forum for disseminating propaganda and abuse, ignoring it if the UN did anything out of line with Soviet policy and using it in situations when it profited Moscow or its clients'. Shevchenko wrote that 'in most respects, the Soviet Union disdained the UN. The one exception resided in the desire to use it to shelter KGB spies and to vent out our propaganda': pp. 161 and 293.

Shevchenko, a UN under-secretary-general, asked for political asylum in the United States in April 1978.

10. Alexander Dallin, 'The Soviet View of the UN' *International Organization*, vol. XVI, no. 1, winter 1962, pp. 20-36.

11. Y. Khilchevsky, 'International Organizations: Problems of Effectiveness and Universality', *International Affairs*, Moscow, December 1981, pp. 110-19.

12. Presumably created by Western-oriented UN secretariats' officials.

13. Quoted by Oscar Schachter, in Robert S. Jordan (ed.), *Dag Hammarskjold Revisited*, Carolina Academic Press, Durham, NC, 1983, 'The International Civil Servant' p. 42. See also his discussion of the meaning of neutrality, pp. 42-5.

14. *New York Herald Tribune*, 17 April 1961.

15. Rubinstein, pp. 259-60, 276.

16. Khilchevsky, pp. 115-16.

17. Mohammed Bedjaoui, *Fonction publique internationale et influences nationales*, Edn. Pedone, Paris, 1958, pp. 225-8.

18. 'The Personnel Policy of the UN', *UN Bulletin*, vol. XIV, no. 6, 15 March 1953.

19. 'Statement of Mr Khrushchev at the XVth Session of the UN General Assembly', UN Doc. A/SR.862, A/SR.882.

20. Jean Siotis, *Essai sur le Secrétariat international*, Lib. Droz, Geneva, 1963, p. 148.

21. Shevchenko, pp. 218, 221.

22. Concerning China, Kurt Waldheim recalls in his memoirs that a secretariat official, on his own initiative, had reassigned a Chinese employee, moving him to a more important position. Within twenty-four hours of his being informed, the Chinese ambassador visited the official with a protest. His response to the explanation given was blunt: 'Who wants a more important job? We were not consulted on this. We don't believe in being pushed around. As far as we are concerned, he will stay where he is': Waldheim *In the Eye of the Storm*, Weidenfeld & Nicolson, London, 1985, p. 46.

23. See *International Herald Tribune*, 28 February 1986, and UNESCO Staff Association *Opinion*, no. 23, 28 February 1986. The Soviet Union had already called for the dismissal of US staff members of UNESCO in 1984: *International Herald Tribune*, 19-20 May 1984.

24. See Theodor Meron, *The UN Secretariat: The Rules and the Practice*, Lexington Books, Lexington, Mass., 1977, pp. 28-34; Thomas Bayard (pseud.) 'L' Attitude des Etats d'Europe de l'Est à l'égard des secrétariats des Nations Unies', *Revue belge de Droit international*, Brussels, 1984-1985/2, pp. 676-8.

25. As of September 1985, 96.8 per cent of Soviet nationals serving the UN were on fixed-term contracts, non-career, and for the entire socialist bloc, 96.3 per cent. For the UN secretariat as a whole, the percentage of fixed-term appointments in relation to total staff was 37 per cent at 31 December 1986. See 'By breaking the Rules, Moscow Keeps a Tight Grip on the UN', *Heritage Foundation Backgrounder*, July 23, 1986, p. 5; and UN Doc. ACC/1987/PER/R.35/Rev. 1, *Personnel Statistics*, 14 September 1987.

26. Khilchevsky, pp. 115-17.

27. For instance, in WHO, approximately 20 per cent of professional staff and higher categories are on secondment from their national civil service. The percentage of fixed-term appointments in relation to total staff in 87 per cent for WHO headquarters and established offices: see UN Doc. *Personnel Statistics*, p. 23.

28. There are no UN organizations headquarters in socialist countries.

29. See ICSC study on the 'Concept of Career, Types of Appointment, Career Development and Related Questions', UN Doc. A/37/30, Annex I, and General Assembly Resolution 37/126 IV of 17 December 1982. The 'Group of 18' has also taken a pro-career stance: it has recommended that staff members should be

eligible for permanent appointments after having served three years in the UN; the General Assembly had recommended the same measure, but after five years: Resol. 37/126.IV.5. The Group, in an open challenge to the socialist countries, recommended by a majority decision that at least 50 per cent of the nationals of any member state working in the secretariat should be employed on a permanent basis: UN Doc. A/41/49, 1986, Recommendations 45 and 47.

30. See UN Doc. JIU/REP/81/10, p. 10, for a discussion of the career vs. fixed-term appointments issue.

31. For headquarters and other established offices, the percentage of permanent contracts in relation to all staff was on 31 December 1986: UN, 63 per cent: FAO, 48 per cent; ILO, 57 per cent; UNESCO, 12 per cent; WHO, 13 per cent. UN Doc. *Personnel Statistics*, p. 23.

32. Rubinstein, pp. 279-82. The information was derived from interviews with officials of international secretariats.

33. For instance, in WHO, the assistant-director-general in charge of administration, budget, finance and personnel, an American citizen, has been in position from 1971 to 1988. During the same period, the post of assistant-director-general for certain programme activities has been filled in succession by three Soviet medical officers.

34. Shevchenko, p. 221.

35. 'The Personnel Policy of the UN', p. 5.

36. For instance, the UN, FAO, ILO and WHO accept 'free' applications, from non-civil servants, directly from the candidates, without any government intervention. On the other hand, IAEA, ITU, UNESCO and UPU want all applications to be routed through, or endorsed by, the relevant member state's authorities.

37. UNAT Judgment No. 192 of 11 October 1974, Sections IX and XV.

38. ILOAT Judgment No. 431 of 11 December 1980, Section D.

39. Geographical distribution may require that the organization ask the government's help in obtaining more applications from nationals of that country. It does not entail 'consultations before making appointments', which imply clearance by governments of all applicants for UN employment.

40. UNAT Judgment No. 333, 8 June 1984, pp. 2 and 14, Section XI.

41. Shevchenko, p. 225.

42. UN Doc. ICSC/18/R.33 of 24 August 1983, para. 116.

43. UN Resol. 35/210 of 17 December 1980 established a target of 40 per cent of all vacancies arising in professional posts subject to geographical distribution in 1981-2 for the appointment of nationals of unrepresented and underrepresented countries. It reaffirmed that no post should be considered as the exclusive preserve of any member state, or group of states. However, it allowed the replacement of staff members by candidates of the same nationality, in respect of posts held by staff members on fixed-term contracts, whenever this was necessary to ensure that the representation of member states whose nationals serve primarily on fixed-term contracts was not adversely affected. Desirable ranges for each member state were to take into account 3,350 posts, UN membership, population and budgetary contribution factors with upper and lower limits.

44. Alexei Roschin, 'How the UN Got Started', *International Affairs*, October 1986, p. 129.

45. UN Doc. JIU/REP/81/10 and JIU/REP/82/9.

46. Hammarskjold stated to the *New York Times*, 19 October 1960: 'I get lists of candidates. We pick out those who seem to fit the vacancies, and then, it happens, too often in some cases, that after a short time of employment, without any pre-warning, those recruited go home again, or may be withdrawn. In fact, it is in some cases difficult to keep such a pace of recruitment as to balance the pace

of withdrawal'. Quoted by Rubinstein, p. 269.

47. UN Doc. JIU/REP/82/11, December 1982, p. 5.

48. UN doc. JIU/REP/82/9, July 1982, p. 12.

49. ILO Doc. GB.230/19/4, June 1985, 'Declaration of the Socialist Countries on the situation in ILO'.

50. Judgment No. 192 of 11 October 1974.

51. UNAT Judgment No. 333 of 8 June 1984.

52. One wonders if the imposed 'special leave' and the order not to enter UN premises did not change the character of these relationships, or if the application for asylum, which caused these administrative measures, did not change the former three-party secondment relationship (Soviet Union, UN, Yakimetz) into a normal two-party contractual relationship (UN, Yakimetz).

53. UN Doc. ST/AFS/SER.A/238 of 19 January 1954.

54. UN Staff Rule 104.4 only requires 'a staff member who intends to acquire permanent residence status in any country other than that of his or her nationality or who intends to change his or her nationality to notify the secretary-general of that intention before the change in residence status or nationality becomes final'.

55. Yakimetz's performance was rated 'excellent'. His chief had recommended the extension of his services in view of his 'long and outstanding record in the UN.'.

56. The Court was of the opinion that (1) the Tribunal did not fail to exercise jurisdiction vested in it by not responding to the question whether a legal impediment existed to the further employment in the UN of the applicant after the expiry of his fixed-term contract on 26 December 1983 (unanimously), (2) the Tribunal did not err on any question of law relating to the provisions of the UN Charter (by eleven votes to three). See ICJ Reports, Advisory Opinion of 27 March 1987.

57. *New York Times*, 4 January 1984.

58. ILOAT Judgment No. 191 of 15 March 1972.

59. See David Ruzié, 'Le Non-renouvellement des contrats à durée déterminée et l'ingérence des Etats (à propos de l'Affaire Ballo)', *Annuaire francais de droit international*, Paris, 1972, pp. 378-91.

60. ILOAT Judgment No. 431, 11 December 1980.

61. See Theodor Meron, '*In re* Rosescu and the independence of the international civil service', *American Journal of International Law*, vol. 75, 1981, pp. 910-25.

62. Shevchenko, pp. 131-2, 232.

63. Shevchenko states that these 'kickbacks' covered almost all the expenses of the Soviet Mission in New York.

64. Information received informally from UN staff members.

65. Alain Pellet, 'A propos de l'affaire Dumitrescu à l'UNESCO: Note sur l'indépendance des fonctionnaires internationaux', *Journal de Droit international*, 1979, no. 3, p. 572.

66. T Meron, '*In re* Rosescu', p. 921, note 34.

67. General Assembly Resol. 37/126, 11, 17 December 1982.

68. UN Staff Regulations 1.2, 1.3, 1.5 and 1.7.

69. UN Doc. COORD/CIVIL SERVICE/5, 1954, 'Report on Standards of Conduct in the International Civil Service'.

70. See 'UN Infested with Spies—and Everybody Knows It', *International Herald Tribune*, 4 September 1979. The article states that about 200 FBI or CIA agents are assigned to counter-intelligence. Other countries allegedly involved in spying operations in New York are China, Israel and Yugoslavia, according to the article. The fact that most headquarters of UN organizations are situated in Western countries (New York, Montreal, Paris, London, Geneva, Bern, Rome, Vienna) explains, but does not justify, the active utilization of these organizations by information services of East European countries, and particularly by the Soviet

Union.

71. According to 'Soviet Espionage: Using the UN against the US', *Heritage Foundation Backgrounder*, no. 453, 9 September 1985, the total number of Soviet and Soviet-bloc nationals in New York amounted in 1984 to 1,204 persons, including 575 staff members of the UN secretariat.

72. Shevchenko, pp. 131-2, 242, 300-1.

73. A. de Borchgrave, 'Geneva's Soviet Agents', *'Newsweek'* 7 May 1979.

74. Bedjaoui, pp. 225-8.

75. Ch. Rousseau, 'Chronique des faits internationaux', *Revue générale de Droit international public*, 1967, no. 4, pp. 792-3.

76. Ch. Rousseau, 'Etats-Unis et URSS', *Revue générale de Droit international public*, 1979, no. 1, pp. 167-8, and 1979/4, p. 1034.

77. According to *Le Messager*, Thonon, 7 July 1978, Boukreev had referred to his sick mother, although she had died two years earlier. See also *La Tribune de Genève*, 5 and 6 August 1978.

78. Such allegations were made regarding Geli Dneprovsky, appointed director of personnel of the UN Office in Geneva in August 1978, and Vladimir Lobachev head of the UN Conferences and General Services Division, also in Geneva. The latter was replaced in 1979 by Yuri Ponomarev, another Soviet citizen. See Borchgrave's article.

79. *La Tribune de Genéve*, 6 July 1978.

80. *The Times*, 23 May 1980.

81. Rousseau, 'Chroniques', *Revue générale de Droit international public*, 1983, p. 865, and *Le Monde*, 15 December 1984.

82. Zacharov paid $1,000 for documents about a US Air Force jet engine. See International Herald Tribune, 25 August 1986 and 12 September 1986.

83. See *International Herald Tribune*, 9 October 1986, which refers to Vladimir Kolesnikov as a 'KGB China Expert'.

84. See *note verbale* from the US Mission to the secretary-general, 13 December 1985, UN Doc. ST/IC/85/74, Ann. (1986) and Thomas M. Franck, 'Unnecessary UN-Bashing Should Stop', *American Journal of International Law*, Washington, DC, vol. 80, no. 2, April 1986, pp. 336-7.

85. *International Herald Tribune*, 10 March 1986 and 9 October 1986; *UN Chronicle*, August 1986, p. 106. In December 1987, Mikhail Katkov, second secretary to the Soviet Mission to the UN in New York was detained by the Federal Bureau of Investigation on charges of espionage. He was to be expelled: International Herald Tribune, 19-20 December 1987.

86. Morozov, p. 179.

Chapter 5

The once-pampered international civil servant: an overpaid bureaucrat?

> In those days, there was no question of any pension rights or of security
> of tenure. They joined in the spirit of adventure, in the proper spirit of
> venture into the unknown, attracted as they were by the political
> philosophy of the League[1]

League of Nations personnel cannot all have been pure idealists: some were no
doubt also attracted by the high salaries offered by the new organization, as
many candidates have been attracted to UN employment on account of its
initially generous employment conditions.

Were the League employees and are the UN organizations' staff overpaid?
In order to answer this question one needs to relate international emoluments
to other international or national comparators. In practice, UN emoluments
are only compared with national standards, the professional and higher
categories with the United States Federal Service, and general service salaries
with the best local employers in the duty station.[2] General service staff are
support staff, essentially recruited locally; they include secretarial and clerical
personnel, administrative assistants and manual workers. Professional staff
are university trained generalists or specialists assigned to programme or
administrative areas. Higher categories include directors, heads of secretariats
and their assistants.

The salary scale for the professional and higher categories effective on 1
April 1987 is shown in Table 5.1. There is a salary scale for general service
staff in each duty station, reflecting the best local employment conditions. The
professional scale is an international scale applicable, subject to post
adjustments, to professional and higher categories staff in all duty stations.
The professional salary scales are based in US dollars, while general service
salary scales are expressed in local currencies.

In theory, there is no 'right' remuneration. In the national private sector,
pay and benefits are determined by reference to the firm's objectives, policies
and type of activities, government regulations (for instance, minimum wages,
compulsory benefits and protection), labour supply and demand, the type of
manpower employed in the firm, the firm's ability to pay, the margin of
profit, the state of the economy, the cost of living, union demands and
competitors' practices. In the public sector, governments are theoretically free
to choose the applicable rates, but in practice they need to relate them to
private-sector rates and practices, in order to remain competitive.

The 'high' UN salaries have been criticized in recent years by both East and
West, by reference to the salaries and benefits applicable to professional and

Table 5.1 *Salary scale for the professional and higher categories showing annual gross salaries and net equivalents after application of staff assessment, April 1987 (in US $)*

Level	Rate	I	II	III	IV	V	VI	VII	VIII	IX	X	XI	XII	XIII
Under-secretary-general USG	Gross	94,802												
	Net D	64,535												
	Net S	58,290												
Assistant secretary-general ASG	Gross	85,609												
	Net D	59,203												
	Net S	53,887												
Director D-2	Gross	69,093	70,819	72,561	74,336									
	Net D	49,406	50,441	51,487	52,552									
	Net S	45,376	46,297	47,228	48,175									
Principal officer D-1	Gross	59,373	60,972	62,551	64,140	65,739	67,340	68,895						
	Net D	43,461	44,453	45,432	46,417	47,393	48,354	49,287						
	Net S	40,039	40,934	41,819	42,708	43,585	44,440	45,270						
Senior officer P-5	Gross	52,718	54,003	55,261	56,511	57,778	59,023	60,276	61,521	62,775	64,016			
	Net D	39,290	40,112	40,912	41,687	42,472	43,244	44,021	44,793	45,571	46,340			
	Net S	36,282	37,019	37,736	38,436	39,146	39,843	40,545	41,242	41,944	42,639			
First officer P-4	Gross	42,356	43,575	44,795	46,038	47,313	48,515	49,718	50,918	52,178	53,455	54,686	55,901	
	Net D	32,605	33,409	34,215	35,014	35,830	36,602	37,369	38,137	38,944	39,761	40,549	41,308	
	Net S	30,282	31,009	31,738	32,455	33,185	33,876	34,563	35,251	35,973	36,705	37,410	38,095	
Second officer P-3	Gross	34,329	35,480	36,625	37,736	38,877	40,040	41,202	42,340	43,377	44,398	45,448	46,500	47,573
	Net D	27,294	28,067	28,822	29,556	30,309	31,077	31,843	32,594	33,279	33,953	34,637	35,310	35,997
	Net S	25,475	26,177	26,860	27,523	28,205	28,899	29,593	30,272	30,891	31,501	32,117	32,719	33,334
Associate officer P-2	Gross	27,608	28,533	29,451	30,382	31,337	32,284	33,239	34,181	35,136	36,117	37,082		
	Net D	22,675	23,323	23,965	24,610	25,259	25,903	26,553	27,193	27,840	28,487	29,124		
	Net S					23,623	24,209	24,800	25,383	25,971	26,557	27,133		
Assistant officer P-1	Gross	20,953	21,916	22,690	23,542	24,408	25,282	26,192	27,056	27,905	28,725			
	Net D	17,936	18,557	19,187	19,800	20,424	21,047	21,684	22,289	22,883	23,458			
	Net S	16,906	17,477	18,056	18,620	19,193	19,766	20,350	20,905	21,450	21,976			

Steps

D = Rate applicable to staff members with a dependent spouse or child.
S = Rate applicable to staff members with no dependent spouse or child.

Source: UN Doc. A/41/53, 1987, p. 244

higher-categories staff. Government pressures have stopped the growth of these salaries and pensions and even reduced some benefits, while the depreciation of the US dollar has further eroded UN professional emoluments and pensions.

Executive heads and staff associations now complain that the governments' pressures on UN emoluments are, in turn, excessive, which may prejudice the recruitment of qualified employees as well as damaging the morale and effectiveness of serving staff.

In September 1987, the Federation of International Civil Servants' Associations (FICSA) said that in major duty stations, the real value of professional salaries had fallen by 20 per cent or more since the early 1970s, a trend aggravated in the last three years by the post-adjustment (cost of living) freeze imposed by the General Assembly. In July 1987 the post adjustment was negative in thirty-three duty stations: staff then receive even less than the base salary, which itself has not increased since 1975.[3]

Origin and principles of UN professional remuneration

UN principles of salary administration were inspired by the League's practice. Confronted in 1920 with the need to recruit staff for a new institution in a high cost of living area (Geneva), and considering that League officials originally had neither tenure in their positions, nor retirement pensions, Sir Eric Drummond, the League's first secretary-general, set salaries at the level of those paid in the British Civil Service, then the best-paid national civil service among the major members of the League, with an extra allowance to compensate for expatriation.

The rationale was that international officials, like national officials, should receive salaries guaranteeing them and their families complete financial independence, the prerequisite for sustained good work. This condition should take into account the fact that these officials are permanently or semi-permanently expatriated. Many of them must be in a position to secure for their children an education in their own countries in order to prepare them for a normal existence at home. Salaries cannot therefore be fixed on a level of national civil service remunerations but should be equal to those drawn by national diplomatic officers on posts in foreign countries.[4]

The Noblemaire committee approved Drummond's initiative in 1920 on the grounds that it would be 'most unfortunate if the scale of salaries were fixed at a rate which made it impossible to obtain first-class talent from those countries where the ordinary rate of renumeration is above the general average'.[5]

The Noblemaire principle, still in force today, was that since there should be no difference in salary on the grounds of nationality, the conditions of service of the international staff must be such as to attract citizens of the country with the highest pay levels.

It was acknowledged that League emoluments were generous but not excessive if compared with those of diplomatic officials abroad instead of the salaries paid to officials at home. Ranshofen-Wertheimer noted that

the erroneous application of the yardstick of national salaries led to false comparisons, paradoxical evaluations and to polemics the heat of which can be explained only by the background of general European impoverishment and envy. The Bulgarian member of the financial section, for instance, received a salary which was in gold a multiple of the Bulgarian prime minister's pay. The standard of living of the gentleman in Geneva was nevertheless incomparably lower than that of his first magistrate at home. ... The majority of the League's higher officials spent their salaries in full.[6]

In fact, League and UN professional salaries have been based on a comparison with the highest paid *home* civil service of any member state, and not on a comparison with any state diplomatic service. UN staff associations have long argued that the latter comparison, which would be more beneficial to UN staff, is the fair and relevant one. A recent study made by FICSA shows that, on the basis of total compensation including expatriate benefits, in Geneva, UN remuneration is only about 80 per cent of that of US civil servants. In field duty stations, such as Bogota, it is only 54 per cent of the US total compensation.[7]

The UN Preparatory Commission recommended in 1945 that the salaries and allowances of UN staff should compare favourably with those of the most highly paid home and foreign services, due account being taken of special factors affecting UN service: among these, the relatively better position of national civil services in terms of a guarantee of stability and security of employment and the more limited promotion prospects to the highest posts in the international secretariats.[8]

The validity of the Noblemaire principle has been reaffirmed by various salary review committees appointed by the General Assembly between 1949 and 1972, and, on the recommendation of the International Civil Service Commission (ICSC), by the General Assembly in 1984, as 'the basis for the determination of the level of remuneration for staff in the professional and higher categories'.[9]

In 1946 an American observer found that the proposed salary levels for the secretariat staff were substantial.[10] The senior UN posts would provide a salary considerably above the top administrative level in the US federal government and far in excess of salary levels in all but a handful of countries. He felt that such high salary levels, supplemented by the very liberal system of allowances, retirement provisions, leave and other conditions of service, would make the UN an extremely attractive place for employment. It would thus be possible for the UN to attract persons with the highest level of training, experience and competence to be found in member countries. The hope was then that the high quality of the staff would more than justify the very generous terms of employment.

By the late 1970s the mood was changing: the previous whole-hearted support for the UN salaries was fading. Other observers injected a note of caution and a warning.[11] They noted that manpower costs for the UN system amounted in 1975 to 74 per cent of the regular budget. The international civil service was compensated on the average 37 per cent more than the US federal personnel in similar grade positions. Total compensation was considerably above the national rates of Sweden and the Federal Republic of Germany. Differences with such countries as Haiti or Grenada were enormous. The very high UN salaries tended to arouse the resentment of Foreign Service officers towards UN bureaucrats, regardless of their nationalities. They were likely to colour their attitudes on multilateral diplomacy, thereby stimulating conflict rather than harmony in the ideals of the UN. Costs, especially in terms of personnel, were already of concern to the major contributors.

Reversing the trend: attacks and pressures

Criticisms were more vocal and pressures more insistent in the 1980s. They came from government representatives and also from UN bodies. The United States led the attack in 1982 by challenging the international Civil Service Commission (ICSC) recommendation for an increase in net base salaries for the professional category. The US representative to the Fifth Committee[12] argued that the ratio of compensation enjoyed by UN staff in relation to the comparator US Federal Service was 135 to 100, and not 118 to 100, as estimated by ICSC. In either case, that level was higher than required by the Noblemaire principle; technically, no increase was justified. Secondly, he said that the best case for an increase would be a demonstration that the UN could no longer recruit and retain good employes; he had found no evidence of such difficulties, but rather that the UN remained an extremely attractive employer. The UN post adjustment system gives UN employees inflation-proof salaries and shields them from the income-limiting effects of the world-wide economic difficulties. Finally, the key question, a financial and political one, was whether member states and the UN itself could afford a pay increase which would cost about $40 million for all the UN organizations. It was unlikely that most member states would vote a budgetary increase in view of the difficult global economic situation. Everywhere citizens and governments were making hard choices involving regrettable sacrifices. The proposed salary increase forced just a choice, as it could only be compensated by programme cuts. The General Assembly rejected the increase, thus choosing financial support for programme delivery in preference to increased staff costs.[13]

Again, in 1985 the US representative identified twin objectives: an adequately compensated international civil service, but one whose pay levels do not attract the attention of the world because of their excessive nature.[14]

Japan called the UN pension scheme 'too generous and in some respects superfluous'. The spokesman for the European Economic Community regretted the failure of the staff representatives, ICSC, the Joint Staff Pension Board and the Administrative Committee on Coordination (ACC, the executive heads of the UN organizations), to draw attention to the excessive growth of pensionable remuneration and benefits, which had resulted in major expenditures on the part of the member states.[15] Eastern European countries joined and supported the Western democracies in a common assault against excessive salaries and pensions. In November 1985 the Soviet Union representative asked that staff costs be curbed. He accused ICSC of 'serving only the covetous interests of the international bureaucracy'.[16] For him, the vast majority of its recommendations tended to increase already-inflated incomes of international staff at the expense of member states. The ICSC had become an organ 'blatantly pandering to the international bureaucracy'. A special committee of government experts should help the General Assembly find out the truth about the remuneration of international civil servants. The Bulgarian representative concurred: the ICSC had become a driving force in escalating personnel costs.[17] Soviet representatives asserted that the UN pensions also were overinflated: they had more than tripled over the past ten years, whereas those of the comparator service had only doubled. Another intergovernmental committee should review the UN pension system in all its aspects and the composition of the Pension Board should be revised to give more weight to member states' representatives.[18]

The Joint Inspection Unit's criticisms

In two trenchant reports on staff costs, in 1984 and in 1985, two inspectors of the UN Joint Inspection Unit (JIU) reflected the concerns and claims of the Western democracies and Eastern European countries.[19] The inspectors noted that the UN secretariat had recently become the target of mounting criticism because of the rapid increase in its costs which, paradoxically, was accompanied by declining efficiency. It was urgent and imperative to take serious measures in order to improve the secretariat's performance and to contain budget growth. Reference was made to 'inefficient and largely overpaid' UN professional staff, to grade-creep, and to excessive bureaucratization. Was the expansion of UN staff by 20.4 per cent during the last decade really necessary? The 1984 report recommended that the General Assembly should not increase either salaries or post adjustments for professional and higher categories at its next session. The 1985 report criticized an ICSC decision on post adjustments, alleged to reflect the interests of the staff only. In a strange formulation, the ICSC decision was said not to be 'objective' because the interests of member states had not been taken into account; more precisely, one could say that the decision was not acceptable to member states and therefore not realistic. The report was critical, in general, of ICSC's 'arbitrary' actions, its inadequate methodology. The proposal to create a special committee of governmental experts in order to assist the ICSC in reviewing the UN remuneration system, the central task of the Commission, was a clear indication of distrust of the ICSC. Finally, the report was highly critical of staff representative bodies 'alleging to be the masters of the organizations', who proclaim the right to strike, whose main thrust of activities is directed at getting still higher salaries and new financial benefits, and who promote the independent nature of the international civil service in order to make it its own domain. The UN administration was accused to vigorously supporting these staff bodies, not as a legitimate staff-participatory management scheme, but because the administration and the staff bodies have common interests; in other words, the UN administration was accused of having abdicated its management responsibilities and to be in full collusion with the staff bodies, in an effort to benefit from higher salaries and allowances. The report wanted all staff activities to be reviewed by the General Assembly. It also challenged the right of the UN Administrative Tribunal to issue final judgments; these should be reviewed by the General Assembly in order not to leave member states to the mercy of any General Assembly subsidiary body, 'in such very important matters as their finances'.

Understandingly, the JIU reports were criticized by FICSA as further damaging the image of the UN organizations and as being replete with errors, inconsistencies, selective quotations, misinterpretations and unsubstantiated conclusions.[20] However, the vitriolic reports seemed to be well received by the main budget contributors in the General Assembly, by expressing a frank, blunt reminder to the UN executive heads that the organizations' financial resources are entirely dependent on the goodwill of member states and that personnel costs should, from now on, be better controlled.

Another inspector criticized the average inadequacy of qualifications of UN personnel, and the indifference shown towards standards of work and competence, which creates a deplorable working environment in which the best staff members no longer find the motivation needed to dedicate themselves to their tasks.[21]

The 'Group of 18' proposals

Created in 1986 on the initiative of Japan, the 'Group of high-level intergovernmental experts to review the efficiency of the administrative and financial functioning of the UN' reviewed both the intergovernmental machinery and the structure of the UN secretariat. Concerning personnel matters, it made a major and spectacular proposal: the overall number of regular budget posts should be reduced by 15 per cent within three years, with 25 per cent being cut at the levels of under-secretary-general and assistant-secretary-general. New recruitment should be made at the lower professional levels (P.1, P.2 and P.3) in order to ensure a 'vigorous' secretariat. Recruitment should be made through national competive examinations.

The Group recognized that personnel policy and management in the UN had suffered as a result of the considerable political and other pressures that have influenced the selection of staff. Consequently, the secretary-general should exercise greater leadership in personnel matters. He should protect the authority of the official in charge of personnel and instruct all other senior officials to refrain from influencing the selection of staff. Implicitly, this advice could also apply to 'influences' from governemnts on the Personnel (now renamed 'Human Resources') Services. Inconsistencies and ambiguities in the Staff Rules and Regulations should be eliminated and a personnel manual introduced. A job rotation system should be developed for professional staff as part of career development plans. Staff members should be eligible for permanent appointments after having served three years in the UN. The leadership of departments and offices should be renewed periodically. Under-secretaries-general and assistant-secretaries-general should not serve more than ten years in their UN post.

On remuneration, the Group of 18 was as critical as the inspectors: the total entitlements (salaries and other conditions of service) of staff members have reached a level which gives reason for serious concern and it should be reduced. The Group proposed to eliminate one benefit, the education grant for post-secondary studies, and to reduce the six-week annual leave credit to four weeks.

Another informal but influential group (the Group of 14) also met in 1986 to study the 'UN Financial Emergency: Crisis and Opportunity'. One of its proposals was an overall salary reduction of 3 per cent across the board, as a financial measure which would produce savings in excess of $10 million a year.[22]

Decisions

Warnings, criticisms and attacks materialized into decisions taken by the UN General Assembly, tending to freeze or reduce professional salaries, benefits and pensions.

Lacking political acumen, the ICSC decided in July 1984 to increase by 9.6 per cent the post adjustment for New York, which would have increased post adjustments in many other duty stations. Half of this increase was applied in August 1984 and the remaining part was due on 1 December 1984. However, on 30 November, because of strong US opposition,[23] the General Assembly requested the ICSC to suspend the implementation of the December increase. This increase would have widened the margin between US rates and the comparator US Federal Service from 17 to 24 per cent, which was deemed excessive. The ICSC had no choice but to bow to the Assembly's demand and to freeze the post adjustment.

The result is that the professional salary scale has not been revised since 1975 and that the cost of living safety valve, the post-adjustment system, has been frozen since December 1984.

In December 1984 the General Assembly approved a new scale of pensionable remuneration for the professional and higher categories proposed by the ICSC. Under the new scale, pensionable remuneration was reduced for all such staff, except at grades P.1 and P.2, thus reducing their future pensions.

Having stopped the escalation of professional staff and higher categories' salaries, the Assembly decided in 1985 to limit the margin range to prevent any excessive future deviation of UN professional rates over US rates: a range of 110 to 120 with a desirable mid-point of 115 was approved. This overturned the decision taken by the ICSC in 1984 that the level of the margin should continue to be determined in a pragmatic manner.[24]

As a consequence of the UN financial crisis,[25] the UN secretary-general decided to defer interim adjustments in the salaries of the general service staff at eight main duty stations. Promotions were also deferred for six months in 1986 and in 1987.[26]

In addition to the salaries and post-adjustment freezes, UN staff stationed in non-US-dollar areas (particularly in Western-Europe) suffered an additional loss in their take-home pay, due to the depreciation of the US dollar. This affected professional salaries, allowances and pensions expressed in US dollars. It was shown that, from 1975 to 1986, whereas take-home pay for ILO staff in New York had fallen 6 per cent behind the cost of living, the lag in Geneva had been 15.1 per cent, as shown in figures 5.1 and 5.2. The figures apply equally to professional staff of all UN organizations.

Successive decisions of the General Assembly have eroded UN pension benefits since 1982. In 1982 the measures included a change in the rate of accumulation through contributory service to qualify for a retirement benefit, raise of the interest rate in the commutation of periodic benefits into a lump sum and change in the system of pension adjustments. Pension contributions for the organizations and for participating staff were increased in 1984 from 21 to 21.75 per cent in a two-third/one-third proportion. A special index for pensioners, reducing pension benefits in certain countries, was introduced also in 1984.

In 1985 the Fifth Committee debates on pensions were overshadowed by the feeling of the major contributors that pension benefits were still overgenerous and that more corrective measures were needed. The Assembly decided to limit the maximum retirement benefit payable to a participant at the under-secretary-general, assistant-secretary-general or equivalent, to 60 per cent of the pensionable remuneration for his level.[27] For the second time in two years the General Assembly adopted in December 1986, for implementation in April 1987, a revised scale of pensionable remuneration entailing reductions ranging, according to grade, from 1.5 to 8.3 per cent by comparison with the preceding scale.[28]

This decrease will affect future pensions, as well as compensation for service-incurred injury, illness or death. The effect of the changes in pensionable remuneration between the scales effective in October 1984, January 1985 and April 1987 is shown in table 5.2.

Staff associations' arguments

Staff representatives have reacted strongly against the erosion of salaries and pensions. The representative of the UN staff associations said in July 1987 that

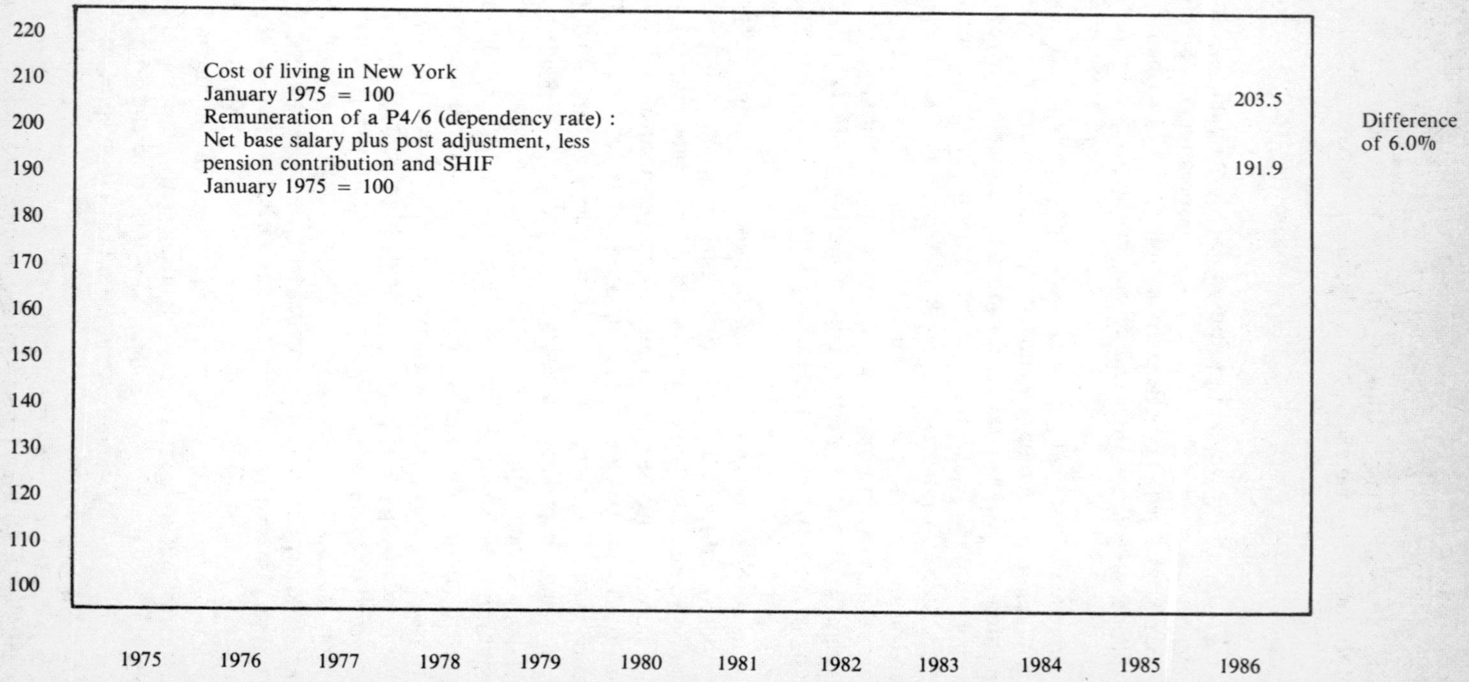

Cost of living in New York
January 1975 = 100

Remuneration of a P4/6 (dependency rate):
Net base salary plus post adjustment, less
pension contribution and SHIF
January 1975 = 100

220
210
200
190
180
170
160
150
140
130
120
110
100

1975 1976 1977 1978 1979 1980 1981 1982 1983 1984 1985 1986

203.5

191.9

Difference of 6.0%

Figure 5.1 Evolution of take-home pay of ILO professional and higher-category staff compared to the cost of living, New York (ILO Liaison Office)

Source: ILO Doc. GB.235/PFA/10/10, February-March 1987, Geneva

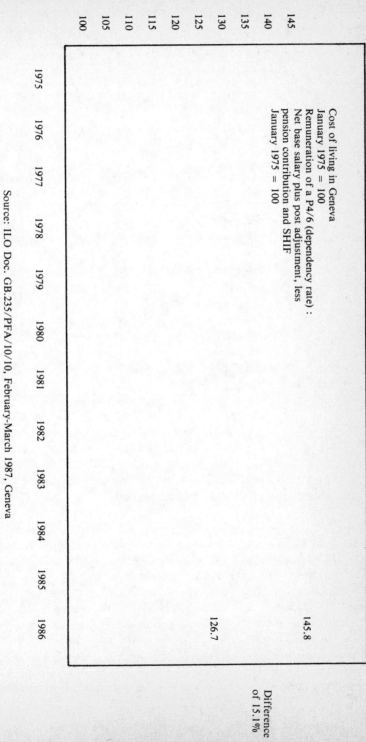

Figure 5.2 Evolution of take-home pay of ILO professional and higher-category staff in Geneva compared to the cost of living in Swiss francs

Source: ILO Doc. GB.235/PFA/10/10, February-March 1987, Geneva

Table 5.2 Comparison of pensionable remuneration

	1 Oct. 1984 US$	variation (%)	1 Jan.1985 US$	variation (%)	Effect 1 Apr. 1987 US$	variation (%)
P-1/Step 1	26,338	+5.4	27,500	+4.4	27,100	-1.5
P-1/Top Step	36,591	+5.4	37,400	+2.2	36,100	-3.5
P-2/Step 1	35,069	+5.4	35,500	+1.2	34,500	-2.8
P-2/Top Step	47,868	+5.4	47,900	-	46,300	-3.3
P-3/Step 1	44,164	+5.4	43,800	-0.8	42,600	-2.7
P-3/Top Step	62,770	+5.4	62,200	-0.9	58,800	-5.5
P-4/Step 1	55,233	+5.4	53,300	-3.5	52,100	-2.3
P-4/Top Step	75,501	+5.4	70,900	-6.1	68,300	-3.7
P-5/Step 1	70,419	+5.4	66,100	-6.1	64,300	-2.7
P-5/Top Step	88,610	+5.4	83,900	-6.3	77,200	-8.0
D-1/Step 1	80,923	+5.4	74,500	-7.9	71,400	-4.2
D-1/Top Step	96,604	+5.4	87,900	-9.9	82,100	-6.6
D-2/Step 1	96,971	+5.4	84,800	-12.6	81,800	-3.5
D-2/Top Step	105,536	+5.4	92,400	-12.4	88,000	-4.8
	124,257	+5.4	103,900	-16.4	98,100	-5.6
	135,800	+5.4	115,700	-14.8	106,100	-8.3

Source: UN Office at Geneva Staff/Coordinating Council
Doc. CCBE/1987/64 of 10 January 1987

the staff of the UN Common System were now facing the darkest moment in their career and in the history of the international civil service, as a result of a steady deterioration of all the working conditions.[29]

FICSA deplored that this deterioration had been based largely on arbitrary and unilateral decisions.[30] Basic principles of labour-management relations, accepted in many national systems, permit employees to negotiate their conditions of service; yet, representatives of the very same nations (i.e the Western democracies) determine entitlements of UN system staff unilaterally. FICSA claimed that the UN staff cannot be denied any longer the right to sit at the bargaining table when their conditions of employment are at stake. The staff representatives stressed the political rather than methodological motives of the reductions. The staff were no longer prepared to bear the brunt of the organizations' political problems.[31] Is it fair and acceptable that remunerations should not only be frozen, but that the take-home pay of professional staff in many duty stations should decrease each month because of the depreciation of the US dollar? Is it fair to defenceless UN pensioners that their pensions should also be reduced for the same reasons?

The associations stressed that such losses were detrimental to the staff and also to the organizations. Several organizations, in particular those with highly technical functions, were experiencing growing difficulties in attracting and retaining the staff they needed to carry out their mandate.[32] The WHO staff representative referred to discussions at the World Health Assembly in May 1987: delegates wondered why certain countries (such as the United States, Japan and the Federal Republic of Germany) were underrepresented in the secretariat. No one doubted that there was plenty of the right kind of expertise available among nationals of these countries. So, why were they not available to WHO? The most obvious answer was that working for WHO was not an attractive proposition.[33]

According to a study of the Geneva staff associations on the reduction in salaries' purchasing power, these reductions amounted, in 1987, to 22 per cent by comparison with July 1971 — when the US dollar suffered its first depreciation — and around 15 per cent by comparison with the last adjustment in basic salaries, in January 1975.

In ILO, as in other UN organizations, a number of long-serving staff members were opting for early retirement in view of the progressive reduction of their prospective pensions in local currency, in spite of longer contributory service. Those who would retire, for example in France, the Federal Republic of Germany or Switzerland in 1988 would receive pensions 20 per cent smaller than those of their colleagues who retired in the same countries in 1986, for equal service time. Besides the personal losses of those concerned, the organizations were losing prematurely a substantial capital of experienced and competent staff.[34]

The embarrassing supplementary payments

The best argument used by the staff associations to demonstrate that the UN professional salaries were now inadequate was the supplementary payments issue.

At the request of FICSA and the ACC, the ICSC addressed this issue in 1979 and following years. FICSA's position was that the practice of some governments of making payments additional to the UN salaries and allowances to international civil servants of their nationality was becoming more frequent. It resulted in discriminatory levels of pay of UN staff by nationality, contrary to the Staff Regulations. The FICSA representative at the ICSC session emphasized in 1980 that national legislation authorizing such payments showed that the emoluments of international civil servants were lower than those of comparably placed national civil servants. The additional payments were necessary in order to encourage the recruitment of nationals of these countries in UN organizations. The conclusion was that UN emoluments were no longer sufficiently attractive to permit recruitment and assignment to any duty stations of competent nationals from all member states.[35]

It was revealed that at least three countries, the Federal Republic of Germany, Japan and the United States had such arrangements. Members of some other delegations said that a limited number of their nationals had also received such supplements on an individual basis.[36]

The ICSC's position was firm on principles but ineffective. The Commission denounced the symptoms but did not draw the logical conclusion, that the UN salary scales were becoming unattractive for candidates from a number of countries, and that, therefore the Noblemaire principle was no longer respected. The ICSC's appeals to member states to stop their practices were to no avail.

In 1980, the ICSC

recommended to the General Assembly that it should call to the attention of all Member States that the practice of making supplementary payments of whatever nature to nationals while serving or in relation to their having served as international civil servants in the organizations of the common system was unnecessary, inappropriate and undesirable. Such payments were, moreover, inconsistent with the provisions of staff regulations and made it difficult for both organizations and staff members to ensure that such regulations were respected and enforced.

The General Assembly noted the report and requested the ICSC to keep the matter under review. In 1982 the General Assembly called the attention of Member States to the fact that the practice of supplementary payments was inconsistent with the provisions of the Staff Regulations and therefore inappropriate.[37]

In 1987 FICSA again requested the ICSC to take up the issue. FICSA stressed the inconsistent position taken by certain major states: on the one hand, they oppose improvements in UN service conditions or even attempt to lower them further, while on the other hand, they make supplementary payments in one form or another to their nationals working in UN organizations. The Chairman of the ICSC sent a request for information to all permanent representatives whose replies (or non-reply) showed, in FICSA's view, that the issue was a source of embarrassment for several member states.[38]

FICSA used the supplementary payments practice to raise doubts as to whether the US Federal Service was still the highest paid and should, or not, remain the comparator in accordance with the Noblemaire principle. FICSA referred to the continuing erosion in US pay, together with the depreciation of the US dollar, against 'positive' developments in other civil services, such as that of the Federal Republic of Germany.[39] Only the ICAO supported the view that there was a case for an increase in the professional scale.[40]

In the present climate of economies and financial constraints it is most unlikely that the General Assembly would agree to a change of comparator, even if amply justified and documented, if such a change would result in a higher salary scale and higher benefits. The rationality of the Noblemaire principle cannot win over political and financial exigencies.

In reply to an enquiry by ICSC, twenty six countries informed the Commission in July 1987 that they did not make any supplementary payments; other countries had not yet replied. The ICSC also asked governments and the organizations if some member states were currently providing staff on the basis of reimbursable or non-reimbursable loans because the organization was not able to pay the equivalent levels of renumeration of staff from certain governmental organizations while working abroad. By July 1987, only WHO (seven cases from the United States and one from France) and the IAEA (twenty seven from the United States, seven from the Soviet Union, six from Japan, five from Canada, four from the Federal Republic of Germany, two from the Netherlands and one each from Bulgaria, Czechoslovakia, Israel, Italy and Finland) declared that there were such cases.[41]

FISCA revealed in September 1987 that supplementary payments were now being made by Canada, Finland, France, Italy, Netherlands, Nigeria, in addition to the three 'pioneers', the Federal Republic of Germany, Japan and the United States.[42]

It is clear that the countries involved prefer to pay additional subsidies to some or all of their nationals employed by the UN organizations, rather than raising the UN salary scales for all professional staff. In doing so, they bury the Noblemaire principle, a principle which all member states have repeatedly endorsed in the General Assembly. They also create an inequality of treatment among professional staff. The practice of supplementary payments recreates a direct link between the international civil servant and his or her government and a financial and moral dependence of the staff member on his or her national authorities.

As stated by the executive secretary of the ICSC, 'the international civil service is further compromised and its independence gravely jeopardized by the (supplementary payments) practice; ironically, even illogically, some of these very member states are advocating reductions of staff benefits'.[43]

Staff responses

The staff associations and their federations have used various information and pressure tactics to try to resist government attacks against their conditions of service and prevent any further deterioration (see also Ch. 7 below).

This has included information campaigns and appeals of the organizations' staff associations directed to their organizations' executive heads and governing bodies. However, as most salary and other employment conditions are decided upon by the Fifth Committee of the UN General Assembly, and not by the governing bodies of the other UN organizations, the more effective pressures had to be applied by FICSA and the CCISUA at the interagency level: the staff interests had to be defended before the Consultative Committee for Administrative Questions (CCAQ), the Administrative Committee on Coordination (ACC), the ICSC, the UN Joint Staff Pension Board and the Fifth Committee.

FICSA initiated and supported financially legal appeals to the two administrative tribunals against the post-adjustment freeze, the reduction in the pensionable remuneration scales and in pension benefits. The appeals have had only a limited success.

FICSA has launched public relations and information campaigns directed mainly at governments' decision-makers, such as heads of states or governments, and permanent representatives to the UN organizations, and at public opinion.

World-wide protests of UN staff in most duty stations were held on 4 June 1986 and on 22 October 1987. One-day strikes were held by ILO and GATT staff resprctively on 20 February and 14 April 1987 to protest against pensions and salary deterioration.

The attitude of the executive heads

The executive heads of the UN organizations are placed in a difficult, conflictual position. On the one hand, as the senior administrators of the organizations they are responsible before their governing bodies for the effective management of their secretariats. They should rationalize, control and restrain expenditures of public monies, and in particular staffing costs, which amount to more than three-quarters of the organizations' budgets. In the interest of economies and in order to limit or reduce the expenditures of member states, they may have to reduce their staff, limit or reduce staff salaries and benefits. While some executive heads might be prudent and austere managers, others might be tempted to expand the programmes and activities of their organization, mainly in the interest of the Third World, encourage budget and programme growth, and find themselves in the unpleasant position of Mr M'Bow, the former director-general of UNESCO. This second alternative has all but been eliminated since the 1980's as totally unacceptable to the main contributors to the UN budgets. The other and more plausible alternative attitude is an appreciation that reasonable, competitive salaries and benefits and pensions are required to attract suitable candidates and retain competent staff members in the organization. Additionally, financial compensation is one important element, albeit not the only one, of motivation. In consequence, the executive heads and their senior administrators cannot afford to let member states continually erode various parts of the UN remuneration package without reacting: the levels of salaries, benefits and pensions may have been excessive in the past, but they have now reached the level of being uncompetitive, detrimental to the motivation of the staff and therefore to the effectiveness and prestige of the organization.

Before the 1984 wave of criticisms, ACC was trying to obtain an increase in the salary scale for professional and higher-categories staff, which had remained unchanged since 1975. The 1982 ACC recommendation was repeated in 1984. The ACC said that professional salary scales and the UN pension scheme constituted the cornerstones of the common system; in particular, the Pension Fund is a fundamental element of the broad contract between the organizations and their staff. The staff's confidence in the organization's ability to provide on a stable basis for old age, invalidity and survivors' pensions was essential for the mutual confidence in the system.[44]

The tune changed in March 1985. Strongly influenced by the debates in the Fifth Committee in the autumn of 1984, the CCAQ adopted a new, very cautious approach:

Considering that the action of the General Assembly reflected, *inter alia,* the policies of austerity and financial restraint being pursued by a number of Member States, especially as regards the emoluments of public servants, the organizations should be responsive to those preoccupations. The appropriate course of action would be to exercise restraint in examining any proposals to improve the conditions of service of staff in the professional and higher categories, and to concentrate on preventing any further erosion of the fundamental principles and objectives which had long governed the salary system.[45]

In October 1986 the executive heads felt that restraint was not productive: they needed to be outspoken. Following the recommendations of the Group of 18, the ACC said that

to seek to solve financial difficulties at the expense of staff entitlements would be extremely shortsighted and counterproductive, and would have widespread adverse implications for the common system... salaries for professional and higher categories have remained unchanged for the last eleven years ... cost-of-living adjustments have been frozen for the last two years, while pension entitlements have been the object of successive reductions in the past four years. Moreover, conditions of service and life of international staff in the field have further deteriorated over this period, and in many cases of local staff, compensation is proving to be clearly inadequate. Although executive heads can still, fortunately, count on the sense of duty and professional conscience of their staff, the generally negative attitude towards the international civil service and repeated questioning of conditions of service, create feelings of insecurity and discouragement. From the long-term point of view, it is far from assured that the international civil service would attract and retain staff of the required highest calibre. ACC considers that mediocrity will ultimately be the price of further reductions in staff entitlements.[46]

In February 1987 the executive heads of the specialized agencies based in Geneva called on the ICSC to take urgent steps to compensate adequately professional staff in Geneva for the losses in take-home pay due to currency fluctuations,[47]

This statement was issued in response to a request by the staff associations and unions of the Geneva organizations.[48]

In April 1987 the ACC examined with 'deep concern' major problems relating to salaries, pensions, leave and other staff entitlements which had emerged in connection with the current financial situation and the resulting process within the UN. Members of the ACC

> reported to the commitee on areas in which they had perceived sharp declines in staff morale due to an increasing erosion of the terms and conditions of service, recently aggravated by currency fluctuations. They noted that a principal asset of the organizations of the common system has always consisted of the expertise, experience and commitment of its staff members. The erosion of such terms and conditions makes the retention of experienced staff and the recruitment of sufficiently qualified new staff more and more difficult, particularly at the field level, thus seriously hampering programme execution. The Committee requested the Secretary-General to present its views to the International Civil Service Commission and the General Assembly, urging them to find solutions that will honour the just expectations of the staff and restore the credibility of the common system.[49]

In July the ACC added that the executive heads were faced with an increasing number of resignations and early retirements of senior advisers, technical specialists and programme managers, depriving the organizations of valuable expertise. The ACC acknowledged that UN emoluments for field service were in most locations far below those provided by the comparator (US) civil service to staff working in the same conditions. For the ACC the erosion of UN conditions of service resulted from: (1) a freeze in emoluments and a substantial decline in purchasing power: (2) at most headquarters and other duty stations in Europe, progressive reductions in local currency take-home pay, resulting from the weakening of the US dollar; (3) at most field duty stations, reductions in spendable income due to inflation and continual devaluations; (4) across-the-board cuts in pensionable remuneration and pension benefits, aggravated by the recent decline in the local currency value of pension benefits at certain locations; and (5) the postponement of reviews of a number of allowances that require updating.[50]

The WHO director-general was more outspoken. In front of the World Health Assembly in May 1987, he said that he was concerned not only about the financial insecurity of the organization but also with the financial insecurity of the staff. Not only were staff being unilaterally deprived of what they thought were acquired rights, but the way it was being done was insulting, as if they were totally unproductive bureaucrats. Staff were shocked and depressed by the growing attack upon their conditions of employment and the 'contemptuous refusal' of the normal dialogue between staff and employers.[51]

The international civil service victimized?

Some observers have wondered whether the persistant attacks on international staff's employment conditions are not really addressed to multilateralism. Anderson believes that governments' efforts to restructure, reform, improve cost-effectiveness, reduce expenses and staff may be a subterfuge for bringing about 'mediocracy' and incompetence in the secretariats, thus ensuring that the UN organizations have no chance of success.[52] Another possibility, writes Anderson, would be that powerful governments want to control the organizations from inside the secretariats by replacing an independent international civil service with men and women 'dependent on directives from a select few capitals which perpetuate bilateralism as the expression of 'power politics'. And what better way to accomplish this that to make the international civil service as originally conceived as unattractive and unrewarding as possible'.

Even if some governmental leaders and influential groups may have such objectives, it is unlikely that all, or even most, member states' representatives have been implementing such a Machiavellian and devious plan. More simply, UN salaries, benefits and pensions have been set to a relatively high level from the 1940s to the 1970s. The economic difficulties of many countries, US criticisms and financial withholdings, problems of programme delivery, politicization and management deficiencies in some organizations have leagued together to bring to a halt the previous, continuous growth of the organizations, including increases in staff numbers and costs.

It appears that the pendulum has now swung too far in the direction of austerity and cuts. The ICSC and member states should take heed of the executive heads warnings and restore the reputation of the organizations as, again, decent employers. Decent employment conditions, stability of take-home pay, timely cost-of-living adjustments, decent and reliable pensions are basic prerequisites to a dynamic human-resources management strategy and to employees motivation.

The morale and effectiveness of the international civil service depends to a large extent on the respect of such basic requirements and on trust in the good faith of employers. All the other elements of effective management, — including effective leadership, worthy and achievable objectives, expertise, good planning, staff participation, career development, good communications, teamwork and hardwork — can only be built on this infrastructure.

Notes

1. Statement of a former League official, in 'Memorandum on the Composition, Procedure and Functions of the Committees of the League of Nations, Proceedings of the Conference on Experience of International Administration', Carnegie Endowment for International Peace, Washington, DC, 1943, p.14.
2. It would be interesting to compare UN emoluments with those offered by the World Bank, the International Monetary Fund, the European Economic Community, the Organization of American States and other regional intergovernmental organizations, as well as with salaries and benefits offered by private-sector multinational firms. The principles and evolution of the UN remuneration scheme are also described in Chapter 11 of H. Reymond and

S. Mailick's *International Personnel Policies and Practices,* Praeger, New York, 1985.

3. Doc. FICSA *Spotlight,* no. 19, 29 September 1987.
4. Richard N. Swift, 'International Salary Administration in Search of Principles', *Public Administration Review,* no. 3, May-June 1970, p. 238 and note 13.
5. See the *Balfour Report* (Annex 57a) adopted by the Council of the League on 19 May 1920 (Annex 57b) and the report submitted by the Fourth Committee to the Assembly on the conclusions and proposals of the Commission of Experts appointed in accordance with the resolution adopted by the Assembly of the League of Nations on 17 December 1920.
6. Egon F. Ranshofen-Wertheimer, 'International Administration Lessons from the Experience of the League of Nations', *American Political Science Review,* vol. XXXVII, 1943, p. 875.
7. Doc. FICSA *Spotlight,* no. 19, 29 September 1987.
8. See UN Doc. 'Common System', vol. 4, no. 2, June 1983, *Bulletin of the ICSC.* These factors were enumerated by the 1949 Committee of Experts on salary, allowance and leave system.
9. Resol. 39/27 of 30 November 1984.
10. Donald C. Stone, 'Organizing the UN', in *Public Administration Review,* vol. VI, 1946, P. 126.
11. Werner J. Feld and Lewis B. Kilbourne, 'The UN Bureaucracy: Growth and Diversity', in *International Review of Administrative Sciences,* Brussels, 1977. pp.332-3.
12. Statement by Senator J. Bennett Johnston on 16 November 1982. See Press Release USUN 128-(82), US Mission to the UN, New York.
13. General Assembly Resol. 37/126 of 17 December 1982.
14. Statement by Gerald B.H. Solomon on 22 November 1985. Press Release USUN 167-(85), US Mission to the UN, New York.
15. Statement by the Delegation of Japan to the Fifth Committee on 20 November 1985 and Statement of M. Pirson (Belgium) on 15 November 1985, UN Doc. A/C.5/40/SR.37. See also Heritage Foundation's contribution: 'A U.N. Success Story: The World's Fattest Pensions', *Heritage Foundation Backgrounder,* no. 378 of 11 September 1984 and Andrew Borowiec's 'Catching the UN's Gravy Train' in the *Washington Times Insight,* 24 March 1986.
16. Statement of V.V. Shustov to the Fifth Committee on 18 and 25 November 1985, UN Doc. A/C.5/40/SR.19 and SR.38, and Soviet Mission to the UN Press Release of 18 November 1985.
17. Statement by Mr Gitsov to the Fifth Committee in UN Doc. A/C.5/40/SR/63, 14 December 1985.
18. Statement of V.V. Shustov to the Fifth Committee on 7 November 1984 and of Mr Zacharov on 21 November 1985: UN Doc. A/C.5/40/SR.44.
19. Inspectors A.S. Efimov (Soviet Union) and N. Kaddour (Syria) — see UN Doc. JIU/REP/84/12 and JIU/REP/85/8.
20. See Doc. FICSA/CIRC/340, 25 October 1984, Annex II.
21. Maurice Bertrand in 'Some Reflections on Reform of the UN', UN Doc. JIU/REP/85/9, 1985, pp. 11-12.
22. The co-chairmen of the Informal Consultation on 'UN Financial Emergency-Crisis and Opportunity', held at the UN Plaza Hotel, New York, 8-10 August 1986, were Sadruddin Aga Khan and Maurice F. Strong.
23. *Heritage Foundation Backgrounder,* no. 416, 13 March 1985, p. 8.
24. Yves Beigbeder, *Management Problems in UN Organizations,* Frances Pinter, London, 1987, pp. 85-7.
25. Beigbeder, pp. 147-51.
26. *FICSA News,* Doc. FICSA/N/88, 5 March 1987.
27. Beigbeder, pp. 99-103.
28. General Assembly Resolution 41/208 I, 11 December 1986. See also ILO Staff

Union *Bulletin*, no. 923, 4 March 1987.

29. Representing the Coordinating Committee for Independent Staff Unions and Associations of the UN System, CCISUA. See Doc. UNOG—Coordinating Council, CCBE/1987/14, 15 July 1987.

30. *FICSA News*, Doc. FICSA/N/88, 5 March 1987.

31. See ILO Staff Union *Bulletin*, no. 923, 4 March 1987, and FICSA/N/88, 5 March 1987.

32. Doc. FICSA/N/88, 5 March 1987.

33. WHO Staff Association *Spotlight*, no.3, 16 June 1987.

34. ILO Staff Union *Bulletin*, no. 923, 4 March 1987.

35. UN Doc. A/35/30, 1980, para. 119.

36. UN Doc. ICSC/26/R.11, para. 6. According to the *International Herald Tribune*, 21-2 November 1987, Thérèse Paquet Savigny, a Canadian recently appointed as UN under-secretary-general for Public Information, said that she could not afford to take the job without an additional $88,000 (paid by her government) on top of her regular $117,000 UN salary.

37. UN Doc. A/35/30, 1980, para. 121, Resol. 35/214 C of 17 December 1980 and Resol. 37/126, Section III, para. 2, 17 December 1982. See also UN Doc. ICSC/26/R.11, 11 June 1987.

38. Doc. FICSA/N/91, 8 September 1987. Kofi Annan, assistant-secretary-general, Office of Human Resources Management in the UN said that some member states have been quite hypocritical: they subsidize their nationals and then claim that other staff are overpaid. See UNOG Staff Coordinating Council, Doc.CCBE/1987/28 of 24 September 1987.

39. Doc. FICSA/N/89, 23 April 1987.

40. UN Doc. ICSC/26/CRP.10, 2 July 1987.

41. UN Doc. ICSC/26/CRP.10, 2 July 1987.

42. See FICSA *Spotlight*, no.19, 29 September 1987. The *Diplomatic World Bulletin*, 19-26 October 1987, said that a UNICEF questionnaire also revealed that France, the Federal Republic of Germany, Italy and Japan were subsidizing their nationals in UN employment.

43. UNOG Staff Coordinating Council *Information*, Doc. CCBE/1987/27, 18 September 1987.

44. UN Doc. A/39/30, 1984, Annex II.

45. UN Doc. ACC/1985/6, 27 March 1985.

46. ACC Decision 1986/19 in Doc. FICSA/CIRC/447, 31 October 1986.

47. WHO Geneva Staff Association *Bref*, no. 64, 24 March 1987.

48. Temporary measures were taken by ICSC in March 1987 to establish a local currency floor and ceiling in order to provide a minimum protection of the take-home pay of staff in countries where the US dollar has significantly depreciated in relation to the local currencies. See WHO Doc. A40/INF.DOC./13, 11 May 1987.

49. WHO Doc. A40/INF.DOC./13, 11 May 1987.

50. UN Doc. ICSC/26/CRP.5, 6 July 1987.

51. WHO Staff Association *Spotlight*, no. 3, 16 June 1987.

52. Ron Anderson, 'International Civil Service Victimized', *UN Special*, Geneva, March 1987.

Chapter 6

International staff's immunities:
an effective armour

When one of us is imprisoned, none of us is free.[1]
In December 1986 the UN General Assembly adopted a resolution deploring the growing number of cases where the functioning, safety and well being of UN officials had been adversely affected, including cases of detention in member states and abduction by armed groups and individuals, and the increasing number of cases in which the lives and well-being of officials had been placed in jeopardy during the exercise of their official functions.[2]

The Federation of International Civil Servants' Associations (FICSA) announced in September 1987 that some fifty staff members were still detained, imprisoned, reported missing — some having died in detention — or held in a country against their will.[3] Staff representatives found unacceptable that member states which had committed themselves to promote human rights all over the world did not observe the same basic principles in the case of international civil servants providing humanitarian aid and economic development assistance.

Such cases are typical human rights problems, where individuals are denied the right to life, liberty, security, due legal process, freedom of opinion, where some are subjected to torture, to arbitrary arrest or detention.[4]

In the case of international civil servants, another dimension is added. Like diplomats, international officials 'enjoy such privileges and immunities as are necessary for the independent exercise of their functions in connection with the organization, which is indispensable for the proper discharge of their duties'.[5] Any human rights abuse committed by national authorities concerning international officials on the territory of any of the organization's member states thus constitutes a breach of any human rights legal declaration or convention adopted by the state concerned, and also a breach of the state's obligations under the UN Charter and other UN legal instruments

Such cases are humanitarian problems which have caused individual tragedies, the anxiety and suffering of families and friends, the emotion of UN colleagues and expressions of solidarity and support on the part of staff associations. They also raise important questions of principle: the inobservation of the immunity rules by states which have adopted them is a direct challenge to the principles of international law, international cooperation, and to the principle of independence of the international civil service. International administrations and governing bodies have had to take a clear formal position on this issue, while realizing the difficulties of preventing such cases from arising, and of confronting individual states on specific cases.

Furthermore, most of these cases involve political or ideological considerations linked to the type of political regime of a number of countries; interventions by an international organization in response to the violation of the immunity of an international civil servant, particularly if he is a national of the host country, may be interpreted by that country as an interference in its internal affairs, and as a veiled or public condemnation of its political, judicial and administrative system. Hence, international administrations prefer to deal with such cases through discreet, if not secret, diplomatic channels, while staff representatives have chosen to publicize widely such transgressions in order to force the organization into action, to shame the governments concerned and make them react and hopefully correct their ways. Staff associations use similar tactics to those adopted by the human rights non-governmental organizations. Alice Wesolowska, a UNDP staff member released after five years in prison said,'Silence is our greatest enemy — publicity our best weapon'.[6]

Reported cases

Between 1973 and 1980, thirteen cases of arbitrary arrests and four cases of kidnappings were notified. Of course, only the official arrests formally implicate the responsibility of governments, although some of the kidnappings may have been carried out by government-sponsored groups. Sixteen of these seventeen persons were nationals of the country where the arrest or disappearance took place. Five of the seventeen probably died in detention.[7]

In 1981 UNRWA reported twenty-six cases of arrest and detention of agency staff members in the Gaza Strip, the West Bank, East Jordan and Syria.[8] Twenty-two of these were released after short periods of detention. The other four were sentenced to terms of imprisonment. In all cases, UNRWA could not obtain adequate information and was therefore unable to ascertain whether official functions were involved. UNDP reported eleven cases of arrest and detention of staff members or their dependants: in two of these, there was evidence of a clear violation of the international status of the individual. UNICEF reported three cases, two in Afghanistan and one in Mozambique. The organization had been unable to provide functional protection at the time of arrest or during detention, because of the failure of the authorities concerned to provide timely information and access to the staff members. One locally - recruited staff member of the Economic Commission for Africa (ECA) was released from prison in Ethiopia in July 1981 after twenty-one months of detention. Three other locally recruited staff members remained in detention in Ethiopia: one was charged with having participated in 'anti-government activities', another of the three died in detention. The Economic Commission for Latin America (ECLA) reported two cases of arrest or abduction in Chile, never explained to the satisfaction of the UN. UNESCO reported the case of a high official arrested in his home country, the German Democratic Republic.

In 1982 the same organizations again reported cases involving field staff (UNRWA, UNDP, UNICEF, ECA) and one of headquarters staff (UNESCO).[9] Most cases involved arrests and detention of locally recruited staff members in their own country. UNRWA reported eighteen cases in the occupied West Bank, the Gaza Strip, in Syria and in Jordan. In addition, 166 UNRWA staff members were arrested in Lebanon by the Israeli armed forces. UNDP had eleven cases, UNICEF two, ECA six in Ethiopia; in the latter cases, the government characterized the offence in three of these cases as 'political'. UNESCO referred again to the East German case.

In the period 1983-84 a total of eighty four cases of arrest and detention of UN officials in twenty eight different countries were reported;[10] in all but ten of these new cases, either the organizations concerned were able to exercise their right of functional protection through representations made by the UN-designated official, or the staff members were released. For these ten cases, the countries or territories of detention were Afghanistan, Ethiopia, Occupied South Lebanon, the Gaza Strip and the West Bank, and the organizations concerned were UNICEF, FAO, UNHCR, UNRWA and UNIFIL. The FAO and UNICEF detainees in Afghanistan (two drivers) had been arrested on charges of subversion.

In 1985 the UN official report repeated the same sad story: cases of arrests, detention or disappearances totalled eighty nine.[11] The countries concerned were again Afghanistan, Lebanon, the Gaza Strip and the West Bank. The organizations concerned were, again, ECA, FAO, UNESCO, UNHCR, UNICEF and UNRWA.

In 1986 ninety five cases were reported. In most cases the organizations were able to exercise their protection rights, they obtained the release of the detainee or were otherwise able to determine that no question of immunity arose. Of the remaining nineteen cases, seventeen concerned locally recruited UNRWA staff, one UNDOF and one UNIFIL staff members. The countries involved were, again, Afghanistan, Ethiopia and Middle East areas. The case of a Romanian official retained in his home country was also reported.

A staff report published in 1987 a list of eight cases of detention or disappearances in Afghanistan, one in Argentina (presumed dead), one in Bahrain, two (killed) in Chile, one in Equatorial Guinea, three in Ethiopia, one in the German Democratic Rebublic, one (killed) in Guatemala, thirteen detained by Israeli authorities in Lebanon, the Gaza Strip and the West Bank, two in Jordan, six in Lebanon, one in Romania, fourteen (one killed) in Syria or detained by Syrian forces in Lebanon.[12]

From this summary one can identify several categories of cases. One concerns countries or areas of civil war, of military strife such as the Middle East, Ethiopia and Afghanistan. A second category includes countries with authoritarian regimes such as the defunct military regime of Argentina, Chile and Kenya. A third category includes the socialist countries. A few cases will illustrate each category.

Afghanistan, Ethiopia and the Middle East

Mr Nooruddin, a locally recruited FAO driver of Afghan nationality, was taken away on 21 April 1984 by the security authorities at the FAO project compound. The UNDP resident representative requested the Ministry of Foreign Affairs to provide information as to the reasons of Nooruddin's arrest and his whereabouts, and to arrange for a meeting between the detainee and a UN representative. It was later learnt that Nooruddin had been arrested together with a UNICEF driver 'on charges of subversion based on documents'. No meeting could be arranged. Nooruddin was amnestied on 10 July 1985.[13]

In Ethiopia Mr Belay, an ECA local staff member, was arrested in October 1978: his family informed ECA in June 1979 that his clothes had been returned, a clear indication that he had died. Two other ECA locally recruited staff members, Haregwein Desta and Azeb Abay were arrested in 1979. No formal charges against Desta had been made known to the UN, while Abay was charged with having participated in 'anti-government activities'. They were amnestied on 21 June 1985 and returned to ECA service.[14]

As of 17 October 1983, sixty-eight UNRWA staff members were believed to be in detention. In November 1983 most were released by the Israeli authorities. In October 1984 there were still three staff members in detention, two of whom had been in detention for over two years and were removed from Lebanon to a prison in Israel by the Israeli military authorities. For example, Khalil J.M.S. Eteiwi, a teacher in the West Bank, was arrested on 12 September 1983. UNRWA learnt, following several requests, that Eteiwi had been brought to trial before an Israeli military court on the charges of conspiracy and membership of an illegal organization, and that, on 16 February 1984 he had been convicted and sentenced to four and a half years' imprisonment.[15]

A British journalist, Alec Collett, was abducted near Beirut on 25 March 1985 while on an UNRWA assignment; he is believed to have been executed by the 'Revolutionary Organization of Socialist Muslims' in April 1986. The agency's commissioner-general stated that if his death was confirmed, Collett would be the twenty-second person to die in the service of UNRWA since June 1982. The 1986 report of the UN secretary-general stated that the Middle East continued to be the principal focus of arrests and detention of officials by national authorities and abductions by unidentified groups.[16]

Mahmoud Tarjouman, a Syrian staff member of the Economic Commission for Western Asia (ECWA) was arrested by the Syrian security authorities on 16 May 1976. There were no charges and he was put into solitary confinement for five months. He was released in 1978, but again arrested and jailed for seven more years. He was released in June 1985.[17]

Argentina, Chile and Kenya

On 11 November 1976 Viviana Micucci, of Argentine nationality, a WHO/PAHO librarian in Buenos - Aires, was abducted from her domicile at 3.30 a.m. by a group of men in uniform, with her brother and her parents. The parents were released, but neither Viviana nor her brother were ever found. The WHO staff association played a determining role in encouraging an initially reticent regional WHO administration to intervene with the Argentine authorities. However, WHO and UN requests for information remained unheeded. In March 1977 the Ministry of Foreign Affairs informed the UNDP representative that Micucci was not detained by the Federal Police and that all efforts by competent authorities to find her had been in vain. Later efforts by staff associations to end the 'conspiracy of silence' did not produce any results, even after the end of the military regime in Argentina. The WHO staff decided in 1982 to dedicate the entrance hall of the WHO headquarters building in Geneva to the memory of Viviana Micucci, and 11 November was observed as 'Remember Viviana Micucci Day'.[18]

Fernando Olivares-Mori was arrested in Chile on 6 October 1973; Carmelo Soria Espinosa was arrested on 14 July 1976. Both local staff members of ECLA are believed to have been killed. Their cases are still the subject of formal claims by the UN. The Chilean government has denied responsibility in these cases and considers them to be under investigation, in accordance with domestic legal procedures.[19]

Salim Lone, of Kenyan nationality, a UNICEF information officer, was arrested during a visit to his country on 22 July 1986 on suspicion of anti-government activities. Prior to his UN employment he had edited an opposition Kenyan publication and had been convicted for publishing comments critical of the High Court. Representations from the UN and UNICEF led to his release from jail within two days, which was followed by the revocation of his nationality.[20]

Socialist countries

Since 1976 Romania, Poland, the German Democratic Republic and the Soviet Union have been involved in human rights cases of UN officials of their respective nationalities.

Romania On 4 June 1976 Sorin Dumitrescu, a UNESCO director of Romanian nationality, while on official duty travel, was retained in Romania by his national authorities and ordered to submit his resignation from UNESCO.[21] A.M. M'Bow, the UNESCO director-general, refused to accept this resignation. On 12 December Dumitrescu was condemned by a tribunal in Bucarest to the payment of an amount due by him in compliance with decree no. 233/1974, which compels international officials of Rumanian nationality to repay to the state a substantial part of their international emoluments. In March 1977 he was called to military duty for five months. In May he was informed of the reasons for the decisions taken: absence of frequent contacts with the Romanian authorities in Paris, violation of the law concerning foreigners, opening of an account in a French bank, renting of a luxurious apartment. On 13 October Dumitrescu, who had remained in permanent contact with UNESCO, was accused, on this account, of violation of Article 157, alinea 2, of the Romanian penal code, punishing 'treason by transmission of secrets'. This charge was however not followed by a judgment.

The director-general of UNESCO, reacted firmly through direct contacts with the Romanian authorities and public statements, with the unanimous support of the UNESCO Executive Board. The staff association and FICSA also supported the director-general and exerted pressure on the Romanian government by publicizing the affair. On 16 May 1978, Dumitrescu was allowed to rejoin his post at UNESCO in Paris.

Another Romanian national, Liviu Bota, director of the UN institute for Disarmament Research (UNIDIR) in Geneva, was summoned to Bucarest on 24 December 1985 for consultations with the government. He was then not allowed to rejoin his post in Geneva. The Romanian government first said that Bota had been offered a high post in the Foreign Affairs Ministry and that he had resigned from his UN post. UN secretary-general J. Perez de Cuellar refused to accept this explanation and insisted that Bota submit his resignation in person, in Geneva or in New York, as required by UN regulations.[22] In November 1986 the chief Romanian delegate to the UN, Teodor Marinescu, accused Bota of espionage during a debate of the Political Committee of the UN General Assembly in New York.[23]

The Romanian attitude was condemned by the UN Staff Union in New York and by FICSA.[24] Members of the UN Human Rights Committee, meeting in Geneva in July 1987, expressed concern over the Bota case and stressed that he should be allowed to go either to Geneva or New York in order to resolve the situation.[25] The chairman of the Advisory Board on Disarmament Studies and Board of Trustees of UNIDIR had noted with regret Bota's absence, which had impaired the functioning of the Institute.

The UN secretary-general intervened personally in this matter. In his contacts with Romanian authorities, he took the position that Bota remains a staff member of the UN until his resignation, which must be submitted in person. Bota was finally allowed by the Romanian authorities to resume UN employment in Geneva on 12 February 1988.[26]

Poland. Alice Wesolowska, a UNDP staff member of Polish nationality, was arrested on 10 August 1979 by the Polish authorities in Warsaw. She was visiting her relatives, on her way from New York, her last duty station, to a new assignment in Oulan-Bator, Mongolia. After seven months in solitary confinement, she pleaded guilty at her trial by a Polish military court; her sentence on 7 March 1980 was seven years' imprisonment, the seizure of her personal property, the deprivation of her civic rights for five years and a fine. All access to Wesolowska had been denied to the UN: the request of Kurt

Waldheim, then secretary-general, that a UN lawyer be allowed to represent her was denied, as was a parallel request by the International Commission of Jurists in Geneva to have a distinguished Swedish jurist observe the trial. Wesolowska was convicted on charges of cooperation with an intelligence agency of an unnamed member of the North Atlantic Treaty Organization. Another more plausible reason was that Wesolowska had been recruited directly by UNDP, while she was an exchange student in the US, and not through the Polish government. In December 1979 the UN Staff Union held a rally denouncing the detention of Wesolowska and of other staff members.[27] In April 1980 and January 1981 the secretary general submitted an appeal for clemency in her case, which seemed to imply that she was guilty. Also in January 1981 Wesolowska started a hunger strike, which she stopped on the expectation that she might be released. She had denied all charges against her in a petition to the Council of State. After several more interventions by the UN, including an appeal by the secretary general, J. Perez de Cuellar, Wesolowska was finally released on 20 February 1984.

In April 1987, it was reported that the Polish government had prevented Mr Wlodzimierz, a Polish staff member in the UN Council for Namibia, from returning to New York after he was recalled to Warsaw. The Polish authorities have been asked to clarify the position.

German Democratic Republic (GDR). Percy Stulz, a UNESCO director of GDR nationality was arrested in East Berlin, while visiting his country on official duty, on 8 March 1980. He was then hospitalized against his will. His UN laissez-passer had been taken away from him. On 10 March he wrote to the director-general of UNESCO that he was in perfect health and that he wanted to continue his work in the organization.[29] The director-general was advised by governmental authorities that in view of the criminal charges lodged against Stulz alleging anti-state activities, he was obliged to offer his resignation from UNESCO. The director-general replied that he had not waived Stulz's immunity from legal process. Stulz's resignation could only be considered if it was submitted at his duty station in Paris. The UNESCO Executive Board, at its session of April—June 1980, expressed its concern regarding Stulz's continued detention and gave its full support to the director-general for his efforts in pursuing Stulz's release: Hungary, Poland, the Soviet Union and Vietnam voted against this resolution. According to some sources, Stulz was blamed for having had as a subordinate in UNESCO an Ukrainian professor who obtained political asylum in France.[30] Stulz's wife allegedly had helped a person to leave the GDR illegally. In August 1980 Stulz was sentenced by a military court in Berlin to three years' imprisonment. The UNESCO General Conference supported the director-general's position in a resolution adopted on 27 October 1980 on the 'Independence of the International Civil Service' Resolution 25.1).

Stulz was released in the autumn of 1981, after having served two-thirds of his prison sentence. However, he was not allowed to return to his duty station, either to resume his duties there or to submit his resignation in accordance with the UNESCO staff rules, in spite of the director-general's request. The director-general considered that the fact that Stulz was no longer imprisoned constituted a partially positive result; nevertheless, the conditions in which this official was prevented, when deprived of his liberty, from returning to his post, after a short leave in his home country, and the non-compliance with the provisions governing the resignation of a UNESCO staff member, these constituted a violation of the status of the international civil service.[31]

Soviet Union. Yevgeni V. Soloviev, another UNESCO staff member, formerly a Soviet citizen, announced in November 1986 that his wife and daughter, in Moscow, had been prevented from joining him in Paris for five years: the Soviet authorities had withdrawn their passports after they had left France for their annual vacation in the Soviet Union. Soloviev was then told by the Soviet authorities that he had to return to the Soviet Union if he wanted to see them again. The Soviet pressures prompted Soloviev to ask the French government for political asylum in December 1981, which was granted. He acquired French nationality in 1985. Soloviev said that no official reason was ever given for the measure against his family. But he noted that the move came after another Soviet employee at UNESCO, Alexei Pleshakov, sought political asylum in May 1981. Pleshakov and Soloviev had been friends before and during their time at UNESCO.

The UNESCO staff association sent five letters to the Soviet National Commission on UNESCO at the Soviet Foreign Ministry: they were not answered.[32] On 14 November 1986 the Council of the UNESCO staff association noted with profound disquiet that the wife and daughter of their colleague Soloviev had been detained against their will in the Soviet Union for more than five years; it expressed its satisfaction at the numerous representations made by the staff association and FICSA to help to reunite their colleague's family; it noted with satisfaction that the director-general of UNESCO had treated this case in the same manner as other cases of arbitrary detention of UNESCO staff members, in accordance with the principles of independence and integrity of the international civil service; and called for the support of every staff association in the UN system.[33]

In February 1987 a FICSA resolution (No. 40/4) was adopted. It considered that the Soloviev situation constituted a grave violation both of the independence of the international civil service which the Soviet Union had committed itself to respect in signing the UN Charter and the Constitution of UNESCO, and the right to reunification of families recognized by the Final Act of the Helsinki Conference. It appealed to the secretary- general of the UN to intervene and decided to participate in a world information campaign designed to persuade political leaders and public opinion to bring pressure to bear on the Soviet government.[34] At the time of this writing, Soloviev's family has not been reunited.

On another level, it is worth noting that Soloviev is the only Soviet international official having obtained political asylum who has remained in a UN organization; in spite of pressures exerted by the Soviet delegation, the duration of his UNESCO contract was extended. What was not possible in the UN secretariat in the case of Yakometz (see Ch. 4) was done in the present case, in a UN specialized agency, through the determination of its director-general, A.M. M'Bow.

Staff pressures

The staff associations of the UN organizations, through FICSA, have been instrumental and insistent in bringing the problems of security and independence of international staff to the attention of the administrations and of UN governing bodies in order to obtain their open support, and to define in practice what action could or should be taken by the organizations in specific cases. The staff associations have also publicized current cases, bringing public-opinion pressure to bear on the governments concerned, and forcing sometimes reticent administrations to adopt clear positions and act.

Between the creation of the UN organizations and 1979, cases were dealt with, usually discreetly, by the organization concerned, but without clear definitions or principles or procedures.

In 1979, at the urging of its member associations, FICSA took the initiative to request the inclusion of an item on the 'Security and Independence of International Civil Servants' in the agenda of the Administrative Committee on Coordination (ACC), in order to explain the Federation's preoccupation with the increasingly grave threat to the security and well-being of international staff. FICSA felt that some cases could be solved with the support of the entire UN system. FICSA's intervention was successful.

ACC reaffirmed the principle of the strict independence of the international civil service, which should be respected by all governments, stressed the inherent right of international organizations to fully protect their staff members when their security was being jeopardized and requested one of its subsidiary bodies, the Consultative Committee on Administrative Questions (CCAQ) to review the matter.[35]

In 1980, following another FICSA intervention, the UN Commission on Human Rights voted a resolution expressing its concern at reports of infringements of the human rights of UN staff members and the abrogation of rights conveyed under the Convention on the Privileges and Immunities of the UN. The Commission appealed to UN member states to respect their obligations under the Charter, the Universal Declaration of Human Rights, the International Covenant on Political and Civil Rights, and the Conventions on Immunities. It requested the UN secretary-general to use his good offices to ensure the full enjoyment of human rights by UN staff members.[36]

In January 1980 UN officials responsible for security matters were apprised of procedures to be followed in reporting the arrest or detention of UN staff, and of the applicable legal provisions.[37]

The legal rights of the UN

Faced with a number of violations of the individual status of their staff members, the UN organizations have had to define the principles and basis for their position and action.

The basic texts governing the status, privileges and immunities of staff members are found in the UN Charter and the constituent instruments of the other UN organizations, the Convention on the Privileges and Immunities of the UN of 13 February 1946, the Convention on the Privileges and Immunities of the Specialized Agencies of 21 November 1947, the Standard Basic Assistance Agreements of the UNDP and Host Agreements concluded between the organizations and the country of the organization's headquarters.

Under Article 105.2 of the UN Charter, 'officials of the Organizations shall similarly enjoy such privileges and immunities as are necessary for the independent exercise of their functions in connexion with the Organization'.[38] Privileges and immunities are therefore linked to the staff member's official functions: they do not cover the individual's other activities.

ACC has given an extensive definition of those 'officials' covered by this protection: staff members, experts on mission, locally recruited employees and, in general, all persons performing functions or services for the UN system.[39] The coverage of local employees is often ignored or dismissed by national authorities: they tend to consider that only internationally recruited staff (professional or general service) are true international civil servants, thus excluding local recruits (mostly nationals of the host country) from any functional protection.

The Conventions on Privileges and Immunities prescribe that UN officials shall

(1) be immune from legal process in respect of words spoken or written and all acts performed by them in their official capacity;

(2) be exempt from taxation on the salaries and emoluments paid to them by the UN organization;

(3) be exempt from national service obligations.

Other immunities and privileges refer to immigration restrictions and alien registration, exchange facilities, repatriation facilities in time of international crisis, duty-free import of furniture and personal effects.

The Conventions specify that the privileges and immunities are granted to officials in the interests of the UN organizations and not for the personal benefit of the individuals themselves.[40] 'The Secretary-General shall have the right and the duty to waive the immunity of any official in any case where, in his opinion, the immunity would impede the course of justice and can be waived without prejudice to the interests of the UN.'

The rights of member states are complemented by obligations: each member state 'undertakes to respect the exclusively international character of the responsibilities of the Secretary-General and staff and not seek to influence them in the discharge of their responsibilities' (Art. 100.2 of the UN Charter).

The organization has its own obligations: it 'shall cooperate at all times with the appropriate authorities of Members to facilitate the proper administration of justice, secure the observance of police regulations and prevent the occurrence of any abuse in connection with the privileges, immunities and facilities mentioned in this Article'.[41]

The rights of functional protection and of intervention have been further elaborated by the organizations.[42] The organizations maintain that when a governmental authority arrests or detains a UN staff member, whether internationally or locally recruited, the UN organizations has the right to visit and converse with the staff member, to be apprised of the grounds for the arrest or detention, including the main facts and formal charges, to assist the staff member in arranging for legal counsel and to appear in legal proceedings to defend any UN interest affected by the arrest or detention. The distinction between acts performed in an official capacity and those performed in a private capacity, which lies at the heart of the concept of functional immunity, is a question of fact which depends on the circumstances of the particular case. The position of the UN is that it is exclusively for the secretary-general to determine the extent of the duties and functions of UN officials.

In order to enable the secretary-general to determine whether an act was done in the course of official functions and, in the affirmative, to decide whether to waive immunity, as well as to enable the organization to exercise its right of functional protection, there must be an adequate opportunity to learn the facts of the case. When a staff member has been arrested or is in detention, the only such opportunity is through access to the staff member concerned.

The International Court of Justice's Advisory Opinion of 11 April 1949 has established the need of protection for the agents of the organizations, as a condition of the performance of its functions.[43] In consequence, the organizations' right of functional protection is also an obligation:

In order that the agent may perform his duties satisfactorily, he must feel that this protection is assured to him by the Organization, and that he may count on it. To ensure the independence of the agent, and, consequently, the independent action of the Organisation itself, it is essential that in performing his duties he need not have to rely on any other protection than that of the Organization (save of course for the more direct and immediate protection due from the State in whose territory he may be). In particular, he should not have to rely on the protection of his own State. If he had to rely on that State, his independence might well be compromised, contrary to the principle applied by Article 100 of the Charter. And lastly, it is essential that — whether the agent belongs to a powerful or to a weak State; to one more affected or less affected by the complications of international life; to one in sympathy or not in sympathy with the mission of the agent — he should know that in the performance of his duties he is under the protection of the Organization. This assurance is even more necessary when the agent is stateless.

The intervention and reporting procedures

At the local level, in case a UN official, or members of his immediate family, have been arrested or detained by national authorities, the UN official in charge of security matters (the 'designated official') will immediately contact the Foreign Ministry of the government concerned and request all relevant information about the arrest or detention, as well as the government's cooperation in arranging, as a matter of urgency, that UN representatives be given access to the individual arrested or detained.

The UN designated official will report the incident by the fastest means of communications to the UN security coordinator at the UN headquarters in New York. The report should, if possible, include the name, nationality and employment status of the persons involved; the time, place and circumstances of the incident; the legal terms and grounds for the arrest and detention; the name of the governmental agency under whose authority the measure was taken; whether access has been granted; and whether consular protection and/or legal counsel is or will be available. An appropriate report should also be sent if the arrest or detention was carried out by an unauthorised or unknown person or persons, rather than by governmental authorities.

No statements concerning the incident should be made to the news media unless previously cleared by UN headquarters.

Further pressures from FICSA

In 1980, the ACC stated again its deep concern at the situation. It considered that any infringement of the security and independence of staff members of UN organizations by a member state is a serious threat to international cooperation: 'The executive heads, who are responsible for the security and independence of the staff under their authority, appeal to governments to give their full assistance in ensuring respect for the principles to which all member states have subscribed'.[44]

A similar appeal was addressed by the General Assembly to the member states in December 1980. The Assembly also requested the secretary-general to report to it on any cases in which the international status of UN staff had not been fully respected.[45]

From then on, a ritual was established: every year, the UN secretary-general submits a report on such cases to the General Assembly, which then adopts a resolution noting with concern the cases and formulating appeals and requests.[46] The resolutions generally call upon member states to respect the privileges and immunities of all UN officials and to resolve outstanding cases. They call on UN staff to comply with the obligations of the staff regulations, with particular reference to regulation 1.8, which states in part: 'These privileges and immunities furnish no excuse to the staff members who enjoy them for non-performance of their private obligations or failure to observe laws and police regulations'.

FICSA recently criticized the secretary-general's reports, a mere listing of cases of violations, for being too bland and sometimes incomplete. On the other hand, FICSA recognized that the reports and the resolutions had enhanced a greater awareness of the problem.

In 1981 FICSA initiated a campaign in favour of Percy Stulz, the UNESCO official detained in East Germany, while praising the action undertaken by the director-general of the organization and the resolutions adopted by UNESCO governing bodies.[47]

In 1982 the FICSA Council discussed the sanctions which the organizations could envisage to apply against the transgressing countries: the withdrawal of UN relations with the country concerned, when a satisfactory and rapid resolution of detention cases was not achieved, or a reduction of the organizations's activities in those countries. Some FICSA representatives felt that the UN withdrawal might be counter-productive, as the organization would then have no means to protect the staff members concerned. In opposition to the organizations' usual cautious stance, the Council agreed that FICSA should give wide publicity to such cases. Some representatives felt that UNDP resident representatives did not do their utmost in cases of arrest or detention of staff members, as they did not wish to jeopardize their relations with the host government. On the other hand, UN staff should be careful not to antagonize the local authorities and to respect the laws of the host country.[48]

In 1983 the FICSA Council cabled the secretary-general to express again its deep concern regarding the continued violation of the rights of UN staff. It advised him of FICSA'S intention to use its network of associations to inform the public through the media in capitals throughout the world of any violations to these fundamental rights 'should your efforts which have been appreciated fail'. FICSA would also use Human Rights Day to remind the public through world-wide media of all unresolved cases.[49]

FICSA'S pressures both on the UN executive heads and on member states were continuing through the threat of 'appeal to public opinion'. In July 1983 FICSA called this issue a matter of life or death and made several proposals to the CCAQ to improve policies and procedures.[50] In 1984 the FICSA Council stated that the UN local representatives must not only be authorized, but required, to intervene immediately in the case of arrest or detention of any UN staff member. FICSA proposed the setting-up of a local pre-constituted emergency committee, which would include the chairman of the Staff Council, to recommend action. Action could escalate from a *note verbale* to the dispatch of a senior UN official. Publicity should be a last resort, as it is irreversible. An effective measure had been to inform the offending government that if it observed the Convention on Privileges and Immunities, it would not be named in the secretary-general's report to the general Assembly.[51]

Fifth Committee debates, November 1986

In his statement to the Fifth Committee, the secretary-general said that independence is one side of the coin and safety, the other. The staff member will remain independent as long as he knows that, in the performance of his official duties, he will be protected from interference or, worse, from prosecution, loss of freedom or death. He deplored that there had been too many cases where this protection was not assured, or where access to the staff member was not granted to the UN representative. A request for access is not intended to give the staff member undue protection, but to make sure that the state has scrupulously respected the international obligations which it has assumed, and that the staff member has respected his duty to be impartial, which excludes any act that might jeopardize the public order of the state in question. The efficiency of the secretariat depends largely on the safety and independence of staff members.[52]

In introducing the secretary-general's report,[53] the UN legal counsel emphasized that locally - recruited officials were entitled to the same degree of protection as international officials. He referred to the many cases of locally recruited staff of agencies on peacekeeping missions in the Middle East. He referred to the cases of Alec Collett and Liviu Bota.

On behalf of the Nordic countries, the representative from Iceland said that the secretary-general and the other executive heads must be given continued support in their efforts to clarify the nature of each case, to secure the necessary personal protection and to restore persecuted UN officials to their normal functions.[54]

The Cameroon representative agreed with the secretary-general that the moral integrity of the staff and its respect for their obligations towards member states were important considerations.

The United Kingdom representative, on behalf of the member states of the European Community, noted with regret the marked deterioration in the situation. He expressed particular concern over the cases of Alec Collett and Liviu Bota. The Canadian representative said that the Bota case involved indefensible behaviour by the government in engaging in his arbitrary detention.[55] The US representative was also concerned over the case of Liviu Bota.

The Romanian representative replied that the way to solve such problems was through discussions between the secretary-general and officials of the countries concerned; in other words, he advocated quiet diplomacy.[56]

The representative from Afghanistan said that his country fully respected the UN Charter and other texts. He reaffirmed the need for absolute respect by the international staff for the laws and customs of individual member states. The individuals quoted in the secretary-general's report had been arrested on charges of engaging in anti-state activities of which the Afghan security forces had undeniable proof. Full rights of defence would be accorded to the detainees and visiting rights granted to UN representatives.[57]

The representative from the Netherlands said that the secretary-general's statement showed how wide the gap was between his notion of how international civil servants and member states should interact and the reality.

In introducing the draft resolution, he said that its sole purpose was to give the secretary-general full support in his efforts to safeguard the well-being and functioning of UN staff. The resolution was adopted without a vote.[58]

The assistant-secretary-general for Personnel Services remarked, somewhat optimistically, that such unanimity should make it possible to ensure that security problems would not arise in the future.[59]

Besides the usual appeals, the resolution asked the secretary-general to continue personally to act as the focal point in promoting and ensuring the observance of the privileges and immunities of UN officials. The secretary general should review and appraise the existing security measures and modify them where necessary.[60]

The associations continued in 1987 their pressures for the respect of the rights of international staff. In February 1987 the FICSA Council again reaffirmed its determination to use all means at its disposal to that end. The FICSA resolution referred with disquiet to the cases of Soloviev and Bota.[61]

FICSA's parallel and rival federation, the Coordinating Committee for Independent Staff Unions and Associations of the UN system (CCISUA) raised this issue in July 1987 at the twenty-sixth session of the International Civil Service Commission (ICSC) and made various proposals for a more coherent policy and more effective protective and reporting procedures. To CCISUA's disappointment, the Commission only requested its secretariat to study the matter.[62]

On 3 September 1987 the UN Sub-Commission on Prevention of Discrimination and protection of Minorities, a subsidiary body of the UN Human Rights Commission, appealed to member states to respect the rights of UN staff members. It asked the secretary-general to strengthen his efforts in this respect and to submit to the next session of the Sub-Commission a detailed report on the situation of staff members and their families detained, imprisoned, missing or held in a country against their will. The Sub-Commission resolution referred in particular to the Bota case.[63]

In October 1987, in his statement to the Fifth Committee, the secretary-general again mentioned his continuing anxiety over the arrest and detention of a number of staff members by certain governments, often without charges. His concern was based on humanitarian grounds, but also in order to ensure that the organization was able to discharge its responsibilities.[64]

The president of FICSA accused the UN secretary-general of not taking any concrete measures to try to obtain the release of more than fifty colleagues detained or who had disappeared; quiet diplomacy was not sufficient. She said that the secretary-general was only initiating routine requests and a routine yearly report. He should act more firmly.[65]

Difficulties of Protection

The principles and the procedures concerning the immunities of UN staff members are clear, but their application raises many problems. While the immunities of national diplomatic personnel are generally recognized and respected (with well-known exceptions), UN personnel, except at very senior levels, are not generally assimilated to diplomats by national customs, police, security, military, administrative or other authorities. UN staff members who are locally recruited and are nationals of the host country are often treated like other citizens and are denied the status of international officials. National diplomats are protected by the principle of reciprocity — we'll do to your diplomats what you do to ours — and more generally by the potential threat of diplomatic, political, economic or military sanctions against the guilty country.

There is no possible reciprocity between a defenceless international organization and sovereign states. What sanctions could an international organization apply to a government guilty of violating the immunities of an international civil servant? Formally, any substantive sanction could only be applied by decision of the organization's governing bodies, which might be reluctant to adopt any effective measures. In substance, is it legitimate to threaten a developing country with cuts or withdrawal of technical cooperation programmes in order to exert pressure to obtain the release of a detained staff member? Should a member state be expelled from the international organization for such transgressions? It is very unlikely that a UN governing body would be willing to go further than voting a resolution appealing to the said government to release a detained staff member or to abide by the UN procedures of access, as has been done in UNESCO. Any other sanction is highly unlikely, on account of the solidarity of groups of states, for instance the socialist group or Third World groups.

The executive head is placed in a particularly conflictual position. He is torn between his functions as a senior international diplomat, elected by member states and responsible to them, and his responsibilities to his staff, including his obligation of functional protection. To what extent can the executive head raise protests against measures taken by a member state with regard to a staff member of his organization, and particularly if the staff member is a national of that country, without negatively affecting the relations of the organization with this state? He may also provoke the hostility of groups of states if he publicly accuses one of them of having reneged on its international obligations. In doing so, he could divide and weaken the organization and jeopardize his present position and future re-election. A.M. M'Bow was perhaps an exception in this respect, whatever criticisms were addressed to him on other grounds: he had an impeccable record of using all private and public diplomatic means at his disposal to come to the rescue of ill-treated staff members and their families. He expressed himself publicly and clearly in the defence of the internationalist principles and was able to secure the support of his governing bodies to his position. Other executive heads have usually pleaded that, in order to be effective, any intervention must be discreet and avoid publicity at all costs. They use the impersonal channels of quiet diplomacy or, at times, those of confidential talks with ambassadors or other national representatives. The UN secretary-general is perhaps in a unique position: his political functions in the field of peace and security, his role of mediator, his good offices require that he should be a neutral intermediary, acceptable to all parties. Should he compromise this position, as an international statesman, in intervening personally on behalf of a detained staff member? This dilemma may explain his reserve, and his careful, legalistic attitude in relation to some of the cases, as opposed to the more determined behaviour of the former director-general of UNESCO, A.M. M'Bow.

These difficulties are made worse by the fact that many cases have political connotations: some of the persons arrested or detained or abducted are suspected of being political opponents of the existing regime, in countries where opponents are considered as traitors or criminals who must be punished or eliminated. The countries concerned, totalitarian or authoritarian states, want to apply their 'justice' to their citizens, without interference by the international organization, and without having to follow the legalistic formalities demanded by the organization. The international defence and protection of human rights implies necessarily an unwanted intervention into the states' domestic jurisdiction, which many states do not tolerate.

The position of staff associations differs from that of the executive heads. Their statutory mandate is to promote and protect the material and moral interests of the international staff and to enhance the notion of a strong, independent international civil service. To defend the freedom and life of staff members, and at the same time to uphold the principles of independence and functional immunity against government pressures, has been considered by all staff associations and unions and their federations as one of their more worthy and essential duties. They are the ones who brought the immunity cases to the attention of the international administrations, who made them define rules and procedures, who publicize the outstanding cases periodically, who intervene publicly with governing bodies and governments on behalf of their detained or disappeared colleagues. They have more freedom of action, within limits, than the UN administrations: the limits, which are not easy to define, are to avoid any action which could harm the cases by antagonizing the governments concerned.

The few cases of ill-treated or killed international civil servants are only a handful in comparison with the innumerable human rights cases in the world; with or without an international status of protection, all the victims have suffered the same injustice, the same persecutions, the same tortures. They should all be defended in and by the various intergovernmental and non-governmental bodies, even if the chances of success are limited.

As to the security problems of international staff, the principles and procedures are now well established. Whatever the political and practical constraints, the executive heads have a duty to actively protect and defend their staff's lives and safety. No doubt the staff associations will continue their creditable pioneering work in this area. Finally, the International Civil Service Commission should also take a firm and public position on problems of of independence and security, and not restrict itself to purely technical tasks.

On 19 October 1987 the secretary-general told his staff, 'I shall seize every chance that I can to intervene on behalf of our detained, restricted or missing colleagues. ... We shall not forget our colleagues, as long as they are denied their human rights'.[66]

Let us hope that this firmness will be applied and shared by all other executive heads and that it will help to resolve some of the outstanding UN human rights cases.

Notes

1. WHO Staff Association *Spotlight*, no.27, 29 October 1987.
2. General Assembly Resol. 41/205 of 11 December 1986.
3. FICSA Press Release, 3 September 1987.
4. Arts. 3,5,9 and 10 of the Universal Declaration of Human Rights adopted by the General Assembly on 10 December 1948, Resol. 217 A(III).
5. Art. 105 of the UN Charter.
6. WHO Staff Association *Spotlight*, no. 27, 29 October 1987.
7. Thomas Bayard (pseud.), 'Arrestations et enlèvements de fonctionnaires des Nations Unies, *International Review of Administrative Sciences*, Brussels, 1/1982, pp. 9-18. See also Paul Tavernier, 'La sûreté et la sécurité personnelle des agents internationaux', in *Les Agents internationaux*, Pedone, Paris, 1985, pp. 325-51.
8. UN Doc. A/C.5/36/31, 4 November 1981.
9. UN Doc. A/C.5/37/34, 8 November 1982.
10. UN Doc. A/C.5/39/17, 15 October 1984.
11. UN Doc. A/C.5/40/25, 25 October 1985.
12. *UN Special*, Geneva, January 1987.
13. UN Docs. A/C.5/39/17 and A/C.5/40/25.
14. UN Docs. A/C.5/36/31 and A/C.5/40/25.
15. UN Doc. A/C.5/39/17.
16. UN Docs. A/C.5/40/25, A/C.5/41/12 and *UN Special*, Geneva, May 1986 and March 1987.
17. *UN Special*, Geneva, April 1987.
18. Bayard, p. 12; *UN Special*, Geneva, November 1984; and WHO Staff Association Doc. 5C31/AGM(1983)/3.
19. See UN Docs. A/C.5/36/31 and A/C.5/37/34.
20. *UN Special*, April 1987.
21. Alain Pellet, see 'A propos de l'affaire Dumitrescu à l'UNESCO: Note sur l'indépendance des fonctionnaires internationaux', *Journal du Droit international* 1979, no. 3, pp. 570-88.
22. Bota denied that he had resigned and accepted another post in Bucharest, in a telephone interview with a Swiss journalist: see *UN Special*, November-December 1986. See also *International Herald Tribune*, 1 July 1986.
23. *International Herald Tribune*, 2 December 1986.
24. *Le Monde*, 10 May 1986, FICSA Resol. 40/4 in Doc. FICSA/C/40/10, 7 May 1987.
25. UN Press Release HR/2005, 14 July 1987.
26. UN Doc. A/C.5/41/12 and *UN Special*, Geneva, October 1987, *Le Monde* of 16 February 1988 and FICSA *Spotlight* of 17 February 1988.
27. During the rally, former UN staff member Shirley Hazzard strongly denounced the Soviet Union and Poland. The Soviet representative to the UN then accused

the Staff Union of 'grossly slanderous attacks' on the Soviet Union and other states and asked that the staff members guilty of committing this provocative act be punished: *International Herald Tribune,* 15 February 1980; *Le Monde,* 9-10 March 1980; *Newsweek,* 17 March 1981; the *Diplomatic World Bulletin,* 10 March 1980 and 23 March 1981; and UN Docs. A/C.5/36/31, A/C.5/37/34 and A/C.5/39/17.

28. *Diplomatic World Bulletin,* 27 April 1987.
29. Bayard, pp. 14-16; UN Docs. A/C.5/36/31 and A/C.5/37/34.
30. *L'Express,* Paris, 28 June 1980; *Le Monde,* 26, 28 March and 11 June 1980.
31. UN Doc. A/C.5/37/34, para. 34.
32. *International Herald Tribune,* 5 November 1986; and *Le Monde,* 22 November 1986.
33. UNESCO Staff Association Circular STA/86/38 of 20 November 1986.
34. Doc. FICSA/C/40/10, 7 May 1987
35. UN Doc. CCAQ/PER/E.128, 10 December 1979 and ACC Decision 1979/23.
36. Resol. 31(XXXV1). See also UNESCO *Opinion,* 24 March 1980
37. All UN staff members were informed of these provisions and procedures in December 1982: see UN Administrative Instruction ST/AI/299, 10 December 1982.
38. The diplomatic privileges and immunities granted to League of Nations officials under Article 7 of the Covenant were conferred upon them 'in the interest of their duties. They furnish no excuse to the officials who enjoy them for non-performance of their private obligations or failure to observe laws and police regulations'. Officials of the Secretariat invoking these privileges and immunities had to report to the secretary-general who would decide whether they would be waived. See League of Nations Staff Regulations, Art. 1.3.
39. UN Doc. A/C.5/36/31, para. 3.
40. The UN Convention may be found in *ICJ Acts and Documents*, no. 3, 1977. The Convention of the Specialized Agencies may be found in *WHO Basic Documents*, 1984.
41. Art. V, Sections 17 to 21 of the Convention on the Privileges and immunities of Immunities of the UN and Art. VI, Sections 18-23 of the Convention of the Specialized Agencies.
42. UN Doc. A/C.5/36/31.
43. *ICJ Reports*, 11 April 1949, pp. 183-4.
44. ACC Decision 1980/4 in UN Doc. ACC/1980/PER/30, 24 June 1980.
45. General Assembly Resol. 35/212, 17 December 1980.
46. See UN Docs. A/C.5/36/31, A/C.5.37/34, A/C.5/38/17 and /18, A/C.5/39/17, A/C.5/40/25, A/C.5/41/12 and General Assembly Resols. 35/12, 36/232, 37/236, 38/230, 39/244, 40/258 C and 41/205.
47. FICSA Resol. No.10 in Doc. FICSA/C/34/20 of 6 March 1981.
48. Doc. FICSA/C/35/25, 5 April 1982.
49. Doc. FICSA/C/36/19, 21 April 1983, Annex X, Appendix III.
50. UN Doc. ACC/1983/PER/27, 7 July 1983. See also UN, UNDP and UNICEF proposals in UN Doc. ACC/1983/PER/26, 7 July 1983.
51. Doc. FICSA/C/37/13, 26 March 1984.
52. UN Press Release SG/SM/743, GA/AB/9, 17 November 1986.
53. UN Doc. A/C.5/41/12 and Corr. 1.
54. UN Doc. A/C.5/41/SR.32, 21 November 1986.
55. Ibid.
56. UN Doc. A/C.5/41/SR.33, 21 November 1986.
57. UN Doc. A/C.5/41/SR.32 of 21 November 1986.
58. UN Doc. A/C.5/41/SR.39, 1 December 1986.
59. UN Doc. A/C.5/41/SR.37, 26 November 1986.
60. Resol. 41/205.

61. Doc. FICSA/C/40/10, 7 May 1987, Resol. 40/4.
62. Doc. UNOG Staff/Coordinating Council *Information,* CCBE/1987/35 of 16 October 1987.
63. Resol. 1987/21 adopted by eleven votes to two, with two abstentions. The Sub-Commission is a subsidiary of the UN Commission on Human Rights. It is composed of independent experts appointed in their personal capacity. See FICSA *Spotlight*, no. 17, 24 September 1987. The issue was raised by the French expert, Louis Joinet.
64. UN Information Circular No. 3446, 20 October 1987.
65. *Le Journal de Genève*, 22 September 1987.
66. UN Press Release SG/SM/815, 19 October 1987.

Chapter 7

Militant unions: facts and fallacies

As seen in previous chapters, the staff associations and unions, and their federations, are staunch defenders of the internationalist concept of the international civil service against governmental pressures. They have consistently promoted the career concept and the internal rule of law through access to the administrative tribunals. As shown in Chapter 5, they have been active in seeking better employment conditions, salaries and benefits and in protesting against any erosion of these benefits. As seen in Chapter 6, they have publicized member states' violation of staff members' immunities and reported on staff abductions and killings.

Some or all of these staff representation activities may have caused recent attacks against their role and their functioning. The staff associations have been accused of excessive militantism, of encroaching upon management prerogatives and of exerting an abusive influence over the UN administrations: the latter two accusations are really addressed to the administrations rather than to the staff associations.

Who initiated these attacks and what are their apparent or real reasons? What are the status and roles of staff groupings in the UN organizations? What are the limits to their militantism? What are their means of action, and are these effective? We will first try to answer these questions by reference to the statutory international staff associations. Short references will then be made to a new and unorthodox type of staff grouping, the national associations and to associations of UN retirees.

The attacks against staff associations

As noted in Chapter 5, the Joint Inspection Unit (JIU) issued a first report on 'Staff Costs' in 1984,[1] referring to mounting criticisms addressed to the UN secretariats because of the rapid increase in their costs, accompanied by 'declining efficiency'. It also raised doubts about the justifiability of the present high levels of remuneration, maintaining that UN staff were largely overpaid. The report mentioned the staff representatives' view that the remuneration of professional staff was inadequate and their active campaign for higher salaries. The report recommended that the General Assembly should not increase either salaries or post adjustment for professional and-higher-category staff at its next session. The reports had been prepared by Inspectors Alexander S. Efimov (Soviet Union) and Nasser Kaddour (Syria).

The UN secretary-general reacted by saying that the assertions regarding the so-called persisting inefficiency of the secretariat were, in his view, entirely unsubstantiated. He could not accept such a generalized accusation which does not do justice to the vast majority of dedicated and efficient UN staff.[2]

FICSA also reacted strongly, feeling that the report's scope was not limited to the UN secretariat proper, as shown by its title, but really affected the staff of all the UN organizations in the common system. FICSA said that the two inspectors' repeated attacks on the efficiency and integrity of the staff serving throughout the system was damaging the image of the UN organizations. FICSA was dismayed by the report's unsubstantiated conclusions, conflicting with those of other UN bodies; for FICSA, the report was replete with factual errors and misquotations.[3]

The second JIU report[4] tried to justify the Unit's intervention and recommendations on remuneration, basically in opposition to the positions of the Administrative Committee on Coordination (ACC) and of the International Civil Service Commission (ICSC), as providing to governments an independent, critical view of this issue. But a large part of the report was a violent attack against FICSA and against UN staff representation activities. It also challenged the authority of the UN Administrative Tribunal (UNAT) to issue judgments which are 'final and without appeal'.

FICSA was accused of 'taking the UN General Assembly to court' through financing mass appeals against the General Assembly decisions to freeze post adjustments and to reduce pension benefits. The inspectors felt that there were no legal grounds for appeals: clearly, this was a decision to be taken by the Tribunal and not by JIU. The inspectors thought that the General Assembly was entitled to review the Tribunal's judgment, in spite of all legal evidence to the contrary. They said that the General Assembly had no intention of leaving member states to the mercy of any subsidiary body (such as the UNAT) in such very important matters as their finances. In other words, the staff's appeals to the Tribunal were not legally justified, but if the Tribunal still decided in favour of the appellants, its decision would be overruled by the General Assembly.[5]

The inspectors accused the UN administration of vigorously supporting the staff bodies because the administration and the staff representatives were the one and only group of international civil servants with common interests. The UN administration was thus accused of being in collusion with staff representatives in claiming higher salaries and more benefits. For the inspectors, staff activities involved too many staff members, both from the associations and from the administration, spending too much of their working time in too many meetings on problems not directly related to the staff bodies' terms of reference. This introduced a disorganizing element into the normal functioning of the secretariat, adversely affecting its efficiency. The main thrust of the staff activities was directed at getting still higher salaries, benefits and pensions. Staff bodies were promoting the 'independent nature of the international civil service' in order to make it its own domain. This tended to transform the service into a closed system which would substantially reduce the control by member states. Staff representatives were spreading false expectations among the staff, thus affecting their morale and ultimately the efficiency of the secretariat. The inspectors believed that the international civil service does not need trade unions, since all the UN conditions of employment are regulated and embodied in staff rules and regulations, and as their employer, member states do not attempt to encroach upon them. National trade unions are financially independent, while the activities of the UN Staff Union are mostly financed by the organization's regular budget. Staff representatives claim the right to strike, although strikes are contrary to the spirit and provisions of the UN Staff Regulations and to the 'Standards of Conduct of the International Civil Service' edicted in 1954.

In consequence, the inspectors proposed various restrictive measures: to limit the number of recognized staff representatives to a reasonable size; to limit their working time on staff activities and the number of meetings; to finance all staff activities by the members' fees. The use of strikes should not be allowed in the staff bodies' terms of reference. Finally, the General Assembly, or a special committee, should review the entire range of the staff activities, in order to 'improve the situation'.

One year later, the 'Group of 18' (see ch.5) took up the same theme in one of its seventy-one recommendations: the efficiency of the organization would be increased if clear guidelines were established for the role and functions of the Staff Union, in order to ensure that the union does not infringe upon the managerial responsibilities of the Secretary-General. Staff unions or associations should finance all their activities from their own funds.[6]

The 'Group of 14' (see Ch.5) proposed that staff organizations should in future pay the salaries of their own full-time officials and related office costs. The relevant savings were estimated at $100,000 in 1986, $250,000 in 1987 and $500,000 in 1988/89.[7]

Soviet representatives had previously criticized staff activities. In December 1982 Mr Kudryavtsev (Soviet Union) referred in the Fifth Committee to 'recent disorders created by irresponsible elements in the secretariat' (a short strike by language staff), which had prevented the normal functioning of UN bodies. In order to protect the organization against such irresponsible actions, the staff regulations should state clearly that strikes and other job actions were prohibited in the UN secretariat. Second, all financial costs relating to the activities of the staff organization should be met from contributions by their members and not from the UN budget.[8] In 1985, also in the Fifth Committee, Mr Dashkevitch (Ukrainian SSR) expressed the particular concern of his delegation over the staff associations' attempts to interfere in matters outside their competence, even to the extent of waging a campaign to make the General Assembly answerable through a Tribunal for resisting staff pressures for salary increases. The UN Staff Council was undermining the work of the secretariat.[9] These arguments are identical to those of the Soviet and Syrian inspectors in their 'Staff Costs' reports.

The staff associations' reactions

Both FICSA and the Co-ordinating Committee for Independent and Staff Unions and Associations of the UN system (CCISUA) reacted strongly against the JIU reports. For FICSA the 1985 'Staff Costs' report contained unwarranted and ill-founded attacks on the integrity of staff representatives, the ICSC secretariat and staff members holding responsible managerial positions. The JIU report attacked the very foundations of orderly judicial procedures and the freedom of association of staff in international organizations. For the CCISUA, the report questioned the validity of judgements of the UNAT even before they had been rendered. The inaccuracy of the information on which the inspectors had based their conclusions and the partiality of their views disqualified the report as a basis for serious discussion.

FICSA was, rightly, particularly concerned about the attacks on such fundamental principles as freedom of association and union rights, which are enshrined in the Universal Declaration of Human Rights, the international Covenants on Civil and Political Rights, and on Economic, Social and Cultural Rights, as well as in ILO Conventions. While the inspectors had criticized the UN unions' programmes, the scope of union activity and the structure of the UN Staff Council, FICSA felt, rightly, that the inspectors' real targets were freedom of association and union rights.[10]

Reasons for the attacks against staff associations

The obvious reason is that the major contributors want to limit or reduce staff salaries, benefits and pensions, while the principal and legitimate objectives of the staff associations are to defend and promote the staff's financial interests, to improve its conditions of employment and to ensure security of employment. Criticizing the staff organizations, trying to discredit them, would weaken them; it would help in removing the staff 'obstacle' to the staff costs reduction drive, it would help in silencing the staff's claims and protests.

The attacks linked the UN administrators to the staff representatives: they attempted to discredit both, by showing that both categories were equally interested in increased financial emoluments and better employment conditions. The administrations were accused of giving in to the associations' claims, of abdicating their proper role of reponsible managers who should control strictly, conservatively, all expenditures of public monies.

Weakening the staff organizations could weaken their resistance to cuts in staffing and in emoluments. Describing them as 'militant' trade unions whose activities infringe upon management prerogatives tends to expose their 'abuse of power' and discredit the 'weak' administrations. Alleged militantism would also prevent some staff members from joining the associations.

In fact, some of the staff organizations have more influence than others; some, like the ILO Staff Union, are militant at times, but they are in no way overpowering the UN administrations and their decision-making prerogatives, nor can they reject the governing bodies' decisions. The staff organizations' influence is limited by the degree of tolerance or acceptance granted by the relevant executive heads and by the facilities provided to them by the administrations. There is relatively more union activism in large secretariats than in small organizations; isolated field experts can hardly apply group pressure on the administrations, unless they are grouped in unions, like the UNDP/UNFPA union and the FAO Field Staff Association.

The staff organizations play a useful role in participating in the personnel management of the organizations and in exerting a statutory but limited counter-power to the personnel prerogatives of the executive heads. However, the objectives and interests of the organizations' management and those of the staff organizations are not identical: the UN managers and the staff representatives are well aware that the organizations' interests have to prevail over the staff interests.

Accusations that staff representatives and UN administrators spend too much time on staff activities assume that these activities and the associations themselves are unnecessary, as the UN organizations are good employers.

This paternalistic argument ignores the modern management theory and practice of encouraging more employee participation, rather than less, in both private - and public-sector enterprises, as a prerequisite for more staff involvement and commitment, a better motivation leading to more effectiveness. Condemning the staff organizations for promoting the 'independent nature of the international civil service' and trying to limit the powers of the administrative tribunals expands the criticisms from the technical field of the determination of the appropriate remuneration to the ideological and political field of the concept and nature of the international civil service. It changes the nature of the criticisms, which then reflect the socialist countries' views of the international civil service and their rejection of the internationalist concept.

The UN staff associations and the administrative tribunals uphold explicitly the traditional and statutory concept of the international civil service, its independence and integrity. They promote the security of employment and the career concept, they defend, in different ways, the status of the international staff against governments' interferences. As seen in Chapter 6, the staff associations have publicized cases of arrests, detention and disappearances of international staff, thus exposing the violations by a number of governments of international instruments. As several socialist states are among those who have violated the immunities of UN organizations' staff, their attacks against the staff organizations may stem in part from a wish to silence and punish the accusers.

Attacks against staff organizations and the administrative tribunals are attacks against the international concept of the international civil service. The UN secretary-general realized the seriousness of this campaign. He expressed his disagreement with the inspectors' criticisms against staff representatives and the administrative tribunals. He also expressed his firm support for the system and operation of staff representation in the UN.

No doubt there may be abuses and excesses of staff representation systems in some of the organizations; it is up to each executive head to monitor and control the way the system operates and to curb deviations and abuses. However, the principle of staff consultation and participation is valid and should be defended.

Staff representation in UN organizations

Following the example set by the ILO in 1928 and the League of Nations in 1930, the UN organizations recognized from their creation the right of their staff to form associations and the right of staff representatives to be consulted on, and to participate in, discussions concerning personnel policies and employment conditions.[11]

In the UN, 'The Secretary-General shall establish and maintain continuous contact and communication with the staff in order to ensure the effective participation of the staff in identifying, examining and resolving issues relating to staff welfare, including conditions of work, general conditions of life and other personnel policies'.[12]

The Staff Regulations state that staff representative bodies are entitled to initiate proposals in the same fields. They must be organized in such a way as to afford equitable representation to all staff members, by means of biennial elections. Joint staff—management machinery is established at both local and secretariat-wide levels to advise the secretary-general on the same questions.

In the UN, staff members may form and join associations, unions or other groupings. However, formal contact and communications from and to the UN administration are conducted only through elected staff councils. Staff participation is generally assured by the means of a secretariat-wide joint staff-management body composed of an equal number of staff representatives and of representatives of the secretary-general, and joint advisory committees.[13] Staff representatives participate in various joint advisory bodies such as an Appointment and Promotion Board, the Joint Disciplinary Committee, the Joint Appeals Boards, the Joint Committees on career development, post classification, health and security, catering services, staff mutual insurance, staff benevolent fund, the UN Joint Staff Pension Committee and Board.[14]

The functions of staff representatives are official. Depending on the number of staff represented, they may be released full-time to carry out their staff representative duties, or half-time or less. The organization provides them facilities for the holding of meetings, secretarial assistance, office space and supplies, the reproduction and distribution of notices, bulletins, their posting on bulletin boards, telephone and cable communications (subject to budgetary considerations).[15]

It is therefore true that the UN provides its staff representative bodies with material support and that the fees of the associations' members do not cover all the real costs incurred by the staff bodies. In turn, the support of the organization limits somewhat the independence of the staff bodies and goes against an extreme militantism.

As a measure of decentralization, heads of departments and offices are expected to hold monthly meetings with their unit representatives on such matters as staff welfare, working conditions and efficiency, the application of staff rules, problems and crises.[16]

The other UN organizations have comparable provisions in their Rules and Regulations: they all recognize the freedom of association and the right to staff consultation and participation as an integral part of the organizations' management. In this sense, staff bodies and staff representatives are an indispensable cog-wheel as well as a lubricant in the whole administrative machinery of the organization, which explains and justifies the support in kind and facilities given to the staff bodies by the UN administrations.

The underlying assumption is that the participation of the staff members in the definition or revision of their employment conditions, in the review of the working conditions and in the promotion of their welfare, will result in a well-informed commitment and dedication to the organization's objectives and activities. Through an open and constructive collaboration of the elected staff representives with management officials, staff problems will be identified, their causes diagnosed, and reasonable solutions will be found and agreed upon. Staff-management cooperation will improve the quality of the organizations' human-resources management; a better-motivated, satisfied and loyal workforce will contribute to a more effective organization.

Staff associations and unions deal with questions related to each organization, such as working conditions, recruitment and career questions. However, the major salary, allowances and pensions matters are reviewed and decided upon either at the administrative interagency level — the Consultative Committee on Administrative Questions (CCAQ) and the Administrative Committee on Coordination (ACC), by the ICSC, the UN Joint Staff Pension Board or by the Fifth Committee of the General Assembly. In view of the progressive centralization of decision-making in these matters, the organizations' associations have had to group themselves. The main federation are FICSA, created in 1952, which represents twenty seven staff associations of, mostly, specialized agencies, and CCISUA, created in 1982, representing mostly staff of the UN secretariat and associated bodies.[17]

Clearly the UN associations are here to stay. The question remains as to whether their militantism is excessive and must be curbed, whether they have a hold on the UN administrators, whether they disorganize the organizations by their action, and in particular by strikes.

There is no doubt that staff participation in management has its benefits, but it also has its costs: meetings, discussions, negotiations with staff representatives take time for both staff and management representatives and are therefore costly. Decisions may be delayed on account of the consultation process. The hearing and review of staff claims at the organization and interagency levels takes time and requires management to prepare postion papers, rebuttals or to change their initial positions. Public pronouncements of staff associations on politically sensitive topics may at times embarrass the organizations. There are direct and identifiable costs in the payment of the salaries of a few staff members for staff representation duties, secretarial and other material assistance. The position of the organizations is that these costs are well worth the benefits of staff representation and participation: the absence of such mechanisms would be likely to have more pernicious, hidden or open, effects, more damaging to the organizations than the open, participative way. That there may be occasional excesses of the democratic participation is also recognized: these should be controlled by the administrations concerned.

The inspectors' allegations that the staff organizations have undue power are excessive. In fact, the UN staff associations are subjected to many constraints and limitations.

Limitations to the staff associations' powers

In contrast to national trade unions, international staff associations have a built-in limitation: their statutory loyalty to the organization. As international civil servants, the staff representatives are committed to accept and promote the objectives of their organization, to discharge their international functions and regulate their conduct with the interests of the organization alone in view, as required by their oath of office.[18] The ultimate objective of national socialist or communist trade unions in Western democracies may be to contribute to a political, social and economic revolution: their representatives may refuse any collaboration with the enterprise, with management representatives considered as capitalist exploiters and class enemies. UN staff representatives accept their organization as it is, they support its internationalist objectives, they fully accept the authority of their executive head, they collaborate with management representatives in order to assist and improve the administrative functioning of the organization: they are loyalists, some of them are reformists, they are not revolutionaries. In consequence, the UN staff representatives are limited in action and in words by their international allegiance.

As international civil servants, UN staff representatives have an obligation of reserve and 'utmost' discretion. They must avoid any kind of public pronouncement which may adversely reflect on their status, integrity, independence and impartiality.[19] Consequently, they should not take to task an identified member state for reneging on its international obligations; they should not criticize countries or groups of countries for their politics, ideology, social or cultural mores, even if these countries' positions have an impact on the staff's status or employment conditions. They can only address their employers, the organizations' member states, as an anonymous collectivity. In recent years, FICSA and a few staff associations have deviated from this idealized 'neutral civil servants' position; for example, they have openly citicized the United States for the withholding of its contributions to UN budgets, as well as other states guilty of having violated staff members' immunities. FICSA has also lobbied national delegations to the Fifth Committee in an attempt to obtain their support in salary, pensions and other employment issues. The *Diplomatic World Bulletin* (14-21 December 1987) reported FICSA's 'outrage' over the appointment of a Romanian as a judge in the UN Administrative Tribunal, while the case of Liviu Bota (see Ch. 6), a senior UN official retained in Romania, remains unsolved. In an unusually strongly - worded statement, and as an unusual public interference with the General Assembly's power of appointment, FICSA said that it viewed this election as a provocation to the staff: 'If the UN wants its statements and resolutions to be taken seriously by member states, it would be better served by giving the example of a dignified and courageous behaviour within its own premises as well as of solidarity vis-à-vis the staff'.

Placed under the authority of their executive head, staff representatives owe him respect: they will avoid any direct criticism of their secretary-general or director-general. Their claims and reproaches will generally be addressed to the collective and anonymous 'administration'. In the national context, trade unionists readily attack the chief executive officer by name. As an exception, FICSA has recently criticized the UN secretary-general for his alleged lack of firmness in trying to obtain the release of detained staff members.

In contrast with national administrations, international organizations are fragile: they have been created by member states and member states can destroy them. If they cease to satisfy the national interests of their members, members may withdraw from the organization, thus weakening it, or the organization may be disestablished. International civil servants are no more indispensable and permanent than their organization — a weak position from which to negotiate, fight or strike.

The associations' reluctant members

Militant trade unionism is rejected by many staff members of UN organizations for various reasons. For reasons of principles: the interests of the organizations, financed by public funds, must prevail over the material interests of its employees. Staff working time should only be spent on the organizations' official business. For reasons of professional status: many medical officers, engineers, economists, political officers, accountants and other specialized professionals have a natural reticence towards unions, group action, meetings: they prefer to associate with their own professional groups, and, if they become dissatisfied with their employment conditions, they leave the organization, rather than trying to make the organization change its ways. Also, the managerial and independent nature of the work of many professionals leads them to identify with 'Management'. For reasons of tenure: personnel seconded from national civil services or other institutions, project staff and specialists who will only work in the organizations for a few years have no particular interest in promoting their career in the international civil service and in improving its employment conditions. For reasons of satisfaction: in spite of the recent erosion of UN salaries and pensions, part of the staff still consider themselves relatively well paid and treated decently: they do not want a forceful spokesman. The cultural and political diversity of the staff and their dispersion in many geographically distant duty stations adds to the difficulties of unionization in international organizations.[20]

Another reason for the staff's lack of interest in unionization is that some of them feel that staff organizations are not effective (which is partly the fault of the absentees): the staff representatives are deemed to be powerless when faced with decisions taken by the administrations or by the governing bodies. Some feel that staff representatives are being used by the administrations as a form of participative tokenism.

These reservations explain that the level of participation of UN staff members in staff associations is relatively low. Elections to the ILO Staff Union Committee for 1985-7 showed a voting participation of 35.58 per cent. Elections to the WHO Staff Committee for 1985-6 showed a voting participation of 33 to 36 per cent. At the 1986 Annual General Meeting of the WHO Staff Association, less than 10 per cent of the headquarters staff attended.[21] The elections to staff participation bodies at the UN Office at Geneva had a participation of 19.3 per cent.

Another problem is to find volunteers for staff representatives' positions. At the WHO headquarters, all candidates for election to the Staff Committee were elected in 1985, and ten out of eleven candidates in 1986. Some staff members are reluctant or unable to add staff representation activities to their busy professional schedules. Some do not believe in such functions for reasons given above. Some fear that such functions will affect their professional reputation, their career or promotion prospects, or that they will be identified as troublemakers by the administration and exposed to sanctions.

All these factors add up to a mood of apathy, which has been denounced by FICSA, and not to a spirit of hard militantism.

Strikes

Trade union militantism is best expressed by strike action, the ultimate weapon of pressure. In the national context, violent or orderly strikes, effective or lost, have traditionally been a symbol of the blue-collar workers' power and solidarity. However, the economic climate, unemployment and the strikes' economic and social consequences for the public have made union leaders and workers think twice before initiating strikes. Workers have realized that strikes may weaken or destroy their enterprise's competitive position, at the risk of loss of jobs.

Many countries do not allow their civil servants to strike. In some countries, civil servants' strikes are permissible but they are subject to various conditions or restrictions: recent strikes in French state enterprises have been highly unpopular because they have inconvenienced the daily activities of part of the active population and because civil servants are considered as relatively privileged — in contrast with the private sector, they have full security of employment, decent salaries and an array of open or hidden benefits.

International civil servants, even though they have no security of tenure, are generally believed to enjoy generous, tax-free, emoluments. Their role is usually peripheral or secondary to the main national economic and social activities and concerns. They have no hold on the public at large, as do, for instance, unionized French electricity workers. As 'privileged' employees, working on obscure tasks, they have no possibility of attracting the support of public opinion. On the contrary, most governments represented in the UN organizations' governing bodies, and particularly those of socialist countries, react with great hostility against strikes by international civil servants.

In spite of these considerations, a few strikes related to salary issues have taken place in the UN organizations: a half-day strike in FAO on 12 May 1970; a covert strike of guards and telephonists at UN headquarters on 12 October 1970.[22] A one-week strike took place at the UN Office at Geneva from 25 February to 3 March 1976, resulting in salary increases for general service staff of 11 to 15 per cent. The high cost of these increases caused staff reductions in ILO and drew criticisms from the Joint Inspection Unit (JIU), member states and the local Geneva press. When the JIU publicized the costs (approximately US $25.3 million for the period April 1975 to December 1977 for all the organizations in Geneva), member states lost confidence in the capacity of the Geneva UN administrations to resist staff demands. The governing bodies of WHO and ILO then requested the more trustworthy International Civil Service Commission (ICSC) to undertake another salary survey. On the basis of its results, ICSC recommended salary reductions in the general service salary scale of between 15.9 to 19.5 per cent.[23]

The initial success of the one-week strike had turned to ashes: the initial financial advantage had disappeared, member states were irate, public opinion hostile and the determination of salary scales for general service staff had been entrusted to the ICSC. Negotiations had been possible with the UN administrations; it was impossible to negotiate with the ICSC. The staff associations had learnt that the times were not propitious for a real strike of international staff. Later work stoppages were usually limited to symbolic demonstrations of one day or less.

From industrial action, the staff associations then turned to legal action, a quieter, more discreet and, they hoped, more effective method to defend their rights and remuneration.

Staff recourses to the tribunals

The staff associations have long trusted the UN and ILO administrative tribunals; however, their trust has been somewhat shaken by the tribunals' recent decisions on salaries, post adjustments and pensions matters. The associations cannot appeal as collective bodies to the tribunals: only complaints from individual staff members are receivable. The associations have often initiated or supported individual test cases.

The right of appeal to independent tribunals provides the staff of UN organizations with a necessary counterweight to the powers and prerogatives of the executive heads, and to politically - inspired administrative decisions taken without consultation by the UN General Assembly.[24] The tribunals exercise their control over the proper application of rules and regulations to individual cases and censure improper motives. They have reinforced the staff's security of employment by reducing the contractual element in the legal situation of UN staff and by stressing the career expectancy concept. They promote the independence and security of the international civil service, as prescribed by the UN Charter.

The tribunals have sustained the right of association and censured its violations. *In re* Robinson the UN Administrative Tribunal (UNAT) was the first tribunal to affirm that the right of association was recognized for the staff of the UN:[25] it was an indispensable element of that right that no action should be taken against a staff member on the ground that he was or had been active in the association. In the Robinson case the appellant's contract had not been renewed, but the administration had not given any reason for this decision. In his action as staff representative, the applicant had taken part in discussions and representations in which he had been opposed to the administration on important and controversial issues. The Tribunal found that the administration's failure to adduce a reason for non-renewal of the appointment in this case, was contrary to the appellant's right of association and that this entitled him to financial relief.

In re Garcia and Marquez (No.2), the ILO Administrative Tribunal (ILOAT) recalled that the Pan American Health Organization (PAHO)/WHO Staff Regulations and Rules accept the principle of freedom of association and require the director to make provision for staff participation in the discussion of policies relating to staff questions.[26] The staff association has the right to ask their membership for voluntary financial contributions. The organization may give financial assistance to the association in the furtherance of activities beneficial to the staff provided that the membership of the association also contributes substantially to such activity. By each contract of appointment, the organization accepts as part of the contractual terms the obligation not to infringe the right to associate. In this particular case the director was ordered by the ILOAT to withdraw the requirement that the staff association's communications to be dispatched through the organization's facilities should first be submitted to the administration for discussion and correction. This curtailment of facilities by the establishment of administrative censorship was considered as a breach of the right to associate.

The non-recognition of the 'non-local association' by the FAO administration was censured by the ILOAT. *In re* Connolly-Battisti (No.7), the Tribunal said that it was for the staff to organize itself and not for the director general to organize it.[27] It was generally accepted that the existence of a good and efficient staff association was essential to good staff relations. The FAO administration's harassment of the non-local association was contrary to the principle of freedom of association. Every measure taken in pursuance of this plan was tainted with illegality.

Freedom of association implies freedom of action of the staff representatives under certain conditions. *In re* Van der Ploeg, the ILOAT said that a UNESCO staff representative should enjoy freedom of action and expression on the sole condition that he respect the obligations incumbent upon him as an official of the organization, and those incumbent upon international officials generally, and that he observe secrecy in respect of deliberations of joint bodies in which he takes part, or confidential information communicated to him by virtue of his trade-union position.[28] He should be allowed reasonable time for discharging his functions as an officer of the association, albeit without jeopardizing the smooth working of the organization. Therefore any administrative decision motivated solely by his position as an officer of the association or by any activities carried out in that capacity, while respecting his obligations, would be tainted by an error in law.

In re Di Giuliomaria, the director general of FAO had justified his summary dismissal of a staff representative by the latter's alleged insubordination and impertinence, misrepresentation of facts and incitement to agitation and by his injurious language, amounting to serious misconduct.[29] The Tribunal found that the staff representative had not abused his rights of criticism, nor had he used injurious or defamatory language. The Tribunal required the organization to pay financial compensation.

Comforted by the tribunals' repeated support of the associations' rights, but defeated by the 1978 salary reductions in the Geneva salary scales for general service staff, the staff asssociations tried to obtain from the tribunals the recognition of the staff rights to collective bargaining in remuneration issues, rather than the platonic right to consultation embodied in the organizations' Rules and Regulations.

In an 'Opinion' given by the ILOAT judges on 16 May 1978, the judges advised that, under contract law, the application of the new, reduced salary scales to ILO officials would not infringe their rights under their contracts of employment and under the Staff Regulations. However, they advised that in labour law (which is not applied by the tribunals under their statutes), this decision would, if taken without prior negotiations with the ILO Staff Union, be a breach of the agreement concluded between the ILO administration and the union in April 1976.

Misinterpreting the opinion of the judges, the staffs of other agencies believed that the Tribunal would also rule in their favour in the test cases which they had filed. This proved wrong, as the tribunals rule in 'contract law' only.

In re Belchamber the UNAT rejected the UN staff member's complaint.[30] The Tribunal found that there was a uniform practice of consultations with the staff representatives prior to revisions of the salary scales of general service staff in Geneva, but that the staff representatives failed and neglected to avail themselves of the several opportunites offered for such consultations. In the circumstances, the Tribunal decided that there had been no breach of an obligation on the part of the UN and that the salary scale promulgated in January 1978 was not vitiated. The UN Tribunal also found that there is no statutory or express contract obligation to 'collective bargaining' with the staff representatives prior to the introduction of a salary scale for general service staff at Geneva and only consultations are required. The ILO Tribunal rejected similar complaints filed by staff members of ICITO/GATT, WHO and WMO on similar grounds: the breach of an obligation to negotiate, if any such obligation existed, would not be a non-observance of the complainant's terms of appointment, or of any staff regulations. Reverting to labour considerations, the Tribunal remarked that the breach of a labour agreement would be sanctioned by the occurrence of the labour trouble which the agreement was designed to avoid, and not by legal means. In other words, the staff have no valid legal case unless (1) the organization's staff regulations are revised to include an obligation to negotiate salaries and (2) the next salary agreement includes a judicial or arbitration clause. In reality, negotiation rights are acquired as a result of a balance of power between labour an management rather than judicial recourses.[31]

The 1985 FICSA Council approved a Legal Defence Strategy in response to decisions taken by the General Assembly in 1984: to freeze the post adjustment in New York and in other duty stations; to change the scale of pensionable remuneration for the professional and higher-category staff without transitional measures; and to reduce pension benefits. For each decision to be challenged, FICSA provided model letters of appeal and encouraged individual appeals. The staff associations or federations are not entitled to file appeals to the Tribunals: only individual staff members have this right.[32]

In spite of the high legal expenses (more than $250,000), the results, up to date, are disappointing. A first legal and moral victory, albeit limited, was achieved when the UNAT Judgment No. 370 rescinded on 6 June 1986 the UN decision not to grant payment of a post adjustment increase for professional staff in New York which was due on 1 December 1984. Citing a procedural illegality, the Tribunal ruled that the UN should pay the increase for the four months from 1 December 1984 to 31 March 1985 — back payments, totalling between $2 million and $3 million, were temporarily withheld due to legal and political hurdles and to the UN financial crisis.[33] The Tribunal judgment satisfied the associations only in part, as they had claimed that the UN decision was illegal and in consequence that the post adjustment increase should be paid as from 1 December onwards, and not be limited to four months.

Another time-limited victory was obtained with the UNAT Judgment No. 395. In this case, which concerned the non-implementation of cost-of-living adjustments for general-service staff in Vienna and New York, the Tribunal ordered the secretary-general to pay to each of the appellants the adjustment due from 1 February 1986 to 9 May 1986, that is for a period of three months and nine days. The Tribunal considered that the secretary-general's decision of 20 March announcing the suspension of the adjustment was ambiguous, and that, in any event, to withhold the adjustment due on 1 February went against the principle of non-retroactivity. However, the General Assembly resolution of 9 May 1986 was regarded as being a clear message to the staff that the adjustment was not to be paid. The Tribunal declared that it could not question the sovereign power of the General Assembly, but it interpreted the will of the latter restrictively in order to protect the acquired rights of the staff.

In both judgment Nos. 370 and 395, the staff claims were satisfied only for a short period of time on the grounds of procedural illegalities. In substance, the Tribunal did not condemn the relevant decisions taken by the General Assembly.

Complaints to the UNAT against the imposition of a cap on the local currency equivalent of the 'dollar track' pension benefits at 120 per cent of those benefits calculated directly in the local currency and on the application of the special index for pensioners, were rejected in Judgements Nos. 378 and 379. FICSA found some small consolation in the Tribunal's determination that a UN staff member, participant in the UN Pension Fund, is entitled to the Pension Fund adjustment system as part of conditions of service. While admitting some room for discretion, the Tribunal stated that the adjustment system must not be arbitrary, must be reasonable and aimed only at protecting the purchasing power of pensioners.[34]

The appeals against the reductions in pensionable remuneration as of January 1985 and the freeze of post adjustment on Geneva, Paris and Rome were rejected by the ILOAT in June 1987.[35] On pensionable remuneration, the Tribunal found that despite the new scale, international civil servants still stand to get bigger pensions than the best-paid national civil servants. It concluded that, notwithstanding the financial injury to the complainants, there was no breach of an acquired right: the organization did not act in breach of its obligations. One purpose of the impugned decisions was to put the Fund on a sounder financial footing. The decisions did not create any form of discrimination, they broke no promise, they did not apply retroactivity to the complainants, and although they caused financial injury to the complainants, the reasons for the decisions were objective and, all things considered, the degree of it admissible. Concerning the freeze of post adjustments, the Tribunal found that the ICSC exercised authority delegated to it by the General Assembly. The Tribunal is not competent to rule on the lawfulness of Assembly resolutions.

While a few other cases are pending, it is unlikely that the staff associations will 'win' other collective claims in the future. The Tribunal can hardly challenge General Assembly resolutions, particularly if a favourable decision would result in payments amounting to millions of dollars. Legal redress is more likely to be obtained on questions of principle, of retroactivity and acquired rights, on individual problems of interpretation of rules and regulations, on individual entitlements to remuneration or benefits, or other questions of employment conditions. 'Taking the Assembly to court' through group action has not been very effective, except for limited 'victories' based on procedural grounds. It has been very costly for FICSA and its member associations, and it has caused negative reactions on the part of some influential member states. Any further recourse will have to be studied very carefully in law and in fact before the staff associations avail themselves again usefully of the judicial process.

Other means of action

Staff associations have other means of action besides strikes and legal recourses. They try to apply pressure on their executive head by submitting to him claims, complaints, petitions, appeals and proposals by resolutions voted by staff assemblies, by publishing the staff views in circulars and in staff journals. Most staff associations have access to one of their governing bodies. They can submit to that body a written and/or oral statement, in some cases followed by a question-and-answer period with the governments' representatives.

However, as most important employment and salary decisions are taken by the Fifth Committee of the General Assembly, the staff associations' federations, FICSA and CCISUA, have found it even more important to present the staff views at the interagency level. Since the early 1970s, FICSA attends all meetings of the Consultative Committee on Administrative Questions (CCAQ).[36] Since 1975 FICSA has been invited to address the Administrative Committee on Coordination (ACC)[37] and is the staff spokesman at the ICSC meetings. Since 1980 FICSA has been allowed to submit a document to the Fifth Committee, and since 1981 an oral statement. FICSA participates in the UN Joint Staff Pension Board meetings as an observer. CCISUA has been admitted to ICSC since 1982, to ACC and to the Fifth Committee since 1983.

On 4 June 1986 FICSA organized a world-wide protest against the deterioration of the staff's conditions of service, which was followed by the staff of UN organizations in most duty stations.

Also in 1986 FICSA addressed letters to the heads of state of the fourteen major contributors to the UN budget. Replies were discussed with the permanent representatives of member states in Geneva, New York and Washington and contacts established with high-level government officials. In Geneva FICSA officials met with the permanent representatives of non-aligned countries and other influential personalities. FICSA's aim was to direct public relations and information campaigns mainly at decision-makers and at public opinion.[38]

Staff action in 1987

Seen from Geneva, UN staff associations were active in 1987, and some were militant. A one-day strike was called by the ILO Staff Union on 19 February 1987, to put an end to 'the intolerable deterioration' of professional staff pensions, as a warning to the ILO administration and the ILO governing body.

On 14 April most of the GATT staff went on strike to protest against professional salary and pension losses.[39]

On 25 February the presidents of GATT, ILO, ITU, WHO, WIPO and WMO staff associations and unions wrote to their executive heads a joint letter to request them to find a solution, as a matter of urgency, to the currency fluctuation problem, which erodes the salaries of professional and higher-category' staff.[40]

On 19 May the representative of the WHO staff association addressed the members of the WHO Executive Board: she told them that the most serious and difficult problems confronting the staff were the same as those faced by the organization: scarcity of resources and uncontrollable currency fluctuations.[41]

In July, the WHO staff association launched a campaign to inform US senators and congressmen of the important work being done by WHO.[42] Similar campaigns were launched by other staff associations at FICSA's initiative. A general assembly of WHO staff voted a resolution on 22 October to protest against the constant deterioration in conditions of service: staff and pensioners should no longer be expected to bear the consequences of the political difficulties currently affecting the UN system. WHO's ability to recruit high-quality staff was being damaged.[43] The 22 October 'action day' had also been launched by FICSA and was followed by most staff associations. FICSA wanted to prepare the staff for 'direct action' (strike or other demonstration) in case the 1987 General Assembly decisions on employment conditions were unfavourable to the staff.

In June the CCISUA representative told ACC that there was a staff malaise throughout the UN system.[44] On 22 October the staff of the UN Office at Geneva sent a message to the secretary-general referring to a 'political hurricane' sweeping through the organization and to an escalation of attacks on the staff, their working conditions and their security of employment.[45]

Militant unions or respectful collaborators

Staff associations and their federations are constantly facing this dilemma. They may choose to fight openly, through all means, including lawsuits and strikes, their administration, their executive head and the organization's governing bodies. They then risk being censured by governments and public opinion and accused of being disloyal to their organizations and of not respecting their international obligations. They risk being accused of wanting governments to lavish too much public money on privileged bureaucrats, to the detriment of substantive programmes and development aid.

They may choose to cooperate loyally and quietly with the administrative powers, give advice, engage in consultation and collaboration, accept and explain unpopular decisions. They will then risk being totally ineffective as representatives of the staff interests, losing the respect and support of their members and being taken for granted by their administration.

In practice, attitudes vary in different organizations, depending on the degree of participation, trust and dialogue established between staff and management representatives, and according to the personalities on both sides. Attitudes also vary according to political, economic and financial circumstances. Clearly, the current climate of forced economies at the staff's expense is conducive to more activism on the part of the staff bodies. On the other hand, in the present state of the world economy and in the climate surrounding multilateralism in general and UN organizations in particular, the staff associations have to exercise caution. They would be well advised to choose symbolic actions (one day, or less, strikes, or support of a few well-chosen legal cases submitted to the tribunals) and to continue their effective public opinion and information campaigns addressed to government representatives and the medias. Other more drastic demonstrations may be counterproductive.

National associations

In 1977 an 'association of German Civil Servants in UN Organizations was created. Since then, other national associations have been set up, to represent UN staff members of their nationality in relation to their government. There are now national associations in Geneva for Spanish, French, Dutch, German and Swiss staff members of UN organizations. There is also a multinational African association.

These national associations, in contrast with the international staff associations, are not statutory: they are not prescribed or authorized in the UN organizations' Staff Regulations or Rules. In fact, one may wonder whether their establishment is not in contradiction with the UN Charter, which requires that 'the staff shall not seek or receive instructions from any government' and that 'Each Member of the UN undertakes to respect the exclusively international character of the responsibilities of the secretary-general and the staff' (Art. 100).

The Spanish association identified this problem and included in its statutes that 'in implementing its aims, the association will act in such a way that at no time the independence of the international civil service would be jeopardized as guaranteed by, in particular, articles 100 and 101 of the UN Charter and the relevant provisions of the constitutive acts of the various organizations and the respective Staff Rules and Regulations'.[46] The Spanish association's aims are to defend and promote the collective rights and interests of its members in relation to the Spanish administration, to create and facilitate relations and contacts between its members, and to organize any activity of a cultural, social or recreative nature. Other associations have similar objectives.

The national associations do not normally interfere with the relations between their nationals and the UN organizations which employ them: they have no contacts nor relations with the organizations and their administratioi.s. Their main interests are aimed at facilitating the reintegration of the international civil servants into their home country at the end of their international emplnyment; for instance, some associations have negotiated with their government in order to allow international civil servants to become national civil servants at the end of their international employment, even though they were not national civil servants when they joined a UN organization. Alternatively, the associations have asked that the terminated UN official should be assisted in finding employment in the private sector in his home country, and that they should be entitled to unemployment benefits. Some associations have asked that UN pensions should not be subject to national taxation in their home country. For those still in international employment, the associations have claimed that they should be allowed to start or continue their participation in their national social security, health insurance and retirement schemes, and that they should be allowed to vote in national elections. National civil servants seconded to UN organizations should retain all their rights and credits on return to their national civil service. Some associations have encouraged the creation of national schools in various duty stations and have tried to facilitate the admission of their nationals' children to universities of the duty station or in the home country.

The national associations intervene with and apply pressure on their national mission or delegation to the UN organization, or directly on the home ministries, by visits or written requests. The ministries concerned may include the Ministry of Foreign Affairs, the Ministry of the Interior and the Ministry of Labour.

Why create these national associations, a creation which could not have been even envisaged in the 1950s or in the 1960s? One reason is that the international administrations are unable to deal with the particular national problems of international civil servants of more than 160 nationalities in relation with their national authorities. Second, the international staff associations deal with employment problems of all their staff, without distinction of nationalities, but they are not able to deal with problems of reinsertion or resettlement of international civil servants into their home country at the end of their international employment. Third, the current political, institutional and financial crisis of the UN organizations, linked to the loss of faith in multilateralism, have aroused well-founded doubts on the part of international staff in the security of their international employment and concern over their own, and their family's, future. If their international organization fails to support them, they car. only turn to their own national authorities for help. Hence the creation by the citizens of a few countries of these national associations.

It is difficult to predict whether this phenomenon will spread or, on the contrary, whether the national associations will wither, when they have reached their principal objectives. There are no British or US national associations, perhaps out of respect for the international principles, and perhaps because British and American citizens tend to rely more on their own resources and initiatives than on the goodwill and resources of their government. Citizens from most socialist countries do not need a formal national association, in view of their close links with their governments, and as they are all on secondment from their national civil service.

National associations are a somewhat disturbing phenomenon, in so far as they reintroduce a national element into the international civil service. They may be another sign of the weakening of the internationalist concept.

While national associations should avoid any interference relating to the employment relations of the international staff with their organization, there have been some deviations from this principle. For instance, the German National Association has obtained that supplementary salary payments be paid by the Federal Republic of Germany not only to German civil servants but also to all other German nationals employed by UN organizations. Supplementary payments have been condemned by the UN General Assembly (see Ch.5) and by FICSA.

The French, German, Italian, Spanish and Swiss national associations addressed a resolution on 20 March 1987 to their respective governments, on the basis of their statutory mandate to represent their members' interests vis-à-vis their governments, and 'convinced that Member States of the European Communities have a particular responsibility for the protection of the integrity of the international civil service' (the Swiss association associated itself with this resolution). These associations requested their governments 'to intervene in a concerted manner and with all the weight of their political prestige' with all the relevant UN bodies in order to restore the UN employment conditions, to stop the violations of acquired rights, to protect salaries and pensions against monetary fluctuations and to ensure a real participation of the staff in the preparation of decisions affecting their employment conditions.[47]

Associations of UN retirees

Associations of UN retirees have been created in New York, Geneva, Paris, London, Rome, Copenhagen, Bangalore, Mexico, Chile and Canada, in order to defend the interests of UN retirees and pensioners. The associations' main activities are to keep their members informed of any changes in the UN pension benefits, of variations of exchange rates in relation to the US dollar (which may affect their take-home pension), of changes in the various organizations' health insurance schemes. They advise and help their members in filing claims to the Pension Fund, to UN insurance schemes and to national taxation authorities. They organize social activities. Through their Federation.[48] they serve as a UN pensioners' pressure group in the meetings of the UN Pension Board and of other UN bodies.[49]

The militantism of UN retirees' associations is limited by their composition and nature: retirees do not readily participate in public demonstrations and they cannot associate themselves with strikes. They support and complement the more visible role of the international staff associations. Their power is that of influence and persuasion, by convincing the associations of serving staff that they have an interest in pension issues ('you are all future pensioners!') and reminding UN administrations and governing bodies of prior commitments, social justice and acquired rights.

Notes

1. The full name is 'Staff Costs and Some Aspects of Utilization of Human and Financial Resources in the UN Secretariat', UN Doc. JIU/REP/84/12. See also Chapter 5 above.
2. UN Press Release SG/SM/3609, GA/AB/2288, 26 October 1984.
3. See Doc. FICSA/CIRC/340, 25 October 1984, Annex II, and the attached detailed 'Review' of the JIU Report,
4. UN Doc. JIU/REP/85/8.
5. There are no provisions for the General Assembly to review the judgments of the UN Administrative Tribunal. The General Assembly is bound to implement them, in accordance with the advisory opinion of the International Court of Justice of 13 July 1954: 'The Court therefore considers that the assignment of the budget function to the General Assembly cannot be regarded as conferring upon it the right to refuse to give effect to the obligation arising out of an award of the Administrative Tribunal': 'Effects of awards of compensation made by the UNAT', *ICJ Reports*, 1954, p. 57. On the other hand, judgments of both tribunals are subject to review by the ICJ under different conditions. A judgment of the UNAT may be referred to the Court only by decision of the UN 'Committee of Applications for Review of Administrative Tribunal Judgments', a body composed of member states' representatives. See Yves Beigbeder, *Management Problems in UN Organizations'*, Frances Pinter, London, 1987, pp. 118-19.
6. UN Doc. A/41/49, 1986, Recommendation 59.
7. *UN Financial Emergency: Crisis and Opportunity*, New York, August 1986, Annex A, 6. A. Efimov, who wrote with N. Kaddour the two 'Staff Costs' reports, was a member of the Group of 14. See also Chapter 5 above.
8. See UN Doc. A/C.5/37/SR.53, and *UN Special*, Geneva, March 1983.
9. UN Doc. A/C.5/40/SR.51, 2 December 1985.
10. UN Docs. A/C.5/40/SR.30 and A/C.5/40/26 of 18 October 1985.
11. See Beigbeder, pp. 126-37.
12. UN Staff Regulations, 1983, Art. VIII.
13. UN Staff Rules 108.1 and 108.2.
14. UN Staff Rules, 1984; UN Doc. GPO/87/7, 15 June 1987.
15. UN Doc. ST/AI/293, 15 July 1982.
16. UN Doc. ST/SGB/206, 5 October 1984.
17. Beigbeder, pp. 129-31.
18. UN Staff Regulation 1.9.
19. UN Staff Regulations 1.4 and 1.5.
20. Beigbeder, p. 132.
21. Ibid.
22. Yves Beigbeder, *La Représentation du personnel à l'Organisation mondiale de la santé*, Librairie générale de droit et de jurisprudence, Paris, 1975, pp.169-76.
23. Yves Beigbeder, 'Current Staff Problems in UN Secretariats', *International*

Review of Administrative Sciences, Brussels, 1982/2, pp. 156-7.

24. Staff members of UN organizations may appeal either to the UNAT or to the ILOAT. See Beigbeder, *Management Problems*, pp. 117-25.
25. UNAT Judgment No. 15, 11 August 1952.
26. ILOAT Judgment No. 496, 3 June 1982.
27. In April 1974, the single FAO staff association separated into four groups representing regional and field staff, headquarters professional staff, local and non-local general service staff. Only the latter group was not initially recognized by the FAO administration. See ILOAT Judgment No. 403, 24 April 1980.
28. ILOAT Judgment No. 54, 6 October 1961.
29. ILOAT Judgment No. 87, 6 November 1965.
30. UNAT Judgment No. 236, 20 October 1978.
31. Beigbeder, 'Current Staff Problems', pp. 158-9.
32. See Doc. FICSA/C/39/7, 8 January 1986.
33. One of the applicants applied to the UN Committee on Applications for Review of Administrative Tribunal Judgements to request the ICJ to give an advisory opinion on the validity of the judgement. The Committee rejected the application on 9 September 1986. In the Fifth Committee, in 1986, the Soviet Union and other countries proposed to defer implementation of the judgement to give time to see what could be done about the problem of a subsidiary body (UNAT) imposing a decision on a 'sovereign' body, the UN General Assembly. The United States and the Soviet Union jointly sponsored a draft resolution which requested 'the secretary-general to study the feasibility of limiting the jurisdiction of the Tribunal to deal with applications involving the common system and financial implications in excess of US $200,000'. The Soviet representative declared that the purpose of the resolution was to prevent the General Assembly from becoming the hostage of the tribunal, which is not sufficiently representative of the broad views of the General Assembly. The draft resolution was finally withdrawn. Judgement No. 370 has now been implemented. See Doc. FICSA/C/40/8, 8 January 1987.
34. Doc. FICSA/C/40/8, 8 January 1987.
35. For post adjustments, see Judgement Nos. 825 through 831. For pensionable remuneration, see Judgement Nos. 832 through 838.
36. CCAQ, a subsidiary body of the ACC, meets periodically to discuss administrative, personnel, financial and budgetary questions. All UN organizations are represented by their responsible administrators.
37. The ACC is a meeting of all executive heads of UN organizations. It meets under the chairmanship of the UN secretary-general, usually three times a year.
38. See Docs. FICSA/N/87, 6 October 1986, FICSA/C/40/3, 30 November 1986
39. *UN Special,* Geneva, April 1987.
40. ILO Staff Union *Bulletin,* no. 921, 25 February 1987.
41. WHO Staff Association *Spotlight,* no. 3, 16 June 1987.
42. Ibid., no. 7, 8 July 1987
43. Ibid., no 27, 29 October 1987.
44. Doc. UNOG Staff/Coordinating Council CCBE/1987/8, 23 June 1987.
45. Ibid., CCBE/1987/39, 3 November 1987
46. My translation.
47. See Annex 2 to 'Convocation: Assemblée générale 1987', Association des fonctionnaires internationaux suisses. Information on national associations of international civil servants in Geneva has been gathered by the author from the associations' responsible officials.
48. The Federation of Associations of Former International Civil Servants, UN New York and Geneva.
49. Beigbeder, p. 105.

Chapter 8

Alternative employment schemes

Traditionally, the employment of international civil servants has been based on well-established, statutory, principles and practices. By reference to national civil services, international civil servants should enjoy the security of their employment, a guarantee of their independence; they should therefore hold long-term or permanent contracts. Second, the UN employment system separates staff in three categories: general service, or support; staff (manual workers, clerical and secretarial personnel), themselves divided into local and non-local recruits, professional staff (university-trained generalists or specialists); and higher categories (directors, executive heads and their assistants). Within these categories, equal pay is given to equal work. Third, international salaries and benefits are set by comparison with the best local employers, for general service staff and by reference to the highest paid national civil service (the US Federal Service) for the professional and higher categories. Fourth, staff emoluments are all paid by the international organization and not by outside sources.

All these principles have been either eroded or breached in recent years through the introduction of alternative employment schemes.

A career service?

Recent figures challenge the career dogma. In December 1986 less than half of the professional staff in all the UN organizations held appointments without time limit: 53 per cent had fixed-term contracts. In December 1982 the proportion was 50-50. For general service staff in all the UN organizations, 54 per cent held appointments without time limit in December 1986. The evolution of percentages of appointments without time limit in relation to total professional staff, between December 1982 and December 1986 is shown in Table 8.1 for the main organizations.

Table 8.1 shows wide variations of percentages among these organizations, with very low percentages of appointment without time limit in UNESCO and WHO and decreases in this type of appointments between 1982 and 1986 in UNDP, FAO, UNESCO and WHO.

In 1986 the separation turnover ratio for professional staff was 18 per cent (11 per cent for general service staff) in all the UN organizations. Forty-three per cent of professional staff had less than five years' UN employment and 65 per cent less than ten. These rates show a healthy intake of new entrants rather than an inbred, closed-in bureaucracy.[1]

Table 8.1 Percentage of appointments without time limit held by professional staff in relation to the total number of professional staff, in the main UN organizations, December 1982 to December 1986

Organizations	December 1982	December 1986
UN	61	63
UNDP	71	56
FAO	68	48
ILO	55	57
UNESCO	14	12
WHO	15	13

Source: UN Doc. ACC/1983/PER/32 of 30 June 1983 and ACC/1987/PER/R.35/Rev.1 of 14 September 1987, *Personnel Statistics*

The proportions of 'career' (no time limit) contracts do not tally with the career concept: do the 88 per cent of UNESCO staff and the 87 per cent of WHO staff members on fixed-term contracts feel that they can count on a career with their organization?

Even in the UN secretariat, the 63 per cent proportion of permanent contracts is well below prior targets: the 1949 Committee of Experts of Salary, Allowance and Leave Systems had estimated that 75 to 80 per cent of the personnel should be appointed on a career basis. The 1956 Salary Review Committee had advocated a maximum of 20 per cent for the non-career staff. In 1969, in commenting on the increase from 31.8 per cent in 1969 in the percentage of non-career staff, the secretary-general said that it would be desirable to maintain a ratio of 25 per cent for the non-career staff.[2]

While organizations justify their varying practices by their different needs, the fact is that the original 'all-career' dogma has been exploded. Organizations need a nucleus of career officials and a varying proportion of short-term specialists, technical cooperation experts, staff seconded temporarily from national or international institutions and other temporary employees.

National professional officers (NPO)

NPOs constitute a hybrid, intermediary category between the general service and the professional categories. NPOs perform professional functions but do not have the status and remuneration of UN professional staff. This new staff category is only used by five UN organizations: others have not adopted it, and staff associations have mixed feelings about this scheme, as they have about other unorthodox schemes.

In 1988 UNICEF will employ 436 NPOs; UNDP, 185; UNHCR, 50; and the UN, 24.[3] UNICEF introduced the scheme in 1961, followed by the UN

Information centres in 1965 and UNDP in 1975.

As an explanation of its need for such a category of staff, the UNICEF representative said at a session of the International Civil Service Commission in 1980 that local professionals offered a knowledge of local languages, history, culture and administrative machinery that expatriates did not possess. In many cases they worked more effectively than expatriate staff and they provided continuity and stability to the field offices. The UNDP representative added that NPOs also helped define, design and gather important data on projects and therefore provided an invaluable input to programming. The proper practice was to pay these local professionals according to the best prevailing conditions offered in the government, industries or universities of the country. They should not receive wages considerably higher than those of government officials and other counterparts, such as the UN professional emoluments. Paying them higher salaries would make the local professional reluctant to revert, when the time came, to positions offering significantly lower salaries. UNDP and UNICEF reaffirmed that a need had been demonstrated to exist in many field offices with country programme responsibilities for staff who could perform functions of a nature that called for both professional skills and an intimate knowledge of local conditions, including the social and economic situation, as well as a mastery of the local languages. National professionals complemented the international dimension brought by international staff with a specific knowledge of the country. This new practice was in line with the urging of the General Assembly in 1973 that the organizations 'invigorate the search for innovative and interdisciplinary approaches', and with the UNDP Governing Council's declaration that 'the basic purpose of technical cooperation should be the promotion of self-reliance in developing countries, by building up, *inter alia*, their productive capability and their indigenous resources by increasing the availability of the managerial, technical, administrative and research capabilities required in the development process'. The FICSA representative strongly objected to the employment conditions of this category of staff, clearly a breach of the principle of equal pay for equal work: such staff were carrying out professional duties, but were only paid general service local salaries. It was a way of obtaining low-cost labour. They should be paid according to professional scales.[4]

In spite of this protest, the International Civil Service Commission (ICSC) authorized the employment of such staff under certain conditions: national professionals may be employed only for functions at field offices which by their very nature require national knowledge and experience and so cannot be carried out effectively by international professionals. The duration of such functions should be limited, in so far as the intention is to hand over the projects to the host government or other national institutions when the government so wishes. Nationals should be recruited locally and not be subject to assignment to any duty station outside their own country. Their remuneration should be based on the same principles as governs that of all other locally recruited UN staff — that is the best prevailing conditions in the locality for nationals carrying out functions of the same level.[5]

FICSA's position changed a few years later. One of its members, the UNDP/UNFPA staff association, had come out strongly in favour of the scheme. It reported that the scheme was supported by governments and UN staff in developing countries. National professionals should be viewed as a source for future regular recruitment by UN organizations as junior professional officers.[6]

At the twenty-third session of ICSC in March 1986, FICSA supported the scheme. The Convenor of the Coordinating Committee for Independent Staff Unions and Associations of the UN System (CCISUA) recognized the valuable work performed by NPOs but found elements of exploitation in the scheme.

The chairman of the Consultative Committee on Administrative Questions (CCAQ) said that some organizations found the use of NPOs to be an effective tool, while others did not find them appropriate to their programmes. This illustrated the fact that the UN common system was not a monolithic structure: varied approaches, responding to varying organizational requirements, could be equally viable. The employment of NPOs should not be encouraged or institutionalized on a common-system basis. The Commission maintained its conditional endorsement of the scheme but cautioned organizations against too liberal a use of the category.[7]

The NPO scheme is therefore applied by some and not by all of the organizations; it is not considered as part of the UN common system of salaries; it does violate the labour principle of equal pay for equal work, as well as the principles of universality and uniformity of UN conditions of employment.

On the other hand, the scheme clearly fulfils the particular programme and personnel needs of the few organizations which apply it. The lesser salary costs are attractive for organizations financed by voluntary funds. The developing countries favour the employment of their nationals by the organizations, even at lower rates than the UN professional rates.

In order to resolve the problem of principle, Barnes has proposed as a long-term solution, that the expatriation factor now included in the UN professional salary scales (where it accounts for 10 to 15 per cent) and the post adjustment, be paid as a separate allowance.[8] In consequence, a NPO serving in his home country would receive the same base pay as an international professional; there would then be no need to have a separate category of NPOs

Whether or not such a solution is eventually envisaged, this unorthodox, ill-accepted 'fourth category' will continue to be used.

Two of the reasons for its creation — the use of nationals in UN programmes and the lower salary costs — are at the root of other new and different employment schemes.

New practices

Staff-related costs amount to 70 to 80 per cent of the UN organizations' budgets. In December 1987 WHO calculated the yearly standard budgetary costs of a P.4 officer in Geneva at UN $97,250, and $65,000 for a P.2 officer.

The emoluments of professional staff include the costs of basic salaries, providing a small step increase each year, dependency allowances, post adjustment, assignment allowance, education grant, installation allowance, home leave and other travel, repatriation grant, end-of-service grant, the organization's contribution to insurance and pension fund schemes, and so on. General service staff are entitled to a basic salary, language allowance, non-resident's allowance (for non-local recruits) and so on.[9]

For costs reasons, but also because of changes in technical cooperation needs, the traditional type of UN expert, appointed for one or more years, and sometimes retained for long periods in a succession of assignments, is being replaced, in part, by new forms of employment: short-term consultants, reimbursement loan agreements, special service agreements, special contracts, national experts, UN volunteers, the use of non-governmental organizations and the temporary employment of retirees. Another move in the direction of a mixed national/international status was made with the international employment of staff paid by governments and not by the organizations' budgets: associate experts and some of the seconded staff are among them.

A few examples follow.

Short-term staff, reimbursable loans and special service agreements.

In a meeting of National Recruitment Services held in 1984,[10] it was reported that developing countries increasingly requested the provision of high-level expertise on a relatively short-term basis; in 1984, over 80 per cent of the appointments were for short-term consultants.[11]

Reimbursable loan agreements have been concluded by organizations with private firms or governments. Agreements of this nature provided for the loan or release to the UN of a consultant for short missions rarely exceeding three months. The UN paid the government or firm for the services of the individual, plus an overhead for administrative expenses. The UN paid the travel and *per diem* directly to the consultant.[12] While short-term staff are UN staff members, staff provided under reimbursable loan agreements do not acquire this status.

In 1985 the ICSC encouraged the use of reimbursable loan agreements for specific technical cooperation assignments of limited duration, in order to obtain access to candidates whose career commitments would otherwise preclude the acceptance of a UN appointment.[13]

Special service agreements are concluded by UN organizations with individuals, giving them the status of an independent contractor and not that of a UN staff member. Such contracts become subject to controversy and litigation if they are suspected of being used as a cheap substitute for the employment of a regular staff member, if the services are performed on a full-time basis on the premises of the organization and if the arrangements are extended for long periods, without breaks. These arrangments should only be entered into for the completion, on a limited time basis, of a specific technical or administrative task. The UN Administrative Tribunal has censured the long-term and repeated use of the special service agreement, which may produce 'unintended consequences where work performed is full-time, continuous and in other important respects indistinguishable from the work of individuals in the same office who have the status of staff members.[14]

Congo agents

Following the independence of the ex-Belgian Congo (now Zaire), both a UN military force and civilian personnel were sent urgently, starting in 1960, to the country. The task of the civilian mission was to ensure the continued operation of essential public services and to put into effect a broad and long-term programme of training and technical assistance. Two thousand experts and other civilian personnel were at work in the Congo at the peak of the programme in 1963-4.

All UN organizations participated in this major operational programme, carried out under strenuous and ofter perilous circumstances. In the public health field, most of the 761 foreign doctors who had staffed the Belgian colony's medical services, had left. A WHO advisory team was assigned to the Ministry of Health. In addition, WHO recruited up to 200 French-speaking doctors, sanitary engineers, nurses, radiology and laboratory technicians. The training of health personnel was also organized under WHO auspices; there was not one Congolese qualified medical doctor at the time of the country's independence.[15]

The UN/Congo civilian operation required urgent recruitment and assignment action. It involved operational staff rather than the traditional UN advisory experts. UN/Congo operational staff had to do the work: only a handful of UN staff kept to the advisory role of guiding the newly installed authorities in organizing their ministries and other management functions. In effect, the UN operational staff were government agents recruited and paid by the UN organizations and loaned to the government for set periods.

In order to satisfy the crash programme's requirements, WHO designed 'agents contracts' for operational staff. They were one-year contracts, renewable, between the organization and the agent, but agents were not WHO staff members. They received emoluments approximately equal to WHO staff remuneration, except that they did not participate in the UN Pension Fund. Agents were placed at the disposal of, and were responsible to, the Congo government: their allegiance was to government authorities, it was not international. Disputes were to be settled by arbitration, and not by the normal jurisdiction of the UN and ILO administrative tribunals. All agents contracts were entered into under an agreement between WHO and the Congo government.

Similar contracts were issued by the UN for its operational staff. For instance, judiciary contracts were drawn up between legal specialists and the UN to assist the Congo government in the administration of justice, for instance to exercise judicial functions. This type of contract did not grant the status of UN staff member and did not include Pension Fund participation.

In re Fayad the UN Administrative Tribunal (UNAT) confirmed that the individual party to such a contract did not acquire the rights nor the obligations of a UN staff member, even though the contract was established between him and the UN.[16] His administrative situation was not defined by the UN Staff Rules and Regulations. The clause of the contract according to which the appellant should not seek nor accept instructions from any other government or from any other authority external to the Republic of Congo showed that the appellant had contracted the essential part of his obligations towards the Congolese government. This government, in view of its urgent need to obtain qualified personnel to exercise functions relating to the administration of justice in the Congo, had requested the UN to help it to find qualified personnel. The UN played the role of intermediary and guarantor of the contract, while the services of operational staff were to the government, not to the UN.

In spite of the somewhat ambiguous nature of these contractual arrangements, these special contracts fulfilled their role, which was to recruit and assign urgently a number of operational specialists to assist the Congolese government.

National experts

The essence of UN and bilateral technical assistance, and later technical cooperation, has been to help developing countries help themselves by giving them advisory services, technical know-how and expertise which they do not have, as well as financial and other resources which they may lack. Traditionally, UN experts have been assigned to countries other than their own: if an expert was already working in his home country, the argument was that there was no need for the UN to use and finance his services. Another argument is that no one is a prophet, or an expert, in his own country: he may miss the international aura. Finally, the national expert assigned to his own country can hardly be expected to act independently from his national authorities and to be impartial: how could he assume independent international functions in and for his home country?

This traditional position has been totally reversed: besides international experts and international consultants, national experts have been appointed by the UN organizations in increasing numbers: from fifty in 1978, their number is estimated at several thousands.[17]

Like national professional officers, they are paid on the basis of local salary rates and not on the basis of the UN professional rates. Unlike them, they are not UN staff members. This is another hybrid employment scheme which establishes a potentially long-term contractual relationship usually reserved for staff, while assuming the form of a contract intended for the purchase of services. It utilizes and finances nationals in their own country, thus nationalizing, in a broad sense, a part of the UN international technical cooperation programme.

The Joint Inspection Unit (JIU) found in 1978 that this scheme was used with hesitancy by some organizations (UN, WHO, ILO, FAO), except where such posts were of an operational (as against advisory) nature.[18] JIU gave the following arguments against the use of nationals as UN-financed experts in the country where the project is located:

(1) If qualified persons are available, they should be employed and paid by the government as national project staff.
(2) The employment of nationals as experts might be detrimental to the international character of the UN contribution and might lessen the flow of fresh ideas from abroad.
(3) It may raise conflicts of interest and loyalties. Arguments in favour of making greater use of national experts include the following:
(1) UN funds should be used to provide the best-qualified persons to fill expert posts. If such persons are nationals of the host country and happen to be available, it would be short-sighted to deprive the project of their services.
(2) Delay in the filling of expert posts is a serious problem. Employment of qualified local nationals, when readily available, would usually be much quicker than international recruitment.
(3) Host country nationals are already familar with the culture, traditions, language and administrative practices of the host country. National experts therefore make a useful contribution and complement the work of international experts who rarely possess such intimate knowledge.
(4) The experience that national experts gain through work at UN-assisted projects is likely to remain in the host country as a permanent asset after the project ends, and may be used in other work. Foreign experts, when they leave, take the experience which they have acquired with them.
(5) The new practice of international cooperation which encourages local subcontracting and purchasing, should also apply to the employment of nationals as experts.
(6) Under the principle of government management of projects, all experts receive policy supervision from the national director, and conflicts of interest and loyalties would therefore be no greater for a national than for a foreign expert.

Another unquoted but compelling reason why UN organizations should employ national experts is that the government of a developing country may lack the financial resources for this employment.

JIU concluded in favour of the scheme. It recommended that the appointment of nationals of host countries to some expert posts should be an accepted feature of the UNDP system. Such appointments should be subject to agreement by the host government and to the understanding that national candidates must have qualifications comparable to those of candidates from outside the country.

In 1980 a Working Party on National Experts advised the organizations on principles and practices which could be applied to the scheme.[19] Its report expressed the hope that such appointments be used sparingly as a transitional tool until such time as governments can undertake direct recruitment in this context. The group drafted a Model Service Agreement, which was to relate to the project agreement approved by the government and the UN organization. The project document should include the following standard provision:

> The government agrees to the recruitment of national professional staff required for the implementation of this project... These services constitute an addition to the regular resorces of the Government and will be available only for the duration of UNDP's participation in the project, Thus UNDP's resources will be used to finance nationally-recruited professional staff...as an alternative to internationally-recruited professional staff. The remuneration of UNDP-financed staff will be determined in consultation with the Government, and should, at all times, be at the best prevailing rates for comparable functions in the country....All nationals employed locally by the UN agency to perform professional services under this project shall be accorded immunity from legal process related to the performance of his/her duties and inviolability for all papers and documents connected with his/her duties'.

National experts are not UN staff members under the terms of the UN agency's Staff Rules; they do not participate in the UN Pension Fund. Their status is that of a contractor. Their remuneration is paid in local currency. They must abide by standards of conduct of integrity, independence, impartiality, reserve and tact, and they must have full regard for the purposes and principles of the UN and its agencies. No specific national or international allegiance is mentioned in the text of the Model Service Agreement.

The national expert is therefore rendering professional services in a UN/government project as a contractor, not as a UN staff member, for a duration not exceeding that of the project. In spite of his 'non-staff member' status, he is protected by functional immunities. This professional expert is paid according to local rates of pay, which constitutes a saving, for the organization, in relation to UN professional remuneration. The government and the project benefit from this local employment of a qualified person.

The growth of this type of employment, in spite of its obvious contradictions, stems from the fact that it fulfils needs of both organizations and developing countries.

In 1988 the UN Consultative Committee on Substantive Questions (Operational Activities) will review this scheme, in view of the rapid expansion of the use of national experts in UN technical cooperation activities. The Committee and the Administrative Committee on Coordination feel that a clarification of their status within the personnel structure of the UN system and a better harmonization of presently varying agency procedures may be needed.[20]

UN volunteers (UNV)

At the end of 1986 the number of UN volunteers on assignment was 1,125. The second UNV high-level intergovernmental meeting, which met at Maseru from 16-21 November 1986, recommended an expansion of the programme: 2,500 UNVs should be serving by 1989.[21]

A 1961 Resolution of the Economic and Social Council had recognized that volunteer technical personnel provided in response to requests from governments and agencies can play an important role in the economic and social development of developing countries.[22] The use of volunteers in international teams can assist in promoting peaceful relations among nations. Furthermore, volunteers provide additional assistance at low cost.

The resolution set the principles that volunteers would not be assigned to the organizations' headquarters; no volunteers would be sent to a country without prior approval of the receiving country, and any such volunteer may remain only with the permission of such country; volunteers would be international civil servants — they would take the oath of office.

The UNV programme was created in 1970 by a UN General Assembly resolution which defined three additional principles: UNVs should emphasize technical competence and skills; UNVs should adhere to the principle of universality in the recruitment and assignments of volunteers, particularly from developing countries; and its activities should be guided by the needs of recipient countries.[23]

A second resolution adopted in 1976 gave UNV its mandate in the field of youth, designating UNV as a 'major operational unit of the UN for the execution of youth programmes', especially of pilot projects to increase the participation of youth in development.[24] A third resolution, voted also in 1976, requested the UNV administrator to develop activities in the field of domestic development services (DDS), that is governmental and non-governmental organizations concerned with development at the grass-roots level.[25]

The UNV programme is financed by voluntary contributions. US$1.12 millions were received in 1986 from eighteen countries, 1987 pledges amounted to $1.1 million.[26] Total resources available in 1986 totalled $5.12 million, including funds carried over from previous years, interests and other income. Resources for 1987 were estimated at $5.24 millions.

In 1986 the UNV programme administered 13,750 man-months of UNV expertise. In April 1986, 1,267 volunteers were either serving or had accepted appointment, with 537 additional posts established and under recruitment. Activities continued from previous years on the African and Asia-Pacific regional projects, involving thirty-seven countries, in the area of domestic development services. Youth projects included a youth and self-employment project in Bangladesh, a self-employment and entrepreneurship development programme in Sri Lanka, a technical-assistance programme for non-governmental organizations and DDS organizations in Zambia, assistance to vocational training programmes for youth in Zaire, and technical assistance to the government of Papua New Guinea in setting up a national youth scheme.

Another important project was the UNV large-scale regional project of emergency assistance to drought-affected countries in Sub-Sahara Africa. It was found that UNVs represented a particularly appropriate resource for emergency relief, as volunteers are experienced professionals who can be mobilized on short notice and who are willing and able to function under difficult living and working conditions. Out of fifty three UNVs having completed their assignments, twenty six had been requested by the host countries to continue their work under other financial sources: their services had been appreciated.

Most volunteers (80 per cent), unlike other categories of UN personnel, come from developing countries and work in the least-developed countries. The roster of UNV candidates contains abouth 3,000 names in more than 100 fields. Their skills range from accountants to youth workers, economists, from mechanics and librarians to statisticians.

Volunteers are normally appointed for two years under special employment conditions; they are not subject to UN Staff Rules and Regulations. They receive a monthly living allowance ranging from $395 to $755 for single volunteers, and from $540 to $1,020 for volunteers with direct dependants, depending on the cost-of-living in the duty station. Free-of-charge housing is normally provided, as well as free-of-cost life and health insurance. Annual leave is granted; appointment and repatriation travel is paid by the UN. A resettlement allowance is paid on return to the home country.

Although the scope of this programme and the number of UN volunteers are still relatively modest (the number of US peace corps volunteers is 5,200), the UNV programme is a successful experiment in international voluntary work. One of its assets is the use of skilled persons who can supplement or replace other, more expensive and/or appropriate types of project personnel. Another positive aspect is for the UN to use the good will and idealism of volunteers for multilateral development activities. The image of the UN in developing countries can also benefit from the limited remuneration and benefits granted to volunteers, in contrast with the more generous employment conditions (in relation to most developing countries) enjoyed by UN experts. The UNV programme is a very useful complement to UN organizations' technical cooperation programmes; it should grow and develop to a more significant and influential level. As stated by the ICSC, UNVs represent an enormous future potential to the UN organizations.[27]

Associate experts

Associate experts are junior experts considered as international civil servants under a special status: they are nominated by donor countries, and remuneration, at lower levels than UN total remuneration, is reimbursed by the donor countries to the UN organizations.[28] Associate experts are 'national experts' from industrialized countries, assigned to developing countries. This arrangement therefore involves four parties, the funds' and candidates' provider (the donor country), the facilitator (the UN organization), the associate expert and recipient country.

The associate expert scheme was conceived as a means of involving young professionals from developed countries in the development process and of providing them with field experience at the expense of the donor country, their own country.

All parties benefit from the scheme: donor countries are paying for the associate experts' field experience, which may qualify the latter for future UN employment or for assignment on bilateral aid. The donor countries also benefit from improving their image as providers of assistance to the Third World. Recipient countries benefit by the additional technical cooperation staff thus provided. The UN organization can utilize additional staff without costs and may recruit some of them, after their tenure as associate experts, as full-fledged experts, with a full knowledge of their capacities. The associate expert gains irreplaceable field experience in a supervised, trainee, status.

The UN organization plays the role of employer and trainer. The organization identifies the country and the programme where an associate expert can be usefully assigned, defines his tasks, undertakes the selection, recruitment, appointment, orientation, assignment and follow-up. The organization monitors the in-service training of the associate expert and assesses its results.[29]

At the end of 1984 there were approximately 1,000 such young professionals, fully financed by donor countries. Donor countries are, at present, limited to a group of Western industrialized countries; the Netherlands were the first country to sign an agreement with the UN for the provision of associate experts in 1958.[30] Other donor countries include Austria, Belgium, Denmark, the Federal Republic of Germany, Finland, Italy, Japan, Norway, Switzerland, Sweden and the United Kingdom. Neither the United States nor socialist countries participate in this scheme.

By agreements concluded with the UN organizations, the donor countries specify the conditions of employment and the type of assignment of the associate experts. Most agreements prescribe that assignments are to be to field projects in developing countries. Candidates should normally not be older than 32 or 35; they should be university graduates with limited practical experience. They are appointed at grades P.1 to P.3; they are paid the relevant UN salary rates but some of the UN allowances may be excluded. Most donor countries have excluded participation in the UN Pension Fund. Initial contracts are for one or two years; they are rarely extended beyond three years.

Training plans and reporting procedures are defined.

Associate experts are another useful complement to UN technical cooperation programmes, as well as an effective training scheme for young professionals from developed countries. Some donor countries (Belgium, Denmark and the Netherlands) have financed, in addition, the assignment and training of nationals from developing countries as associate experts: this expansion of the original purpose of the associate experts' scheme would be even more beneficial to development activities.

Seconded nationals

A few member states provide to the UN organizations the services of national civil servants or professionals working in national institutions for specified periods of time, without costs or with limited costs to the organizations, under non-reimbursable loan arrangements. The benefits of such arrangements are, here also mutual. They are advantageous to the member state and to the individual concerned, as the latter's continuity of national career and his return to his national service are guaranteed. They are advantageous to the organizations which can obtain the services of a qualified individual at no cost, or at less cost than a normal UN employment would entail. The individual concerned and his service or institution may also benefit from the international experience, contacts and exposure acquired: his country will benefit from an image of generosity towards international cooperation and organizations.

Such arrangements usually concern qualified, experienced professional personnel, who can be assigned either to the headquarters or a field position. Agreements have been concluded with a number of Western industrialized countries including Canada, Denmark, France, Italy, Norway and the United States. The seconded individuals are usually 'baptized' as international civil servants and are subject to selected UN Staff Rules and Regulations.

For instance, a few highly qualified young state administrators from France have been recently seconded to the WHO under the French Civil Service 'mobility' arrangements. The seconded individuals receive a WHO contract and sign the international oath of office. They enjoy the functional immunities and privileges. They are placed under the supervision of a WHO staff official. On the other hand, the French government pays the seconded officials their salaries and allowances directly under French administrative rules. In addition, WHO pays them an assignment allowance, an installation allowance and a repatriation grant. Appointment and repatriation travel expenses, as well as duty travel, are assumed by the organization. WHO also provides for health insurance protection. The French seconded officials do not participate in the UN Pension Fund.

Agreements with the US government vary. Some provide that WHO pays to the seconded official his salary and allowances at WHO rates, as well as travel costs, while the US department will pay for insurance costs. Others provide that the seconded official is recruited by WHO without compensation; his US salary and allowances continue to be paid and assumed by his US administration during his secondment to WHO. In some other cases, WHO reimburses the equivalent of the relevant WHO salary and allowances to the US government, an amount which is usually less than the US remuneration, in spite of the Noblemaire principle! Some of the agreements provide for a double national and international allegiance: the seconded US official is directly responsible to a WHO supervisor, while a US federal official will exercise 'administrative cognizance' over the officer. The extent of this 'cognizance' is not always clear. An agreement states that 'the rules and policies governing the internal operation and management of WHO will apply to the seconded officer': does this include the WHO Staff Rules and Regulations? Another section of the agreement states that 'The rules and policies of both the US Department of Health and Human Services and of WHO governing standards of conduct shall apply to the officer', on the expectation that both sets of rules are compatible. Contrary to normal secondment rules, it seems that in such cases the seconding national administration retains a significant supervisory role over the seconding official; this is directly related to the extent of the financing of the seconded official's remuneration by the releasing organization — beggars can't be choosers.

Other countries have varied schemes which are negotiated with and agreed by individual governments and the organization. The agreements are normally complemented by a contract between the individual concerned and the organization, a contract which requires the individual to sign the UN oath of office.

When seconded officials continue to receive their emoluments, or most of them, from their national authorities, their previous employer, there is a risk that they will feel more 'national' than 'international'. The risk, or the temptation, is similar to that of UN staff members who receive a financial supplement to their UN emoluments from their national authorities.

In practice, in spite of the ambiguous nature of these seconded nationals' contracts and loans, the WHO experience is very favourable. There have been no noticeable problems of double allegiance. The seconded officials have generally worked very competently and loyally in their technical or administrative field, in the interest of the organization.[31]

Other organizations' practices

Although the following practices are those of organizations not belonging to the UN system, they are indicative of new international employment trends.

The Intergovernmental Committee for Migration (ICM) in Geneva has designed an 'Integrated Experts' scheme, under which the Committee arranges for the assignment of German and Italian experts to Latin American countries. To help overcome the considerable difference between the salaries offered in the countries of origin and destination, and to ensure a high professional standard of candidates, the experts receive supplementary benefits from their governments as well as contributions to medical and accident insurance and travel costs, in addition to the emoluments received from the Latin American Institutions. The role of ICM is that of an intermediary and facilitator. ICM receives a detailed request from the recipient country. It then searches for candidates and submits applications to Latin American governments or institutions. The latter select the candidate. ICM may assist with the negotiation of the contract. It deals with travel arrangements.

Under this scheme, ICM's aims are to meet the specific needs of Latin American countries for experts in the various fields of science and technology which cannot be filled by local experts. To these ends, ICM works in close cooperation with the governments of the Federal Republic of Germany and of Italy. Through these programmes European specialists are made available for periods of one to six years to work in public institutions, universities, public services, vocational training schools and other positions of particular interest to Latin American countries. These experts not only work in an advisory capacity but become part of the economic, educational or service structure of the country, working closely with nationals: they are fully integrated in the local working environment.

The ICM scheme of integrated experts is basically bilateral; it remains international only through the middle-man role played by ICM.[32]

CERN, the European Organization for Nuclear Research, also in Geneva, has adopted the model of an open laboratory of scientific research, directed by scientists, controlled by administrators and financed by member states. CERN personnel is divided into two categories, established and non-established staff members. In the first category, about 3,500 'established' staff members are traditional international civil servants who administer the organization and its programmes. Only about sixty of them are physicists; they maintain a scientific continuity. The recruitment of this personnel, including scientists, engineers, technicians, workers and administrators, is made on an international basis, but it is not subject to the 'geographical distribution' (quotas for each member state) requirements of UN organizations. National quotas would be incompatible with the organization's scientific and technical requirements. Recruitment even extends to nationals of countries which are not member states of the organization, such as China, Japan, the United States and the Soviet Union, for scientific reasons: open exchanges of knowledge and research are essential to the organization's scientific progress.

The 'non-established' staff members number about 2,500. They are physicists from national institutions who carry out the organization's research. They are not international civil servants but nationals working temporarily in an technologically advanced international research centre, for their own benefit, for the benefit of their national institution and for the benefit of CERN. This category allows for a rotation of researchers in the organization, in an effort of symbiosis between the organization and the scientific community.

The non-established staff members include fellows, scientific attachés, guest professors. Fellows are young scientists who have completed their studies; they may stay in CERN two or three years with a fellowship stipend. Scientific attachés are older scientists sent by their university or national institute to CERN to join a research team. Attachés may be remunerated by their national institute or by CERN or by both.

Most non-established staff members remain closely dependent on their national institution during their work at CERN; they work in an international organization as national agents. They have a dual allegiance, not to their government and to the organization, but to their national scientific institution and to CERN.[33]

Trends

The trends are clear: new, unorthodox employment schemes have been grafted successfully onto the old international civil service tree. New colours have been added to the original palette of the League of Nations' employment terms. The question as to whether new and·different employment conditions should or should not be invented to meet new conditions and constraints, has been answered positively.

These new conditions are related to 'new dimensions' in technical cooperation, the need to promote self-reliance of developing countries, to give full weight to national expertise and to ensure continuity of development programmes at the country level. On the part of donor countries, and generally of the big contributors to the UN budgets, these new conditions are influenced by their demands to limit or reduce staff costs, their desire to control the use of part of their contributions and the assignment of some of their nationals during their international employment. Developing countries have promoted the employment of their own nationals by UN organizations.

The trends towards an increasing recourse to short-term appointments of experts and consultants has been encouraged by the UNDP Governing Council.[34] The council has also asked for measures to reduce the cost of international experts and consultants' services.

In December 1985 the General Assembly approved the International Civil Service Commision's recommendations regarding the development of recruitment sources. One recommendation, addressed to member states, was to facilitate the secondment of their nationals to the organizations. The Commision also recommended that the organizations consider using reimbursable loan agreements for specific technical assignments of limited duration in the context of technical cooperation activities, in order to obtain access to candidates whose career commitments would otherwise preclude service with the UN common system. It recommended that the organizations make full use of UN volunteers, the associate experts scheme and non-governmental organizations as recruitment sources to develop their rosters. Finally, the organizations should consider retired persons as candidates in technical cooperation fields of work where expertise is scarce.[35]

Alternative employment schemes include short-term contracts, an overlapping of general service and professional grades and salaries, special salary, allowances and pension conditions, the employment of non-staff members, the overlapping of national and international status, the use of volunteers. A summary of selected alternative employment conditions is shown in table 8.2.

Table 8.2 Selected alternative employment conditions

Status	Employment conditions
(1). International status	
Short-term consultants, temporary staff	*Special UN short-term, temporary salary/allowances conditions*
National professional officers (UN, UNDP, UNHCR, UNICEF)	*Local professionals working in their home country at field offices, paid on UN best local rates*
UN volunteers	*Special UN employment conditions, lower than UN rates; stipends*
Associate experts	*Special P.1/P.3 conditions, costs financed by donor countries*
Seconded officials on special conditions	*Remuneration may be paid in whole or in part by seconding country to organization or to seconded official*
(2). Contract with organization, but non-staff member	
Reimbursable loan agreement or special service agreement	*Remuneration paid by organization to institution or individual*
WHO Congo agents	*Government agents—national allegiance*
UN judiciary contracts	*Government agents—national allegiance*
National experts	*Working in their own country, paid on best local rates*
(UN, UNDP, ILO, FAO, WHO)	
ICM integrated experts	*Salaries paid by receiving government, supplement by donor government*
CERN non-established scientists	*Remuneration paid by CERN or by national institution or by both*

The problems of principles and practices raised by some of these schemes will have to be further studied and resolved. Still, their usefulness is clear: they respond to needs of developing and donor countries and their practicality has been demonstrated. In designing and applying alternative employment schemes, the organizations have proved that they can adjust their rules and practices to new circumstances. As international service organizations, their interest is to be able to adapt and expand their employment role in order to satisfy national needs and international aspirations.

Notes

1. UN Docs. ACC/1983/PER/32, 30 June 1983, and ACC/1987/PER/R.35/Rev.1, 14 September 1987, *Personnel Statistics*.
2. H. Reymond and S. Mailick, *International Personnel Policies and Practices*, Praeger, New York, 1985, pp. 99-100.
3. UN Doc. ICSC/26/R.20/Add.1, 7 July 1987.
4. General Assembly Resol. 3176(XXVIII), 17 December 1973, and UN Doc. E/5703, 1975.
5. UN Doc. A/35/30, 1980, paras. 303-310, *Report of the ICSC*.
6. Doc. FICSA/C/39/CRP.43, 10 February 1986.
7. UN Docs. ACC/1986/3, 1 April 1986, paras. 73-80, and ICSC/23/R.19 of 16 April 1986, paras. 162-72.
8. Roger Barnes, 'Adaptation of Personnel Structures of the UN System to Changing Needs: The Problem of National Professionals', *The Adaptation of Structure and Methods at the UN*, The Hague Academy of International Law/ UN University, Workshop, 4-6 November 1985, M. Nijhoff, Amsterdam, 1986, pp. 235-42.
9. UN Staff Rules, Chs. III and VI.
10. UN Doc. *Final Report on the Meeting of National Recruitment Services*, Geneva, 24-8 September 1984, UN Department of Technical Cooperation for Development.
11. The salary costs of a consultant may amount to US $100 to $200 or more per day plus travel costs. Pension Fund participation only applies to contracts of six months or more.
12. *Final Report*, p. 11.
13. UN Doc. A/40/30, 1985, p. xiv.
14. See UNAT Judgments Nos. 233 and 281.
15. *La Deuxième décennie de l'OMS*, 1958-67, pp.53-5, and *Basic Facts about the UN*, 1985, p. II.5a, II.6.
16. UNAT Judgment No. 176.
17. The UN Report JIU/REP/78/3, 1978 counted fifty cases: FICSA's estimate for 1987 is 12,000 (Doc. FICSA/C/41/1, 18 November 1987). Other estimates range from 2,000 to 6,000, depending on the definition of 'national experts'. More comprehensive data will be collected by the UN organizations in 1988: see Doc. ACC/1987/10, 12 August 1987.
18. UN Doc. JIU/REP/78/3, 1978, p. 53-6.
19. UN Doc. ACC/1980/PER/37, 23 December 1980.
20. UN Doc. ACC/1987/10, 12 August 1987.
21. UN Doc. DP/1987/46, 24 April 1987, *UN Volunteers, Report of the Administrator*.
22. Resol. No. 849(XXXII), 4 August 1961, Economic and Social Council.
23. General Assembly Resol. 2659(XXV), 7 December 1970. The oath of office (Pledge of Commitment of UNV) states, 'I pledge to exercise with dedication, discretion and conscience such duties as shall be entrusted to and undertaken by

me as a UNV, to comport myself in accordance with the principles of the UN Charter and not to seek or accept instructions in regard to the performance of my duties from any authority external to the UN System with the exception of work-related instructions from the specific host Government authority to which I may be attached'.

24. Resol. 31/131(XXXI), 16 December 1976.
25. Resol. 31/166(XXXI), 21 December 1976.
26. UN Doc. DP/1987/46, 24 April 1987: *UNV, Report of the Administrator*. In 1986, voluntary contributions to the UNV Special Voluntary Fund were received from the United States, six Western European countries, ten developing countries and China.
27. UN Doc. ICSC/21/R.20, 25 February 1985, para. 48.
28. UNDP uses the term 'Junior Professional Officers' for the same scheme.
29. This evaluation of the Associate Experts Scheme in WHO is due to M. Lafif in an unpublished note on 'Les Experts associés—Réflexion sur une récente évolution', 1986.
30. UN Doc. ISCS/21/R.20, 25 February 1985, and *Final Report*, para. 74.
31. Information obtained by author. In WHO, US seconded officials have worked, in particular, very effectively and loyally for the Smallpox Eradication Campaign. US, Canadian, French, Dutch, Danish and Norwegian seconded officials are now contributing, mostly free of charge to the current WHO Global AIDS programme.
32. See *ICM in Facts*, 1985, and *Transfer of Specialized Human Resources*, ICM, May 1984. As a reversed brain-drain effort, ICM also sponsors a 'Return of Talent' programme to facilitate the return of professionals and technicians, who have acquired training and know-how in industrialized countries, to their own country, or to a country in the region. Under this programme, 4,500 highly qualified Latin American nationals have returned to their region, and 115 African professionals have also benefited from the ICM programme. The European Economic Community will make available to ICM some $8.7 million to assist, over four years, about 550 African nationals to six target countries: see *ICM Monthly Dispatch*, no. 106, 8 December 1987.
33. See J.M. Dufour, 'Recherche scientifique et coopération européenne', in *Les Agents internationaux*, Pedone, Paris, 1985, pp. 81-92.
34. *Final Report*, p. 36.
35. UN Doc. A/40/30, 1985, para. 252, and General Assembly Resol. 40/244 III of 18 December 1985.

Conclusion

> The great privilege in which we share is that of working for the people of the world—all of them—in a brotherhood of service[1]

The principles and practices of the international civil service are the fruit of difficult, subtle and changing compromises between the sometimes conflicting demands or expectancies of member states, international administrations and staff. More generally, international staff, like their organizations, are subject to the demands or influences of such factors as the decisions of sovereign states, the world relations of power, the proposals of internationalist idealism, the political and economic interdependency of nations, claims of Third World countries, global and regional conflicts, ideological oppositions, economic and currency fluctuations, historical events and trends. In other words, international staff are not only the idealistic pioneers and vanguard of a future, more orderly and peaceful world, they are living in the real, present world of conflicts, rivalries and uncertainties: their ivory tower has been assaulted and broken into and they are now exposed to the same constraints and pressures asnational civil servants and ordinary citizens.

The internationalist concept

The traditional concept of the international civil service remains as invented by Sir Eric Drummond: a hard core of international career staff, sworn to political and financial independence from governments, is needed in all the international secretariats. They are to assure the permanency, continuity, memory and will of the organizations. They are to define the organizations' strategies and long-term plans. They are to act as negotiators, mediators, conciliators, middle-men between states, and between states and their organization. They are to define and represent the views and interests of the community of nations, in contrast with individual states' own interests and demands.

In his recent report to the ILO Conference in 1987,[2] the director-general of the organization, Francis Blanchard, said that the main functions of secretariats are not confined to providing services; their main function is to propose courses of action in the pursuit of the organization's objectives. In this they differ significantly from national civil servants who have direct authority to carry out given policies in a coherent societal framework. 'The secretariats of international organizations, which have no such authority, have to help create the basis of agreements by reconciling differences'. Blanchard asserted that, to play their role, the secretariats must enjoy the confidence of the organizations' constituents, a confidence which can only be earned through impartiality, objectivity and respect for all the interests involved. 'These attributes can be secured only by an independent multinational civil service, free from national or other external influence and exclusively devoted to the service of an organization'. The high standards of competence and integrity required of officials must not be made to yield to considerations of nationality or political patronage. Member states should understand that it is to their advantage for the international civil service to be independent and attain a very high standard of quality.

If the organizations need this internationalist hard cord, their varied functions, particularly in the development field of advisory services and operational activities, require a broader array of employment schemes. The trend towards a diversification of staff members' roles, status and employment conditions, has been encouraged in part by the increasing and successful government pressures for a reduction in staff costs. It has also been a result of the stress on self-reliance of developing countries, which has promoted the employment of nationals working in their own countries as UN national professional officers or national experts. Developing countries now provide most of the low-cost UN volunteers. The organizations have also been used to facilitate the appointment and training of associate experts from industrialized countries for assignment to Third World countries. Finally, the employment of seconded national civil servants, paid either by their own government or by the international organization, has shown, together with other unorthodox employment schemes, that staff employed by UN organizations may have the status of a traditional international civil servant, or that of a national working for an international programme under local conditions of employment: there is now a continuum of employment conditions and status, ranging from international to national employment with intermediate positions.

Dag Hammarskjold would not recognize his international civil service, but the political and economic circumstances have changed considerably in the last thirty years. New problems and demands require new solutions. Organizations which cannot adjust to change disappear.

The US and socialist pressures

The McCarthyism of the 1950s is dead: the suspension of the US loyalty clearance in 1986 was a symbolic and practical victory for its liberal opponents. Friends of the US were relieved when the democratic United States finally desisted from applying pre-UN recruitment procedures similar to those of socialist countries.

Thirty years later the US administration and Congress are applying severe financial sanctions against all the UN organizations, in breach of the US international obligations, and without reasonable justification. The US ultimate aim seems to be to punish or destroy the organizations for supporting multilateralism. Its initial, more reasonable apparent intention was to reduce the 'politicization' of the organizations and to encourage budgetary and administrative reform: the UN is becoming 'leaner' (by 15 per cent) and its restructuration is progressing, but the US 'UN bashing' continues, to the detriment of the organizations' programmes and of the US image. Following the US withdrawal from UNESCO, one wonders whether this announces the end of the universality in the UN organizations by the progressive disengagement of the US from the UN network. Will the next US administration attempt to change this course of events?

The socialist views of international organization and of the international civil service have not changed since Khrushchev's shoe-banging at the UN and the Soviet invectives against Trygve Lie and Dag Hammarskjold. The socialist governments still exercise strict control and supervision over the recruitment and employment of their citizens. Most of the UN staff members from most socialist countries still do not respect their international oath of office.

Mikhail Gorbachev has recently announced an unexpected reversal of established Soviet positions towards the UN.[3] He has proposed a number of measures: to set up under the aegis of the UN a mechanism for extensive international verification of compliance with agreements to lessen international tension, limit armaments and for monitoring the military situation in conflict areas; a wider use of UN military observers and UN peacekeeping forces; the Security Council members could become guarantors of regional security; a UN tribunal should be created to investigate acts of international terrorism; a world information programme under UN auspices should familiarize peoples with one another's life; a special fund of humanitarian cooperation of the UN should be established; a World Space Organization should be created; the mandatory jurisdiction of the International Court of Justice should be recognized by all states on mutually agreed upon conditions; a World Consultative Council should unite the world's intellectual élite, and so on.

Do these innovative proposals for a bigger UN role in international affairs announce a real change of the Soviet attitude towards the organizations? Could internal Soviet glasnost and perestroika influence the attitude of the socialist countries' authorities and bureaucracies vis-à-vis the international secretariats and their nationals employed in the secretariats? Could these be trusted to be good socialist citizens *and* good international civil servants?

National and regional fiefdoms

In a related area, the General Assembly adopted in December 1987 a resolution (UN Doc. A/C.5/42/L.24) which may help the secretary-general in destroying 'national fiefdoms' in the secretariat's senior posts. The resolution reaffirmed that no post should be considered the exclusive preserve of any member state or group of states. It requested the secretary-general to ensure that equal opportunity be given to candidates of all member states when making appointments to all posts in the upper echelons. It reaffirmed that the secretary-general, in making such appointments, should strive to appoint only a candidate from a member state other than that of the incumbent to be replaced in order to reinforce the principle of rotation in the upper echelons of the secretariat, unless there are exceptional circumstances.

This resolution would affect not only the national preserves of the US and or socialist countries, but also those of other countries such as China, France or the United Kingdom, which have become accustomed to be treated as the 'owners' of particular senior posts. It will also affect groups of countries, such as African, Asian, or Latin American countries, for which similar expectations have been created. The implementation of this resolution will not be easy, but it will constitute a progress of internationalism in the UN secretariat.

Remuneration, privileges and immunities

Political and economic pressures have eroded the remuneration package of UN employees. At the professional level the Noblemaire principle has lost its luster: is it really and correctly applied when several industrialized countries have to pay salary supplements to their citizens so that they will accept UN employment? Is the US Federal Service still the national civil service offering the best remuneration? Is it reasonable that the budgets of most of the UN organizations, the salaries of their professional staff and UN pensions be calculated in US dollars when that currency fluctuates wildly with neither floor nor ceiling?

The UN secretary-general recognized in 1987 that there were flaws in the application of the Noblemaire principle. He felt that the present remuneration system needed reassessment. All executive heads were deeply concerned by the deterioration in the terms and conditions of service; some suggested that the level of remuneration had become so unsatisfactory that it was almost impossible to carry out certain programmes, especially in the field.[4]

For various technical reasons, the General Assembly decided in December 1987 to request the International Civil Service Commission to undertake a comprehensive review of the conditihns of service of staff in the professional and higher categories, in order to provide a sound and stable methodological basis for their remuneration.[5] Due regard was to be given to:

(1) The need for securing the highest standards of efficiency, competence and integrity in recruiting staff with due regard being paid to equitable geographical distribution.
(2) The need for greater transparency and simplicity in the concepts and and administration of the remuneration system.
(3) The need for sufficient flexibility to respond to varying requirements resulting from different types of appointments and changing circumstances.
(4) The relativity of benefits among duty stations as a factor in staff mobility.

(5) The need for a long-term improvement in the operation of the post adjustment system, including the separation of the effects of inflation and currency fluctuations and a simpler and more accurate reflection of differences in cost of living between the base of the system—New York— and field duty stations

The final review should be presented to the General Assembly at its forty-fourth session in the Autumn of 1989.

Will Noblemaire survive, or will another formula be found which would provide more stability of remuneration, a more simple salary and allowance system and equitable adjustments for cost-of-living and currency fluctuations?

International civil servants do not need extravagantly high conditions of service nor diplomatic privileges; they should receive a reasonable and dependable remuneration. For professional staff, the salary rates could be set by comparison with a number of national civil services, rather than by reference only to the US Federal Service. The US dollar standard could also be replaced by an international value based on a basket of currencies, like the European Currency Unit.

International civil servants have to be protected by functional immunities, as a guarantee of their independence. The unfortunate, recurring cases of violations of these immunities have to be dealt with promptly and diligently by the executive heads, with the support of their governing bodies and of their staff. Staff associations will remain alert to such cases and publicize them, if need be.

Unionism

The organizations have a need for representative staff associations in order to maintain a constructive dialogue between administration and employees. The fears that these groupings may be, or become, too militant or powerful are ill-founded. Staff representatives know the limits of their action: they know that the organizations are fragile, expendable and that states have all the cards in their hands.

Staff associations are needed to protect the staff against political whims, to maintain reasonable conditions of employment, to call on the rule of law in staff-management relations and to enhance the prestige of the international civil service.

The UN secretary-general has recently assured his staff that, at the time of restructuring and staff reductions, it was vital for the staff to be properly informed and fully consulted. Staff views should be sought and taken into account before management decisions are taken on matters affecting staff interests and concerns. The exchange and interplay of ideas among the whole diversity of staff represented in the UN is needed. For the secretary-general it was vital to identify and eradicate those sources of unnecessary friction which undermine harmonious relations and hinder effective operations. Staff-management cohesiveness and mutual respect must be strengthened.

However, the secretary-general warned that the consultation process, which should be standard in modern management and in staff-management relations, does not connote co-management: 'Management is my necessary responsibility as Chief Administrative Officer ... the roles of management and staff are closely intertwined, but they are different'.[6]

'The UN of Tomorrow': Criticisms and proposals on UN personnel management

A recent report of the UN Association of United States[7] referred, among other issues, to the UN 'very troubled' personnel situation. It attributed its causes to various factors: challenges posed by cultural diversity; a lack of clarity, at the level of working staff units, about the organization's mission; and a remarkably low level of interest, on the part of most member states, in ensuring administrative efficiency. For the authors of the report, it is this member states' attitude, which is tolerant of personnel inefficiencies and guilty of fostering them, that is the single most important explanation of this situation.

The report said that no really significant improvement in personnel matters was likely to take place without a fundamental change in the attitude of the UN top leadership: UN secretaries-general have not sufficiently asserted their personnel prerogative in front of challenges by the General Assembly, by governments, staff associations and other sources of influence. The report recommended that the secretary-general should defend his personnel prerogatives; that he should be assisted by a high-level, independent search-and-review committee regarding the election for all posts at grades D.2 and above (to shield him from political pressures); that the General Assembly should discontinue its 'command and compliance' approach to personnel matters and restrict itself to braod issues of policy. Members of the International Civil Service Commission should be required to have substantial experience in the area of personnel management in the public or private sector. On recruitment, external competitive examinations should be extended to grades P.3 and P.4, writing tests and occupation-based oral examinations should be conducted for recruitment at the P.5 and D.1 levels (again to protect the UN administration against political pressure and to verify the capacities of candidates). On tenure, no permanent contracts should be granted before an employee had served for a minimum of six years. Two successive negative performance evaluations should result in dismissal. The performance evaluation form should be replaced by one that rates the performance of specific tasks. All professionals should be evaluated annually. Most of these technical recommendations are reasonable—they should be seriously considered.

On the other hand, one cannot easily change the attitude of member states. One can hardly stop the General Assembly from adopting resolutions on personnel matters. However, the secretary-general can and should assume more personal interest in personnel matters, offer more resistance to member states' pressures on staff selection on recruitment and on promotions. Even though his priority tasks relate to peace and security and other programme issues, the organization's effectiveness depends to a large extent on the quality and motivation of its staff. It seems that J. Perez de Cuellar is convinced of this truth, perhaps more so than his predecessors. The executive heads of specialized agencies are faced with the same dilemma: as stated by Bettati, it is a

> 'cruel dilemma which leads the head of an international administration to warn collectively the states and their interference, while giving in, here or there, to the entreaties of one or several of them, now to preserve the ephemeral budgetary balance or the precarious political consensus, now to compound in subtle measurements the often contradictory exigencies of the principle of an equitable geographic distribution with the principle of the best possible competence of the staff and of the respect of their independence'.[8]

An international organization needs a strong executive head, as well as a competent and pro-active personnel department.

The secretary-general's view

The UN Secretary-General recognized in 1986 that there was need for improvement in the management of the secretariat at all levels.[9]

In April 1987 he made clear that the foundations for an effective reform of the UN required a genuine commitment to the revitalization of the organization by all its members and an end to the current financial uncertainties.[10] 'Improving the administrative and financial functioning of the UN without addressing the fundamental issue of 'efficiency to do what?' would not achieve the desired objective.

The UN reform process, as recommended by the Group of 18, includes the restructuring of the intergovernmental machinery (now under consideration by the Economic and Social Council) and that of the UN secretariat. The latter restructuring is proceeding, together with the 15 per cent staff reduction approved by the General Assembly.

For the secretary-general, this period of restructuring and change provides the secretariat with a major challenge. It provides a chance to adapt the UN after forty-two years, to the role which the world body should fulfil as the world moves towards the twenty-first century.[11]

On 16 October 1987, J. Perez de Cuellar told the Fifth Committee members that he had been deeply impressed by the continued dedication of the staff during the current severe crisis, and by their admirable performance in the face of adverse conditions and, at times, unwarranted criticism.[12]

In the words of Jan Martenson, director-general of the UN Office at Geneva in an address to the staff:

'We are engaged ... in a global enterprise which will make a difference to coming generations. We are the servants of the only existing expression of the international community, implementing international policies in what is a comparatively new experiment in human affairs. All of you ... took up your duties with ... a sense of mission. Over the years ... doubts may perhaps emerge and sometimes the vision fades. At times, we are beset by criticism and uncertain about the future. But ... it is, always will be, a privilege to serve the United Nations. We can take pride in our work and be secure in the knowledge that we are making a real contribution, however incremental, however halting, to the betterment of the human condition.[13]

The international civil service has been threatened in the past and it has survived. The traditional international civil service is now being challenged: in order to survive, grow and tackle new tasks, it needs to adjust to new realities, to accept new modalities, to change threats into opportunities. A new balance has to be found between idealism and realism.

Notes

1. Dr Brock Chisholm, first director-general of WHO, in *Working for WHO*, WHO Doc., Geneva, P. 13.
2. *Reflections on the Future of Multilateral Cooperation: The ILO Perspective*, Report of the Director-General, ILO, Geneva, 1987.
3. Press Bulletin of the Permanent Mission of the Soviet Union in Geneva, no. 169 (1433), 18 September 1987, M. Gorbachev's article on *The Reality and Guarantees of a Secure World*, and Flora Lewis' article 'A Soviet Turnaround May Let the UN Work, at Last', *International Herald Tribune*, 23 October 1987.
4. UN Press Release SG/SM/830, 20 November 1987, 'Statement of the Secretary-General on occasion of Staff Day'.
5. General Assembly Resol. in UN Doc. A/C.5/42/L.18.
6. UN Press Release SG/SM/830.
7. *A Successor Vision: The UN of Tomorrow*, Final Panel Report, September 1987.
8. M. Bettati, 'L'Avenir de la fonction publique internationale: question introductivein *L'avenir des organisations internationales*, Economica, Paris, 1984, p. 190. My translation of the French text.
9. *Report of the Secretary-General on the Work of the Organization*, September 1986, UN Doc. A/41/1, 9 September 1986.
10. *Reform and Renewal in the UN: Progress Report of the Secretary-General on the Implementation of General Assembly Resolution 41/213*, UN Doc. A/42/234, 23 April 1987.
11. UN Press Release SG/SM/830.
12. UN Press Release SI/42/87.
13. UN Doc. IC/Geneva/3403, 20 March 1987.

Bibliography

Abi-Saab, G. (ed.), *The Concept of International Organization*, UNESCO, Paris, 1981.

Bastid, S., *Les Fonctionnaires internationaux*, Sirey, Paris, 1931.

Bayard, Th. (pseud.), 'L'Attitude des Etats d'Europe de l'Est à l'égard des secrétariats des Nations Unies', *Revue belge de droit international,* Brussels, 1985, no. 2, pp. 672-94.

'Arrestations et enlévements de fonctionnaires des Nations Unies', *International Review of Administrative Sciences,* Brussels, 1982, no. 1, pp. 9-18.

Behrstock, J., *The Eighth Case: Troubled Times at the UN,* University Press of America, New York, 1987.

Beigbeder, Y., *La Représentation du personnel à l'Organisation mondiale de la Santé*, Librairie générale de droit et de jurisprudence, Paris, 1975.

Management Problems in UN Organizations, Reform or Decline? Frances Pinter, London, 1987.

'The Withdrawal of the USA from the International Labour Organisation', *Industrial Relations*, Quebec, May 1979, pp. 223-40.

'Current Staff Problems in UN Secretariats', *International Review of Administrative Sciences*, Brussels, 1980, no.2, pp. 149-59.

'Individual Grievance Procedures in UN Secretariats', Quebec, *Industrial Relations,* 1982, no.2, pp.327-42.

'L'Influence de modèles administratifs nationaux sur le système administratif des institutions des Nations Unies', *International Review of Administrative Sciences,* Brussels, 1984, No.2, pp. 148-56.

'Reformes administratives et structurelles des Nations Unies', *Etudes internationales,* Quebec, vol. VIII, no. 2, June 1987, pp. 353-70.

'La crise financière des Nations Unies et les travaux du Comité des Dix-Huit', *Annuaire francais de droit international,* Paris, 1986, pp. 426-38.

Berkov, R., *The World Health Organization: A Study in Decentralized International Administration*, Librairie Droz, Geneva, 1957.

Bettati, M., *Le Droit des organisations internationales*, Presses universitaires de France, Paris, 1987.

(ed.) *L'Avenir des organisations internationales*, Economica, Paris, 1984.

Claude, I.L., *Swords into Plowshares*, Random House, New York, 1971.

Finger, S.M., 'The UN Secretariat Revisited', Orbis, Philadelphia, spring 1981, pp.197-208.

Finger, S.M. and Mugno, J., 'The Politics of Staffing the UN Secretariat', The Ralph Bunche Institute on the UN, the Graduate School and University Center of the City University of New York, December 1974.

Franck, Th. M., *Nation against Nation: What Happened to the UN Dream and What the US Can Do about It*, Oxford University Press, Oxford, 1985.

Gati, T.T., (ed.), *The United States, the United Nations and the Management of Total Change*, New York University Press, New York, 1983.

Graham, N.A. and Jordan, R.S., *The International Civil Service: Changing Roles and Concepts*, Pergamon Press, New York, 1980.

Hammarskjold, D., *The International Civil Servant in Law and in Fact*, Oxford Lecture, 30 May 1961, Clarendon Press.

Heritage Foundation, 'A UN Success Story: The World's Fattest Pensions', *Backgrounder*, no. 378, 11 September 1984. See also UN Studies' in *Heritage Publications*, 1986.

Hoggart R., *An Idea and Its Servants: UNESCO from Within*, Oxford University Press, New York, 1978.

Holly, D.A., 'Bureaucratie internationale et détermination de la ligne générale des organisations internationales: le cas de l'UNESCO', Quebec, *Etudes internationales*, December 1985, pp. 757-70.

Jacobson, H.K., *Networks of Independence: International Organizations and the Global Political System*, New York, Knopf, 1984.

Jéquier, N., (ed.), *Les Organisations internationales entre l'innovation et la stagnation*, Lausanne, Presses Polytechniques Romandes, 1985.

Jonah, J., 'Independence and Integrity of the International Civil Service: The Role of Executive Heads and the Role of States', *New York University Journal of International Law and Politics*, vol. 14, no. 4, summer 1982, The Meller Conference on International Civil Service.

Jordan, R.S., 'What Happened to Our International Civil Service?: The Case of the UN', *Public Administrative Review*, March-April 1981.

   (ed.), *Daq Hammarskjold Re-Visited: The UN Secretary-General as a Force in World Politics*, Carolina Academic Press, Durham, NC, 1983.

Kay. D.A., 'On the reform of International Institutions', *International Organization*, Cambridge, Mass., summer 1976, pp. 533-8.

Langrod, G., *The International Civil Service*, A.W. Sijthoff-Leyden, Oceana Publications; Dobbs Ferry, New York, 1968.

Lewis, S., 'The Defensible UN', *International Perspective*, Ottawa, September-October 1985, p.6.

Lie, T., *In the Cause of Peace*, Macmillan, New York, 1954.

Luard, E., *A History of the UN*, vol. 1, Macmillan, London, 1982.

McLaren, R.A., *Civil Servants and Public Policy: A Comparative Study of International Secretariats*, Waterloo, Ont., Wilfrid Laurier University Press, 1980.

Meron, Th., *The UN Secretariat, the Rules and Practice*, Lexington Books, Lexington, Mass., 1977.

   'L'Indépendance de la fonction publique internationale et son avenir', *L'Avenir des organisations internationales*, Economica, Paris, 1984, pp. 221-40.

Plantey, A., *Droit et pratique de la fonction publique internationale*, Paris, Centre National de la Recherche Scientifique, 1977.

Renninger, J.P., *Can the Common System be Maintained? The Role of the International Civil Service Commission*, UNITAR, New York, 1986.

Ranshofen-Wertheimer, E.F., 'International Administration: Lessons from the Experience of the League of Nations', *American Political Science Review*, vol. 37, 1943.

Reymond, H. and Mailick, S., *International Personnel Policies and Practices*, New York, Praeger, 1985.

Rovine, A.W., *The First Fifty Years: The Secretary-General in World Politics, 1920-1970*, A.W. Sithoff-Leyden, 1970.

   Betrayal from Within: Joseph Avenol, Secretary-General of the League of Nations, 1933-1940, Yale University Press, New Haven, Conn., 1969.

Rubinstein, A.Z., *The Soviets in International Organizations*, Princeton University Press, Princeton, NJ, 1964.

Ruggie, J.G., 'The US and the UN: Towards a New Realism', *International Organization*, vol. 39, no. 2, Spring 1985.

Siddii, J., *Politics of Health: The World Health Organization, 1948-85*, graduate thesis in preparation, Oxford University, Department of International Relations, - to be published in 1989.

Siotis, J., *Essai sur le secrétariat international*, Geneva, Lib. Droz, 1963.

Société francaise pour le Droit international, *Les Agents internationaux*, Paris, Pedone, 1985.

Thant, U, *View from the UN*, Doubleday & Co., New York, 1978.

Urquhart, B., *Hammarskjold*, Knopf, New York, 1972.

Waldheim, K., *The Challenge of Peace*, Weidenfeld & Nicolson, London, 1980.

Weiss, Th. G., *International Bureaucracy*, Lexington Books, Lexington, Mass., 1975.

Zacher, M., *Daq Hammarskjold's UN*, Columbia University Press, New York, 1970.

Index

Index

Index

DATE DUE